THE AudioPro **Home Recording** Course

Volume 2

a comprehensive

multimedia

recording text

by Bill Gibson

MIX PRO AUDIO SERIES · **MIX** BOOKS®

6400 Hollis Street . Emeryville . CA 94608

06 05 04 03 02 01 00 99 98 97   6 5 4 3 2 1

Library of Congress Catalog Card Number: 96-078454

Book design and layout: Bill Gibson
Computer graphics: Bill Gibson
Cover design: Tami Needham
Cover photograph: Susana Millman

Front cover photo: Studio E is a private project audio and video recording facility located
in Sebastopol, California. As home to *Zone TV*, a musical television show, Studio E has
recorded some of the top bands in California. Come visit us at www.studioemusic.com

Production staff:

Mike Lawson: publisher, Lisa Duran: editor, Randy Antin: editorial assistant, Sally Engelfried:
copy editor, Teresa Poss: administrative assistant, Georgia George: production director, Tom
Marzella: production assistant

MixBooks
6400 Hollis Street
Emeryville, CA 94608
(510) 653-3307

Also from MixBooks:

I Hate the Man Who Runs This Bar!
How to Make Money Scoring Soundtracks and Jingles
The Art of Mixing: A Visual Guide to Recording, Engineering, and Production
500 Songwriting Ideas (For Brave and Passionate People)
Music Publishing: The Real Road to Music Business Success, Rev. and Exp. 4th Ed.
How to Run a Recording Session
The Songwriters Guide to Collaboration, Rev. and Exp. 2nd Ed.
Critical Listening and Auditory Perception
Keyfax Omnibus Edition
The AudioPro Home Recording Course
Live Sound Reinforcement
The Studio Business Book
Modular Digital Multitracks: The Power User's Guide
Concert Sound
Sound for Picture

Also from EMBooks:

Tech Terms
Making the Ultimate Demo
Tech Terms: A Practical Dictionary for Audio and Music Production
Making Music With Your Computer

Also from CBM Music and Entertainment Group:

Recording Industry Sourcebook
Mix Reference Disc, Deluxe Edition
Mix Master Directory
Digital Piano Buyer's Guide

MixBooks is a division of Cardinal Business Media Inc.

Printed in Auburn Hills, Michigan

ISBN 0-918371-20-1

Contents

Chapter 5

Acoustic Piano and Rhodes

Chapter 6

Recording Synthesizers

Chapter 7

Panning and Stereo Imaging

Chapter 8

The Total Recording Session

Chapter 9

Mixdown to Master to Product

Audio Examples

CD-1

Chapter 2 Bass Guitar

CD 1: Track 1
Audio Example 2-1 Buzzes and Clacks
Audio Example 2-2 The Controlled Performance

CD 1: Track 2
Audio Example 2-3 Dull Bass Strings
Audio Example 2-4 Boiled Bass Strings

CD 1: Track 3
Audio Example 2-5 Bass Through the Passive DI
Audio Example 2-6 Bass Through the Active DI

CD 1: Track 4
Audio Example 2-7 Bass 1: The P-Bass
Audio Example 2-8 Bass 2: Inexpensive Bass
Audio Example 2-9 Bass 3: Custom P-Bass
Audio Example 2-10 Bass 4: Active Electronics

CD 1: Track 5
Audio Example 2-11 Finger Plucking
Audio Example 2-12 Thumb Plucking
Audio Example 2-13 The Felt Pick
Audio Example 2-14 The Plastic Pick
Audio Example 2-15 The Plastic Pick, Muted

CD 1: Track 6
Audio Example 2-16 Plucking by the Bridge
Audio Example 2-17 Plucking by the Neck
Audio Example 2-18 Plucking Between the Neck and the Bridge

CD 1: Track 7
Audio Example 2-19 Bass Cabinet Miked at the Center
Audio Example 2-20 Bass Cabinet Miked at the Outer Edge

CD 1: Track 8
Audio Example 2-21 The Direct Bass Sound
Audio Example 2-22 The Miked Bass Speaker
Audio Example 2-23 Blending the Direct and Miked Sound

CD 1: Track 9
Audio Example 2-24 Non-compressed Bass
Audio Example 2-25 Compressed Bass
Audio Example 2-26 Snaps Not Limited
Audio Example 2-27 Limited Snaps

CD 1: Track 10
Audio Example 2-28 Mix With 50Hz Boosted on the Bass Track
Audio Example 2-29 Mix Without 50Hz Boosted on the Bass Track
Audio Example 2-30 Alternating Between 2-28 and 2-29

CD 1: Track 11
Audio Example 2-31 Sweeping From 80Hz to 150Hz

CD 1: Track 12
Audio Example 2-32 Sweeping the Cut Between 250Hz and 500Hz

CD 1: Track 13
Audio Example 2-33 Sweeping the Boost Between 250Hz and 500Hz

CD 1: Track 14
Audio Example 2-34 Boost Then Cut at 1000Hz

CD 1: Track 15
Audio Example 2-35 Sweeping the Boost Between 2kHz and 3kHz

CD 1: Track 16
Audio Example 2-36 Panning the Bass

CD 1: Track 17
Audio Example 2-37 Adding Reverb to the Bass
Audio Example 2-38 Solo Bass With Reverb

CD 1: Track 18
Audio Example 2-39 The Stereo Bass Sound
Audio Example 2-40 Adjusting Bass Delay for Mono Compatibility

CD 1: Track 19
Audio Example 2-41 The Bass With Chorus

CD 1: Track 20
Audio Example 2-42 Stereo Synth Bass

CD 1: Track 21
Audio Example 2-43 Synth Bass Direct In
Audio Example 2-44 Synth Bass Miked
Audio Example 2-45 Blending Direct and Miked Synth Bass

CD 1: Track 22
Audio Example 2-46 Sampled Bass Nuance
Audio Example 2-47 Using the Sampled Bass Nuance

CD 1: Track 23
Audio Example 2-48 Key Bass Played by Guitar MIDI Controller

CD 1: Track 24
Audio Example 2-49 Bass Part Played on the Keyboard

CD 1: Track 25
Audio Example 2-50 Guitar-Controlled Key Bass in a Rhythm Section

CD 1: Track 26
Audio Example 2-51 Bass Boosted at 40Hz
Audio Example 2-52 Bass Boosted at 80Hz
Audio Example 2-53 Bass Boosted at 160Hz
Audio Example 2-54 The Previous Three Audio Examples

CD 1: Track 27
Audio Example 2-55 Bass Sound Recorded at 0VU
Audio Example 2-56 Bass Sound Recorded at -3VU

CD 1: Track 28
Audio Example 2-57 Switching Between Stereo and Mono

CD 1: Track 29
Audio Example 2-58 Bass Panned at 9:00 and 3:00

CD-2

Chapter 6 Recording Synthesizers

Introduction

The *AudioPro Home Recording Course, Volume 2* continues with the fundamentals of audio recording in a way that is easy to understand and extremely practical. Each chapter helps you through a specific set of real recording situations. If you've progressed through Volume 1 of this course, you're now ready to complete a recording. Each specific piece of information presented can help you produce a professional musical product.

This is a complete course, designed to progressively build your recording skills. Where I might have introduced a topic in Volume 1 with a minimum of information, the material in Volume 2 offers a deeper insight and understanding of many topics. Read all the printed material and listen carefully to the audio examples provided on the accompanying compact discs. (You'll find the audio examples listed by CD and track number as they appear in the chapter.) The information in each complements the other, and together with the detailed illustrations they offer a complete course. Each part of the course is important to the development of your audio recording skills.

Please refer to the Glossary if you come across a term that's unfamiliar to you. As you've progressed through this course, you have probably learned many new terms and definitions. If you're becoming overwhelmed, slow down and review. You might need to re-examine Volume 1 occasionally just to clarify and solidify your newly gained knowledge. Strive to keep an open mind at all times and take the time to let some of these concepts settle in. Practice the techniques prescribed within until you really feel com-

fortable with each process. New information often seems much more difficult than it is. I've done my best to present this information in the most palatable way possible. Each segment, if viewed as a small data chunk, should be easy to understand. So don't become overwhelmed by the mass of information. Let each paragraph sink in as an understandable bite; the meal will come together by itself.

This material will help you get sounds that are competitive. Persevere! Keep fine-tuning your craft. The techniques described in this course are going to help you make better use of your recording time. Your music will only benefit from your deeper understanding of the studio as a musical tool.

This course is designed and presented from a musical standpoint. That's really what this is all about. Technical manuals are wonderfully interesting, instructive and helpful. I've read most of them over several years of teaching recording classes in Seattle. But this course gives you the fast track to good results in your home studio. Certainly, continue your pursuit of knowledge. For me personally, the more I learn, the more I want to learn. Knowledge itself is a lifelong quest.

Enjoy your music. Music is emotion and feeling. Please hold that high in your considerations while you record. If you let the music live, it will be undeniable. Every truly good recording is full of life and expression. It breathes. It touches the listener's heart. Develop your technique to the point where nothing hides what the music has to say. Enjoy the process!

1 Impedance and Wiring

It's my intent here to add a little depth to your understanding of two topics: high vs. low impedance and balanced vs. unbalanced. This explanation will not be so technically in-depth that only those on a higher mental plane will dare to read it. This a simple, albeit fairly thorough, peek at two very important factors in the recording equation.

Impedance is the resistance to the flow of electrical current. High impedance is high resistance to the flow of electrical current; low impedance is low resistance to the flow of electrical current. If you keep that simple mental picture in mind, the rest of the details should fall into place nicely.

Basic Terminology

Ohm (indicated by Ω): The unit of resistance to the flow of electrical current used to measure impedance

Impedance: Resistance to the flow of electrical current

Z: The abbreviation and symbol used in place of the word *impedance*

Hi Z: High impedance. The exact numerical tag (in Ω) for high impedance varies, depending on whether we're dealing with input impedance or output impedance. It's generally in the range of $5,000\Omega$ to $15,000\Omega$ for output impedance and $50,000\Omega$ to $1,000,000\Omega$ for input impedance. It's important here to understand that hi Z is usually greater than 5,000 to $10,000\Omega$.

Lo Z: Low impedance. The exact numerical tag (in Ω) varies for low impedance as well as high impedance. It's generally in the range of 50Ω to 300Ω for output impedance. It's normal for microphone output impedance to be between 50Ω and 150Ω, and 500Ω to 3000Ω for input impedance. Normal input impedance for lo Z mixers is 600Ω. Essentially, lo Z usually uses small numbers below 600Ω.

Output impedance: The actual impedance (resistance to the electron flow measured in Ω) at the output of a device (microphone, amplifier, guitar, keyboard). To keep it simple, realize that the output impedance is designed to work well with a specific input impedance.

Input impedance: The actual impedance (resistance to the electron flow measured in Ω) at the input of a device. To keep it simple, realize that the input impedance is designed to work well with a specific output impedance. Low impedance and high impedance are not compatible.

Compatibility Between Hi Z and Lo Z

The reason lo and hi Z don't work together is really pretty simple. The most common analogy for explaining the incompatibility between low impedance and high impedance involves a couple of simple water pipes and some water.

In this analogy, water represents electricity and the size of the pipe represents the amount of impedance (Z).

Imagine a very small pipe. The small pipe represents hi Z because no matter how much water (electrical current) is at the entrance (input) of the small pipe, only a limited amount of water can get through the pipe at once. Its physical size limits the amount of water that can pass through the pipe in a period of time.

If you plug the output of a low-impedance mic into the input of a high-impedance amplifier, you have a problem. Imagine the microphone signal traveling through a very large pipe (Lo Z). It's expecting to see a similar sized pipe at the input of a low-impedance amplifier. When it meets the small pipe (Hi Z) at the input of the hi Z amplifier, it's impossible for the complete low-impedance signal to efficiently and accurately enter the small pipe. There's too much resistance to the signal flow; the pipe's too small.

This analogy is very appropriate because

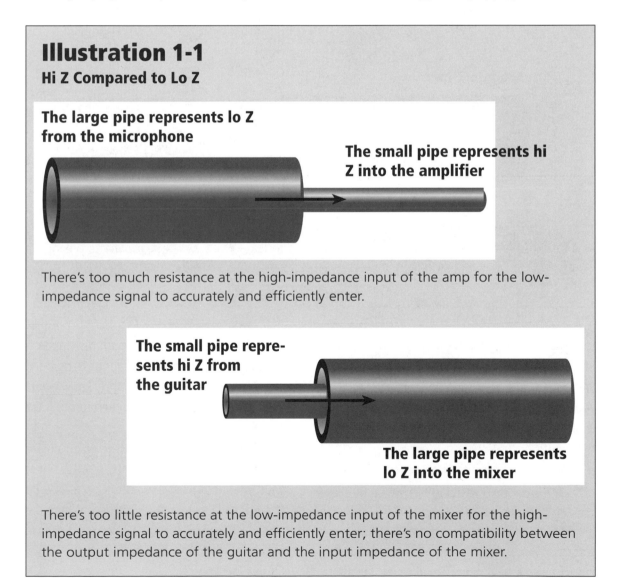

Illustration 1-1
Hi Z Compared to Lo Z

The large pipe represents lo Z from the microphone

The small pipe represents hi Z into the amplifier

There's too much resistance at the high-impedance input of the amp for the low-impedance signal to accurately and efficiently enter.

The small pipe represents hi Z from the guitar

The large pipe represents lo Z into the mixer

There's too little resistance at the low-impedance input of the mixer for the high-impedance signal to accurately and efficiently enter; there's no compatibility between the output impedance of the guitar and the input impedance of the mixer.

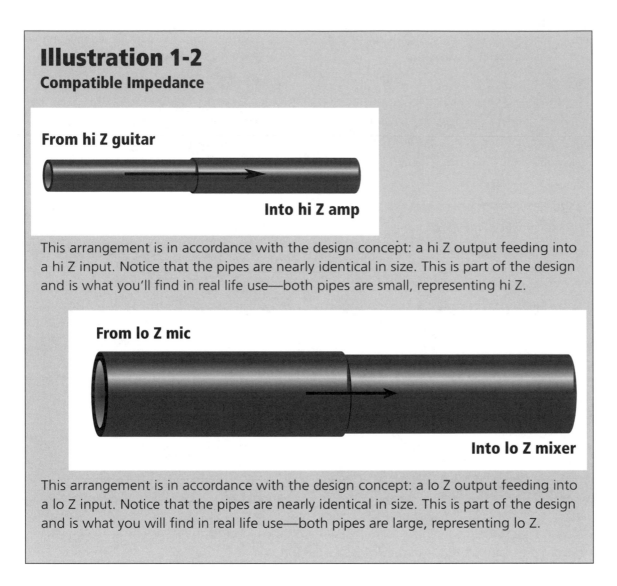

Illustration 1-2
Compatible Impedance

From hi Z guitar

Into hi Z amp

This arrangement is in accordance with the design concept: a hi Z output feeding into a hi Z input. Notice that the pipes are nearly identical in size. This is part of the design and is what you'll find in real life use—both pipes are small, representing hi Z.

From lo Z mic

Into lo Z mixer

This arrangement is in accordance with the design concept: a lo Z output feeding into a lo Z input. Notice that the pipes are nearly identical in size. This is part of the design and is what you will find in real life use—both pipes are large, representing lo Z.

the result of plugging the output of a lo Z mic into the input of a hi Z amp is insufficient level. The amp might be turned up to maximum but you'll barely be able to hear the signal from the mic; there's too much resistance at the amplifier input (Illustration 1-1).

The other incompatible scenario involves attempting to plug a high-impedance output (microphone, guitar, keyboard, etc.) into a low-impedance input (mixer, amp, speaker, etc.). In this case, the hi Z output (small pipe) is expecting to meet a hi Z input (small pipe); in other words, it's expecting to meet high resistance. If the high-impedance output signal is plugged into a low-impedance input, the signal meets practically no resistance and therefore almost immediately overdrives the input.

Practically speaking, when you plug a high-impedance guitar output into a lo Z mixer input, the input level can hardly be turned up before the VU meters read 0VU; even then, the sound you hear is usually distorted because there's not enough resistance at the input (Illustration 1-2).

Illustration 1-3
Line Cable

This illustration shows the construction of typical wire used for unbalanced cables. Notice that the hot lead is stranded wire in the center core, the shield is braided wire isolated from the hot lead by a plastic tube; and around the shield is a plastic or rubber insulating material.

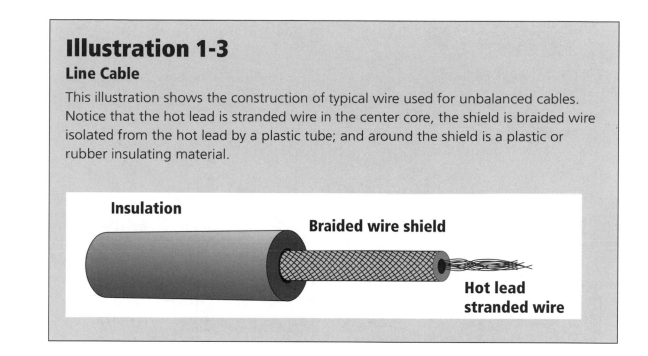

Insulation

Braided wire shield

Hot lead stranded wire

High-impedance outputs are supposed to meet high-impedance inputs; low-impedance outputs are supposed to meet low-impedance inputs. It's not true that the input and output impedance need to be identical. In fact, the input impedance is generally supposed to be about ten times the output impedance, but as I mentioned earlier, we need to keep in mind that high impedance uses high Ω ratings (around and above 10,000Ω) and low impedance uses low Ω ratings—usually below 1000Ω (Illustration 1-3 and 1-4).

We can simply use an impedance transformer—also called a line matching transformer or direct box—to change impedance from high to low or low to high; that's the easy part. We

Illustration 1-4
Wiring Line Cable

This illustration shows the parts of a typical 1/4" line cable. The other common unbalanced connector is the RCA phono plug.

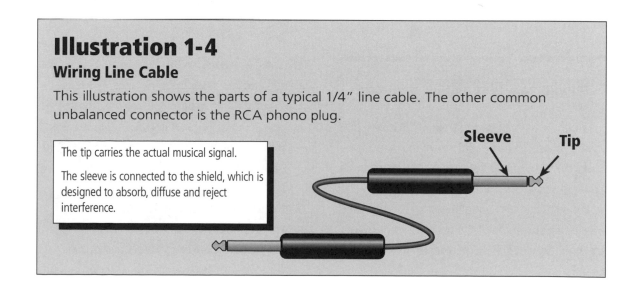

The tip carries the actual musical signal.

The sleeve is connected to the shield, which is designed to absorb, diffuse and reject interference.

Sleeve

Tip

Illustration 1-5
Wire for Balanced Cables

Most wire for balanced cables has three separate leads twisted together in the center core throughout the length of the cable. Two of the leads carry the signal and the third connects to ground. Sometimes there are only two center wires, in which case they are both hot; the sleeve is connected to ground via the braided shield.

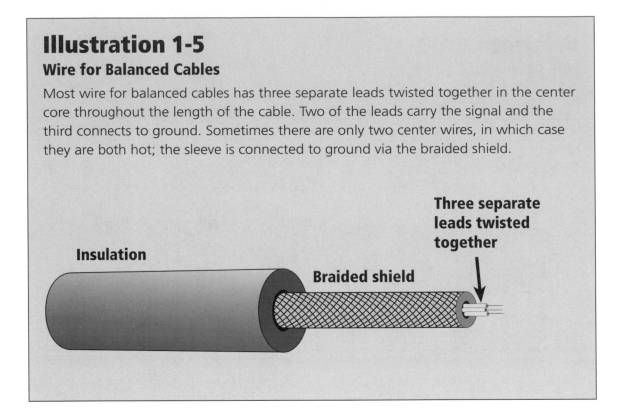

Insulation

Braided shield

Three separate leads twisted together

should, however, strive for a thorough understanding of why we do what we do. This simple explanation of impedance is meant to get you started toward your enlightenment. It is admittedly primary in its depth, but it functions as an excellent point of reference for further technical growth.

Balanced vs. Unbalanced

For the purposes of this course, we'll cover this topic—much like we did with impedance—using simple visual references and non-technical language. Some of the basic differences between balanced and unbalanced wiring schemes are simple, and some of the technical differences are brilliant; let's look at these two types of wiring.

As a point of reference remember this: *Almost all guitars are unbalanced and almost all low-impedance mics are balanced.* If we dissect the cables that connect the guitar to the amp or the mic to the mixer, we'll learn a lot about the concept of balanced and unbalanced wiring.

Basic Terminology

Lead: Another term for wire

Hot lead: In a cable, the wire carrying the desired sound or signal. From a guitar, the hot lead carries the guitar signal from the magnetic pickup on the guitar to the input of the amplifier.

Braided shield: Cables for instruments, mics and outboard gear—pretty much anything other than speaker cable—have one or two wires, or hot leads, carrying the desired signal. Surrounding the hot leads are very thin strands of wire braided into a tube so that electrostatic noises and interferences can be diffused, absorbed and rejected. This braided tube that surrounds the hot leads is called the *shield*.

Unbalanced Guitar Cables

Normal guitar and keyboard cables, also called line cables, contain one hot lead to carry the instrument signal. That hot lead is surrounded by a braided wire shield. The purpose of the shield is to diffuse, absorb and reject electro-

static noises and interference (Illustration 1-5).

This system works pretty well within its limitations. Radio signals and other interference is kept from reaching the hot lead by the braided shield—as long as the cable is shorter than about 20 feet. Once the cable is longer than 20 feet, there's so much interference bombarding the shield that the hot lead starts to carry the interference along with the musical signal. The long cable is acting as a crude antenna and is picking up plenty of transmissions from multiple transmitters. This fact is true even when we study balanced cables; the main difference is that the

Illustration 1-6
Three-point Connectors

Any three-point connector can be used on balanced cables. As long as there's a place for each of the two hot leads and a ground to connect, the system will work. XLR connectors are the most common, but the 1/4" tip-ring-sleeve plug—like the kind on your stereo headphones—is also common. In commercial studios, a smaller version of the 1/4" stereo plug, called the tiny telephone connector, is also common.

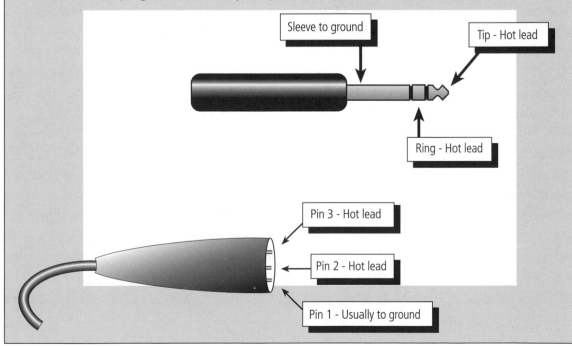

Sleeve to ground

Tip - Hot lead

Ring - Hot lead

Pin 3 - Hot lead

Pin 2 - Hot lead

Pin 1 - Usually to ground

balanced wiring scheme cleverly beats the system by using the system. (Refer to Illustration 1-6 to see the different parts of the connectors used for unbalanced cabling.)

Balanced Cables

Almost all low-impedance mics, as well as some outboard equipment and mixers, use balanced cables. Whereas the length limit of the unbalanced cables is about 25 feet—depending on the position of the moon and the stars—balanced low-impedance cables can be as long as you need (up to 1000 feet or so) without the addition of noise or electrostatic interference *and* without significant degradation of the audio signal. Pretty cool, huh?!

In Volume 1, Chapters 1 and 2 of the *Audio-Pro Home Recording Course*, we talked about phase interaction. We found that if two waveforms are 180° out of phase, they'll electronically cancel each other. It's also true that if two waveforms are exactly in phase, they'll sum, doubling in amplitude. These two theories play key roles in the design of the balanced system.

A cable for a balanced lo Z mic uses three conductors, unlike the unbalanced system that just uses the hot lead and the braided shield. Of these three conductors, two are used as hot leads and the other is connected to ground. Two conductor shielded cables are also very common; the two conductors are the hot leads and the shield is connected to ground.

This is the good part and I'll explain it to you in the simplest illustrative form that I've found. The exact same signal is carried by both hot leads. The only difference is that one lead is carrying a signal from the mic that's 180° out of phase with the other lead. This is very significant; knowing this fact is crucial to the understanding of balanced wiring.

If, at any time, you were to cut the cable and combine those two hot leads, you'd hear absolutely no musical signal from the source since the two hot leads are out of phase; the two sound waves would totally cancel each other. What you would hear would be any noise or electrostatic interference that had been absorbed up to that point. In fact, that noise would be doubled in amplitude from its normal level since both hot leads contain the same interference—completely in phase. The hot leads are twisted evenly throughout the length of the cable intentionally so that they're both subjected to the exact same interference (Illustration 1-7).

Any three-point connector can be used on balanced cables. As long as there's a place for the two hot leads and a ground to connect, the system will work. XLR connectors are the most common connector, but a plug like a 1/4" phone stereo headphone plug with a tip-ring-sleeve configuration is also common. In the larger studios, a smaller version of the stereo phone plug is common: the tiny telephone [TT] connector.

Now let's look at the concept of balanced wiring that lets us use cables of up to 1000 feet in length with no significant signal loss and no interference.

I already mentioned that at the microphone end of the cable, the two hot leads are carrying the signal 180° out of phase so that if the two hot leads were combined anywhere along the cable length, we wouldn't hear any of the desired musical signal. We would, however, hear lots of noise and electrostatic interference.

The completion of the system happens when, at the mixer end of the cable, the phase of one of the hot leads is inverted so that the

Illustration 1-7
Balanced Theory

If the cable were cut anywhere between the connectors and the hot leads were combined, we'd hear no musical signal; we would hear all noise. This is because the hot leads are 180° out of phase coming from the microphone.

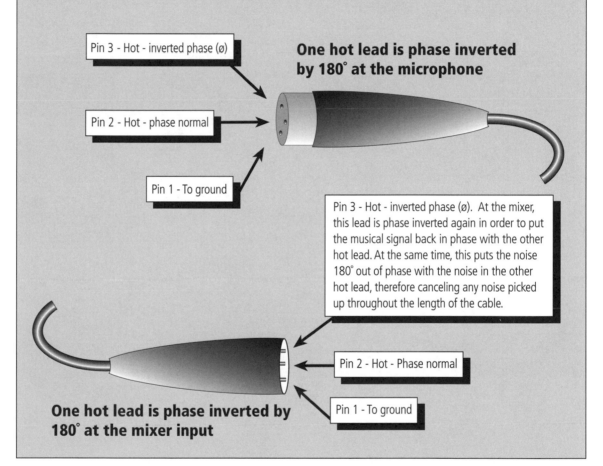

Pin 3 - Hot - inverted phase (ø)

One hot lead is phase inverted by 180° at the microphone

Pin 2 - Hot - phase normal

Pin 1 - To ground

Pin 3 - Hot - inverted phase (ø). At the mixer, this lead is phase inverted again in order to put the musical signal back in phase with the other hot lead. At the same time, this puts the noise 180° out of phase with the noise in the other hot lead, therefore canceling any noise picked up throughout the length of the cable.

Pin 2 - Hot - Phase normal

Pin 1 - To ground

One hot lead is phase inverted by 180° at the mixer input

hot leads are back in phase. Now when they're combined, the signal can be heard, plus there's a doubling in amplitude; this is good.

So, what's the benefit of inverting the phase again at the mixer end of the cable, aside from the fact that the hot leads are back in phase?

Since the noise and interference were absorbed throughout the entire length of the cable—no matter how long the cable—and since the noise is absorbed equally and is in phase on both hot leads, a most interesting thing happens when the phase of one of the hot leads is inverted at the mixer end of the cable. Any noise or interference that was picked up by the cable is totally canceled because one of the hot leads contains noise that's made to be 180° out of phase with the noise in the other hot lead. I love that part!

Conclusion

In summary, the result of balanced wiring is total cancelation of noise and interference, plus a doubling in amplitude compared to the signal in an unbalanced system.

2 Bass Guitar

Bass is an interesting instrument. Its function, in most musical settings, is to give a solid rhythmic and harmonic foundation for the rest of the arrangement. As the engineer, it's your job to get a great bass sound that blends with the rest of the song. It's the bass player's job to play a solid rhythmic part with the correct musical touch. Without both player and engineer working together in any recording situation, things can become difficult.

Electric Bass

Throughout this section I'll refer to certain parts of the electric bass. Refer to Illustration 2-1 for a description of the different parts of this instrument.

A bass player who's unfamiliar with the recording process can cause some problems. Live players usually develop a brutal performance approach to bass. They get used to playing as hard as they can to help themselves feel the beat and to just get into the music. This heavy touch results in a lot of string buzzes and rattles that are usually covered up or forgiven in a live performance. But in recording, the same noises can be both distracting and destructive to an otherwise good song.

A player with a solid but controlled touch can get a great rhythmic feel and a clean sound. Listen to this part. The bassist is playing very

hard and causing buzzes and clacks that will distract from the song.

Audio Example 2-1 Buzzes and Clacks
CD-1: Track 1

Audio Example 2-2 demonstrates the same bass part played in Audio Example 2-1 performed with a controlled touch.

Audio Example 2-2 The Controlled Performance
CD-1: Track 1

As engineers, we don't usually get to pick the bassist for the session, so we need to be capable of getting the best from each situation within the given time restraints.

Offering a couple of politically delicate and emotionally sensitive suggestions can help an inexperienced bassist through a tough situation. If I've learned anything in my years of recording it's that a musician's ego, though often sizable, is usually fragile. It's the "bigger they are, the harder they fall" theory. Be diplomatic and constructive in your suggestions.

I've found that the best way to suggest a change in a musician's approach is to simply play back a take. If you turn the bass track up and the bassist hears a lot of fret buzz and rattle, that says it all. Most of the time, a conscien-

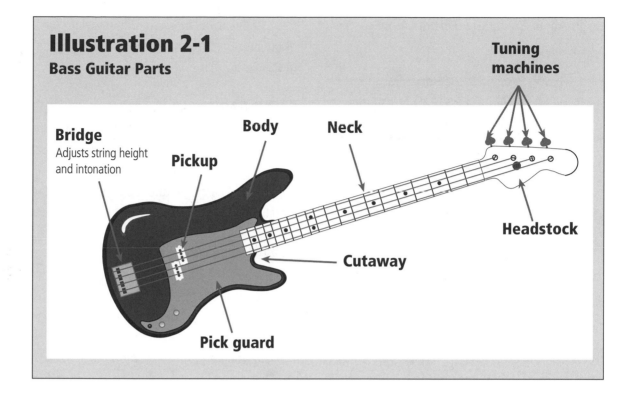

Illustration 2-1
Bass Guitar Parts

Tuning machines

Bridge
Adjusts string height
and intonation

Body

Neck

Pickup

Headstock

Cutaway

Pick guard

tious player will hear and adjust his or her playing technique accordingly. If a suggestion is necessary, having the tape as your reference helps the player instantly understand what you're talking about. As a rule, musicians want to do whatever they can to get a good recording, and they'll almost always do anything within their abilities to accomplish that.

A good player, playing with a solid touch that's completely controlled, makes your job easy. A player who consistently overplays and is out of control makes your job difficult.

Condition of the Bass

If you have any control over the condition of the bass, be sure the strings are in good condition and that the intonation, string height, and pickups are adjusted for the desired sound.

Old, dull sounding strings are rarely good for recording. Some players like old strings for

certain styles, like traditional rock, country or jazz, because they feel that older strings have a smoother sound with less string squeak and rattle. This is true in a certain setting, but most great players that use bass strings for a long time keep the strings very clean and in good condition.

There is a point in the life of any string when it starts to vibrate unevenly throughout its length causing dead spots, or dull sounding notes, and unpredictable intonation at different positions on the neck.

Many players frequently boil their bass strings to clean out the built-up oils and dirt that detract from the clarity of the sound. This can greatly increase the life and clarity of the strings. Audio Example 2-3 demonstrates a bass that I've had around for a while in the closet. It's a good bass with custom pickups and a custom neck and body but old strings. Listen to the bass guitar in Audio Example 2-3 before I boiled the strings.

Audio Example 2-3 Dull Bass Strings
CD-1: Track 2

Listen to Audio Example 2-4 to hear the bass after the strings were removed, boiled and reinstalled. Notice the difference in clarity.

Audio Example 2-4 Boiled Bass Strings
CD-1: Track 2

Poor string height adjustment can cause fret and string buzz, uneven volume from string to string or (if the strings are too high) intonation problems, especially in the higher frets.

Intonation is set by the string length adjustment at the bridge. This is the adjustment that determines the accuracy of the notes at each fret. It is best done by an experienced guitar technician. Inaccurate adjustment of guitar intonation results in an instrument that can be in tune in the open position but out of tune everywhere else on the neck.

If the pickups aren't adjusted properly, the strings might not have even volumes and the sound of the instrument can change drastically. Pickups that are too close to the strings can produce a sound that's muddy or distorted. Pickups that are too far from the strings can produce a signal that's weak or thin-sounding. There's usually a position that gets the right combination of clarity and raw punch for the music.

As the recordist, it's not typically your position to start readjusting these settings on the instrument, but be aware that these are some of the most important factors in finding a great bass sound.

Direct Box/Direct In (DI)

Bass guitar typically sounds best when run directly into the mixer, either through a direct box or plugging directly into line in.

If you're using a direct box, plug into the direct box, then plug the XLR out of the direct box into the mic input of the mixer. See Illustration 2-2 for more about plugging the bass into a direct box. This approach usually produces the best sound and offers the advantageous option of long cable runs from the direct box to the mixer.

In Volume 1 of the *AudioPro Home Recording Course,* you heard examples of both active and passive direct boxes.

To review, a passive direct box simply transforms the high-impedance output into a low-impedance signal suitable for the mic input of the mixer. The bass in Audio Example 2-5 is running through a passive direct box directly into the mic input with no EQ or dynamic processing.

Audio Example 2-5 Bass Through the Passive DI
CD-1: Track 3

An active direct box contains circuitry that, besides matching impedance, enhances the signal. Active direct boxes usually have more high-frequency clarity and more low-end punch. Audio Example 2-6 demonstrates the same bass as the previous example run through an active direct box.

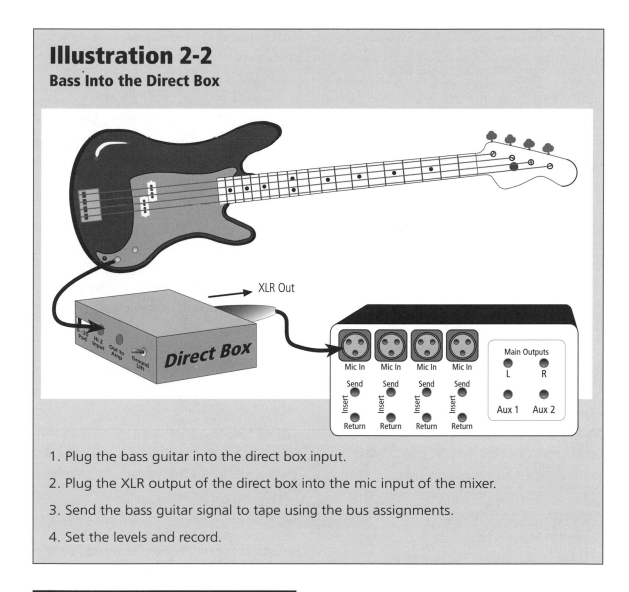

Illustration 2-2
Bass Into the Direct Box

1. Plug the bass guitar into the direct box input.

2. Plug the XLR output of the direct box into the mic input of the mixer.

3. Send the bass guitar signal to tape using the bus assignments.

4. Set the levels and record.

Audio Example 2-6 Bass Through the Active DI
CD-1: Track 3

Refer to Volume 1, Chapter 1 of the *Audio-Pro Home Recording Course,* for a more detailed description of impedance and direct boxes.

The Bass Level

It's almost always best to set the instrument's volume control at maximum. This sends the hottest signal to the board, resulting in a better signal-to-noise ratio.

Many of the newer pickups, especially pickups using active electronics, have very strong output levels. These strong levels can overdrive the circuits of some direct boxes and mixers. If the active bass electronics are overdriving the direct box or mixer inputs, try turning the volume down at the bass until the sound is clean and distortion free.

I've had excellent results plugging basses with active electronics directly into the line input of the mixer, bypassing the direct box. This way, you've eliminated a circuit. Always try to include the least number of circuits in the signal path while still achieving the appropriate musical sound. Fewer circuits in the signal path usually means less noise and less distortion. Many stock instrument pickups produce a weak signal. If your bass produces a low level signal, you might have an insufficient level when plugging into the line input of a mixer that operates at +4dBm. On the other hand, the same bass might work very well when plugged into the line input of a mixer that operates at -10dBV. Each situation is a little different, so you must rely on your ears and an informed decision to guide the way. Know your options and try each of them until you find the sound you're looking for. Start with the method that you expect will work best. As your experience level increases, you'll probably be able to accurately predict the results of several different types of setups. Here are a few rules of thumb I use:

1. If the bass is an early model Fender, Gibson, Ibanez, etc. with stock pickups, use a passive or active direct box and set the instrument volume at maximum.

2. If the bass is a Fender, Gibson, Ibanez, etc. with active electronics, use a direct box and, if necessary, turn the instrument volume down from maximum to keep from overdriving the direct box or the mixer input. Also, try plugging direct from the instrument into the mixer's line input.

3. If the bass has active EMG pickups, plug into line input of the mixer. Also, try plugging the bass into a direct box—but you'll probably need to turn the output of the instrument down.

Instrument Differences

Aside from instrument adjustment, the player's touch and the choice of direct box, choice of instrument is also very important. When you consider that many different manufactures make many different models, it makes sense that the sound difference from one instrument to the next can be so dramatic that even two identical basses made by the same manufacturer can sound different.

Listen to the basses in Audio Examples 2-7 through 2-10 and note the differences in sound quality. Use the chart in Illustration 2-3 to evaluate each instrument's sound. Each bass was plugged into the same mixer input, without EQ, using the same direct box.

Audio Example 2-7 demonstrates a Fender Precision Bass. The Precision Bass, sometimes referred to as the P-Bass, is the all-time most popular bass guitar. It has a good solid low end that provides an excellent foundation for most musical styles. This has become the standard bass sound, and we can use it as a reference for the other sounds.

Audio Example 2-7 Bass 1: The P-Bass
CD-1: Track 4

Audio Example 2-8 demonstrates a very inexpensive bass.

Audio Example 2-8 Bass 2: Inexpensive Bass
CD-1: Track 4

In Audio Example 2-9 you hear a custom built copy of a Precision Bass that uses DiMarzio pickups.

Illustration 2-3
Bass Sound Comparison Chart

	Lows	Mids	Highs	Clarity	Punch	Sustain
Bass 1 Precision Bass Audio Example 1-7						
Bass 2 Inexpensive Bass Audio Example 1-8						
Bass 3 Custom P-Bass with DiMarzio pickups Audio Example 1-9						
Bass 4 Active Electronics Audio Example 1-10						

This is a subjective survey for your own benefit. Rate each instrument from 1 to 10 in each category. "10" is the best or most pleasing; "1" is the worst (annoying, least pleasing or awful). These are the key sound characteristics in most sounds, so practice evaluating other instruments with these same qualities in mind. Once you've rated these bass guitars, you should have a better idea of what you think a *good* bass sound is.

Audio Example 2-9 Bass 3: Custom P-Bass
CD-1: Track 4

The bass in Audio Example 2-10 uses active electronics within the bass itself. Active electronics add punch in the lows and clarity in the highs.

Audio Example 2-10 Bass 4: Active Electronics
CD-1: Track 4

As we study some of these fundamental differences between basses, it's apparent that many of the initial variables can make or break the sound. Recording the bass sound that's right for the song can be tricky. The techniques that we cover will help you out of some tight spots, but your recording life will be much easier if the source is good. Work from the instrument to the tape recorder. Give each point along the signal path detailed attention.

Musical Style

Each style of music has its own appropriate bass sound and playing style. When referring to a player's touch, we're basically indicating the intensity of the right-hand attack. Some players lightly touch the strings, while others pluck with great aggression and fire. Style, in contrast to touch, includes everything about how the notes are plucked or struck, along with how the rhythmic feel is interpreted and the passivity or aggression of the musical performance.

Bass is an instrument that contains many different sounds depending on the style preference of the player. Musicians who play jazz all the time seem to sound just like jazz players when playing jazz. Musicians who play rock all the time seem to fit well stylistically into almost any rock song. Country players sound good playing country music, R&B players sound good playing R&B music, and on and on. We encounter a problem when a player who only knows the idiosyncrasies of one style tries to play another style. It often just doesn't feel right. A player who understands the nuances and correct interpretations of several styles greatly increases his or her value in any musical setting, especially recording. If you analytically listen to many different types of music, you'll be able to discern many of the characteristics that make a particular style correct.

The type of attack used to pluck the bass string plays a very important part in stylist interpretation. Audio Examples 2-11 through 2-15 will help you recognize some of the different ways a bass can be played.

Most parts are played with the first two fingers of the player's right hand. This technique produces a solid low end with good definition in the attack of each note.

Audio Example 2-11 Finger Plucking
CD-1: Track 5

Some players pluck the bass with their thumb only. This usually gives a sound that is fuller in the lows.

Audio Example 2-12 Thumb Plucking
CD-1: Track 5

Some parts are played with a pick. Using a felt pick produces a sound similar to using the fingers but without quite as much low end.

Audio Example 2-13 The Felt Pick
CD-1: Track 5

Using a regular plastic pick produces a sound that has a lot of attack and a clear sound.

Audio Example 2-14 The Plastic Pick
CD-1: Track 5

When playing with a pick, the player might mute the strings slightly with the heel of the right hand, producing a good attack with a tight, solid low note. This is a common sound in country music.

Audio Example 2-15 The Plastic Pick, Muted
CD-1: Track 5

Sometimes when you're recording bass, you'll simply need a sound that's warmer and fuller; other times you might need a sound that's thin with more definition. It's not always possible to bring in different instruments. If you ask the bassist to pluck the strings closer to the bridge, the sound will have less low end and the notes will penetrate through the mix. If the bassist plucks the strings closer to the point where the neck joins the body, the sound will be smooth and warm in the low end, but the definition of each note might decrease.

Asking the bassist to adjust his or her right hand position is a great way to get the raw sound you need for a song. If you need a smooth, sustained, low-end bass sound, you could EQ all day and never get the effect of simply asking the bassist to pick the strings closer to the neck. Or, if you need the bass to cut through the mix a little better, the best solution could be to simply ask the bassist to pluck a little closer to the bridge.

Audio Example 2-16 demonstrates the sound of a bassist plucking back by the bridge. This sound generally works best for punchy rock, fast country, or some R&B songs.

Audio Example 2-16 Plucking by the Bridge
CD-1: Track 6

Audio Example 2-17 demonstrates the sound of a bassist plucking up by the neck. This is generally best for slow ballads that need a full, sustained bass sound to support the rest of the arrangement.

Audio Example 2-17 Plucking by the Neck
CD-1: Track 6

Most bass parts sound best if plucked somewhere between the two extremes demonstrated in Audio Examples 2-16 and 2-17. Being aware of this sound-shaping technique can save you a lot of time and energy. Audio Example 2-18 demonstrates the sound of the same bass as the previous two examples, plucked about halfway between the point where the neck joins the body and the bridge.

Audio Example 2-18
Plucking Between the Neck and the Bridge
CD-1: Track 6

Recording Levels for Bass

Record the bass with the hottest part of the track peaking at about 0VU. If the sound is strong in the low end, it's usually OK to push the bass level to +1 or +2VU. If the bass sound is particularly thin with lots of snaps and pops, record at -1 to -3VU to compensate for the transient attacks.

Mic Techniques

Most of the time the direct sound is best because of its definition and clarity. During mixdown, a direct bass sound is usually hard to beat for defining the low end in a controlled way. Sometimes, especially on harder rock songs, it sounds good to mike the bass cabinet. If a player has a characteristic sound that comes from a unique amplifier setup, miking that setup might be the best way to get the appropriate musical sound to tape.

When miking a bass cabinet, keep the mic close to the speaker cabinet to get a good, tight sound. When the mic is close to the cabinet, you might need to be conservative in adjusting the amp volume. If the amp is too loud, the sound

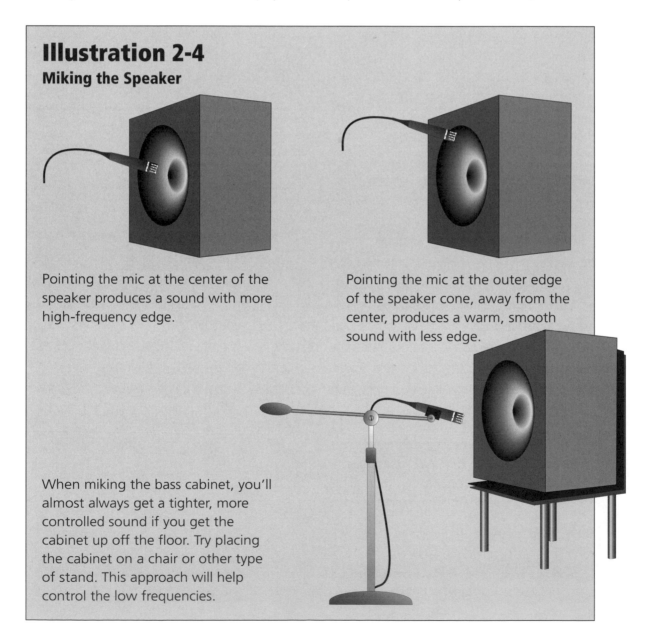

Illustration 2-4
Miking the Speaker

Pointing the mic at the center of the speaker produces a sound with more high-frequency edge.

Pointing the mic at the outer edge of the speaker cone, away from the center, produces a warm, smooth sound with less edge.

When miking the bass cabinet, you'll almost always get a tighter, more controlled sound if you get the cabinet up off the floor. Try placing the cabinet on a chair or other type of stand. This approach will help control the low frequencies.

from the amp could overdrive the mic. Moving-coil mics like the Shure SM57, Sennheiser 421, Electro-Voice RE20 or the AKG D-12E are good for close-miking the bass cabinet and will also handle a lot of volume before they overdrive.

In Volume 1, we found that the guitar sound could really benefit from adding the room ambience to the sound on tape. That's not usually true on the bass. If the bass sound contains too much ambience, the low end of the mix tends to become muddy and unclear. Room ambience isn't usually equal in all frequencies, and your

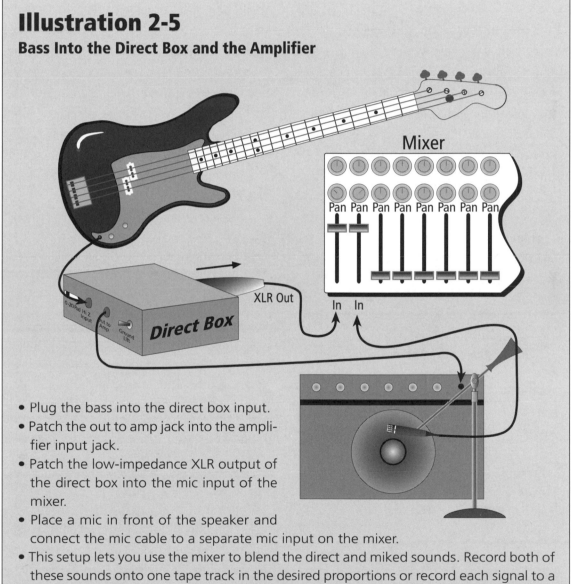

Illustration 2-5
Bass Into the Direct Box and the Amplifier

Mixer

Pan Pan Pan Pan Pan Pan Pan Pan

XLR Out

In   In

0-20 Pad Hi Z Input   Out to Amp   Ground Lift

Direct Box

- Plug the bass into the direct box input.
- Patch the out to amp jack into the amplifier input jack.
- Patch the low-impedance XLR output of the direct box into the mic input of the mixer.
- Place a mic in front of the speaker and connect the mic cable to a separate mic input on the mixer.
- This setup lets you use the mixer to blend the direct and miked sounds. Record both of these sounds onto one tape track in the desired proportions or record each signal to a separate tape track. It's best to record the miked and direct signals to separate tracks if you can spare the tracks. That way you give yourself freedom in the mixdown to blend the sounds in the way that supports the music best.

bass sound can take on a boomy character that's not good for the sound of your mix.

Try to keep the mic within one to three feet of the cabinet. If the cabinet contains multiple speakers that each cover a different frequency range, move the mic back two or three feet from the cabinet to get the full range of the sound.

If the cabinet contains just one speaker or multiple identical speakers, move the mic close to one speaker. Usually one of the speakers sounds better than the others. If so, mike the best sounding speaker. Keep in mind, the center of the speaker has more edge and highs and the outer edge of the speaker produces more warm, smooth lows (Illustration 2-4).

Audio Example 2-19 demonstrates the sound of a bass cabinet with the mic aimed at the center of the speaker from a distance of about one foot. Notice the clarity in the upper midrange.

Audio Example 2-19
Bass Cabinet Miked at the Center
CD-1: Track 7

Audio Example 2-20 uses the same speaker as Audio Example 2-19, miked with the same mic pointed at the outer edge of the speaker. Notice the full sound that comes from miking this part of the speaker.

Audio Example 2-20
Bass Cabinet Miked at the Outer Edge
CD-1: Track 7

When miking a bass cabinet, you'll almost always get a tighter, more controlled sound if you get the cabinet up off the floor. Setting the cabinet on a chair or other type of stand can help control the low end of a miked bass cabinet.

As with guitar, we can combine the direct sound and the miked sound to get the best of both worlds. If we combine the tight, clean sound of the direct signal with the character of the miked signal, we can get a unique sound that adds to the musical feel of the song. It's sometimes possible to pan the direct and the miked sounds apart in the mix, but be careful with this technique. Always check your mix in mono before you commit to panning the two bass tracks apart, and be sure the bass volume sounds balanced between the left and right channels (Illustration 2-5).

Listen to the direct bass sound in Audio Example 2-21.

Audio Example 2-21 The Direct Bass Sound
CD-1: Track 8

Audio Example 2-22 demonstrates the sound of the miked bass speaker.

Audio Example 2-22 The Miked Bass Speaker
CD-1: Track 8

Most of the time you'll keep both the miked and the direct sound panned to center, blending for the sound you want. Listen as I blend the two sounds. You'll hear the direct sound first, then the miked sound. Then I'll pan the two tracks apart for a stereo sound.

Illustration 2-6
Bass Compression - Insert and Line In

You can insert the compressor into the signal path by patching the insert send from the mixer into the input of the compressor, then the output of the compressor to the insert return of the mixer.

It's best to insert the compressor as close to the beginning of the signal path as possible. The best patch point for a compressor is usually just after the mic preamp, as the signal heads to the equalizer.

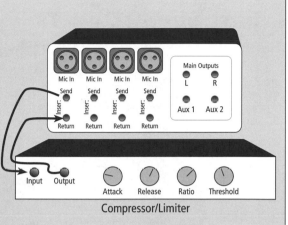

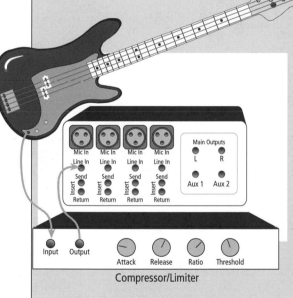

You can also plug the bass directly into the compressor, then plug the compressor into the line input of the mixer. The success of this technique depends on the bass pickups, the sensitivity and impedance of the compressor input and the level compatibility between the compressor output and the mixer's line input. When you use all compatible ingredients, this approach offers good control and a clean-sounding bass track.

Audio Example 2-23
Blending the Direct and Miked Sound
CD-1: Track 8

Compressing the Bass

Bass is usually compressed. There's a big difference in level between notes on many basses. Some notes read very hot on the VU meter and some read very cold. Since the compressor auto-

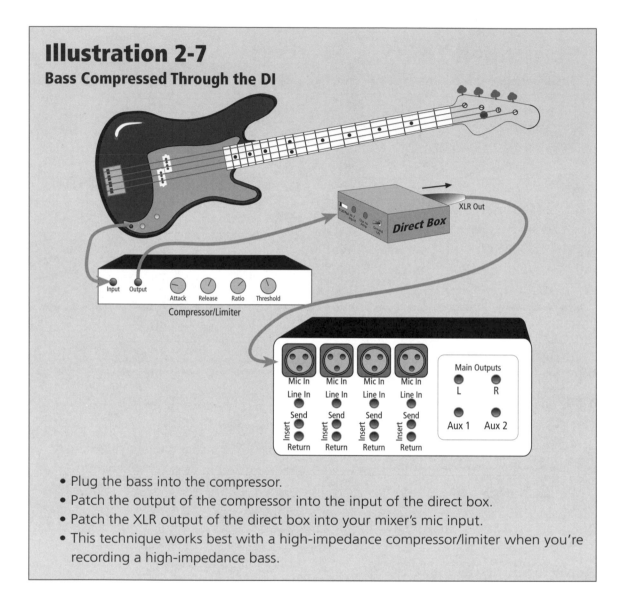

Illustration 2-7
Bass Compressed Through the DI

Direct Box

XLR Out

Input Output   Attack Release Ratio Threshold

Compressor/Limiter

Mic In   Mic In   Mic In   Mic In   Main Outputs
Line In Line In Line In Line In   L   R
Send   Send   Send   Send
Insert   Insert   Insert   Insert   Aux 1   Aux 2
Return   Return   Return   Return

- Plug the bass into the compressor.
- Patch the output of the compressor into the input of the direct box.
- Patch the XLR output of the direct box into your mixer's mic input.
- This technique works best with a high-impedance compressor/limiter when you're recording a high-impedance bass.

matically turns down the signal above the user set threshold, it helps keep the stronger notes under control.

If the bass notes are evened out in volume by the compressor, the bass track stays more constant in the mix and supplies a solid foundation for the song. If the bass is left uncompressed, the bass part can tend to sound especially loud and boomy on certain notes and disappear altogether on others. More consistent levels from note to note typically provide the best founda-

tion for most recordings.

A compressor becomes especially useful if a player snaps a high note or thumps a low note because the level changes can be extreme. Not only does the compressor help control the louder bass sounds, but it also helps the subtleties come through more clearly. If the loud sounds are turned down, the entire track can be boosted to achieve a proper VU reading. As the track is turned up, the softer sounds are turned up, which makes them more audible in the mix. Refer to

Illustration 2-8
Procedures for Compressing the Bass Guitar

1. Set the ratio (typically between 3:1 and 7:1).
2. Set the attack time. The attack time needs to be fast enough to compress the note but not so fast that the attack of the bass note is removed. If the attack time is too fast, the bass will sound dull and lifeless.
3. Set the release time. Start at about .5 seconds. If the release time is too slow, the VCA will never have time to turn the signal back up after compressing. If the release time is too fast, compression might be too obvious, as the VCA reacts to each short sound by turning down and then back up.
4. Adjust the threshold control for the desired amount of gain reduction (typically about 6dB at the strongest part of the track).

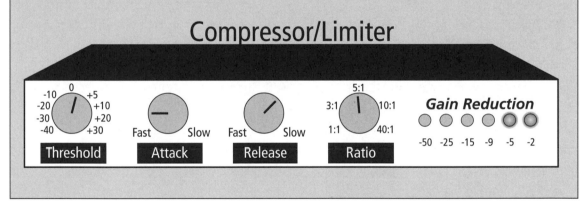

Illustrations 2-6, 2-7 and 2-8 for a detailed description of different setups used to compress bass.

The bass part in Audio Example 2-24 is not compressed. Notice the difference between the loudest and softest sounds.

Audio Example 2-24 Non-compressed Bass
CD-1: Track 9

Audio Example 2-25 uses the same bass used in Audio Example 2-24. This time the bass is compressed with a ratio of 4:1 and gain reduction of up to 6dB. This example peaks at the same level as the previous example, but notice how much more even the notes sound.

Audio Example 2-25 Compressed Bass
CD-1: Track 9

If the bass part is very consistent in level and the player has a good, solid predictable touch, you might not even need compression. I've been able to get some great bass sounds without compression. This only happens when you have a great player with predictable and disciplined technique, a great instrument and the appropriate bass part. Aside from these factors, most bass parts need compression.

If the bass part includes snaps and thumps, consider limiting. With a limiter, most of the notes are left unaffected, but the snaps and thumps are limited. Limiting is the same as compression, but with a ratio above 10:1. See Volume 1, Chapter 2 of the *AudioPro Home Recording Course* for more about compression and limiting.

If the limiter is set correctly, the bass part can be totally unprocessed on everything but a strong thump. The thump might exceed the threshold by 10dB, but if the ratio is 10:1 or higher, the output of the compressor won't show more than a 1dB increase.

Follow this procedure to correctly adjust the limiter:

1. Set the ratio control to about 10:1.
2. Set the attack time to fast.
3. Adjust the threshold so that gain reduction only registers on the snaps and thumps.

The bass part in Audio Example 2-26 isn't limited. Notice how much louder the snaps are than the rest of the notes. Also, note that the normal level is low in order to keep the snaps from oversaturating the tape.

Audio Example 2-26 Snaps Not Limited
CD-1: Track 9

The bass part in Audio Example 2-27 is limited. Notice that now the snaps aren't much louder than the rest of the notes, and the entire part sounds louder because the limiter has squashed the peaks.

Audio Example 2-27 Limited Snaps
CD-1: Track 9

Equalization

Of all the parts of a mix, the low frequencies are the most difficult to deal with, especially at first. If you're listening on large far-field monitors powered by many watts of clean power, it's fun to boost the bass and sub-bass frequencies between 30 and 70Hz. It sounds good and you can physically feel the bass. But this approach presents two primary problems:

1. Most home and car stereos can't reproduce these low frequencies. Your music might sound weak in the low end if it's played on an average system, even though it sounded warm and smooth in the studio.

2. The bass and sub-bass frequencies contain a lot of energy. The low-frequency level can dominate and control the overall mix level. If you've boosted sub-bass frequencies, the VU level of the mix will rise (pretty much in direct proportion to the boost). If your mix is played back on a regular home stereo, these lows will be inaudible. Also, in order to achieve an acceptable listening level, you'll need to turn up the volume. When the volume is turned up, the noise is turned up, so your mix ends up sounding noisy *and* thin in the low end.

Audio Examples 2-28 through 2-30 are all mixes of the identical rhythm track. In Audio Example 2-28, I've boosted 50Hz on the bass guitar by about 6dB.

Audio Example 2-28
Mix With 50Hz Boosted on the Bass Track
CD-1: Track 10

Audio Example 2-29 demonstrates the same mix as Audio Example 2-28 without the boost at 50Hz on the bass track. Both of these mixes peak at the same level on the VU meter, but notice that Audio Example 2-29 seems louder.

Audio Example 2-29
Mix Without 50Hz Boosted on the Bass Track
CD-1: Track 10

Now listen to the two mixes together in Audio Example 2-30. The first eight bars have 50Hz boosted on the bass. The second eight bars have no boost.

Audio Example 2-30
Alternating Between 2-28 and 2-29
CD-1: Track 10

The same results occur if you're just recording the bass track. If you have a question about how much bass frequency to print to the multitrack, print slightly less than you think you might need in the mix. You can always turn lows up in the mix. But if you've recorded to the multitrack with too much sub-bass or bass, the track might be unnaturally noisy because of the artificial levels from the overabundance of inaudible lows.

It's often appropriate to roll off the frequencies below about 40Hz. This can get rid of frequencies that might never be heard but are adding to the overall level of the mix. To add a good low-end foundation to a bass sound, try boosting between 80 and 150Hz. This frequency range will produce a very solid feel, and these frequencies can be heard on almost all systems.

On the bass in Audio Example 2-31, I boost at 80Hz then sweep the boost from 80Hz up to 150Hz.

Audio Example 2-31
Sweeping From 80Hz to 150Hz
CD-1: Track 11

If the bass sounds muddy and thick in the lower mids or upper bass, try cutting at a frequency between 250 and 500Hz. Cutting these frequencies can help a stock P-Bass sound like a bass with active electronics. This is one of the most common requests from bassists. Cutting in this range and running the bass through an active direct box can usually produce the desired effect. In Audio Example 2-32, I'll cut at 250Hz, then sweep the cut from 250 to 500Hz.

Audio Example 2-32
Sweeping the Cut Between 250Hz and 500Hz
CD-1: Track 12

In Audio Example 2-33, I'll boost at 250Hz, then sweep the boost from 250 to 500Hz.

Audio Example 2-33
Sweeping the Boost Between 250Hz and 500Hz
CD-1: Track 13

The frequencies between about 700 and 1200Hz contain the sound of the bass string being plucked, plus harmonics that can help the listener recognize the pitch of the bass notes. In Audio Example 2-34, I boost then cut at 1000Hz.

Illustration 2-9
Panning Time Reference

Panning is often indicated relative to clock settings. If someone says, "Pan the instruments at 9 o'clock and 3 o'clock," they're assuming you'll pan the left side to the 9 o'clock position (straight left) and the right side to the 3 o'clock position (straight right). 10 o'clock and 2 o'clock denote a left/right panning that is less extreme than 9 o'clock and 3 o'clock. 7 o'clock is hard left panning, and 5 o'clock is hard right panning. 12 o'clock is center.

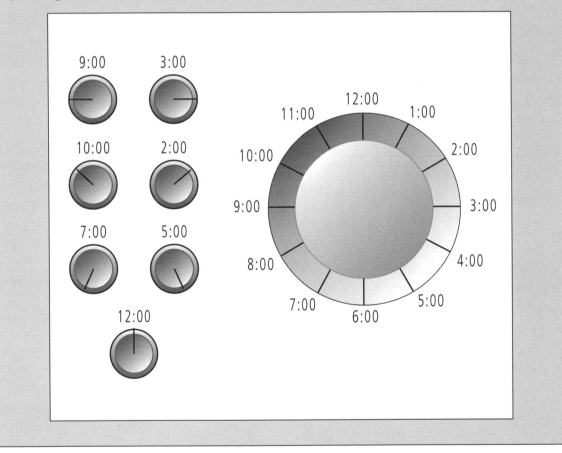

Audio Example 2-34 Boost Then Cut at 1000Hz
CD-1: Track 14

The upper clarity and string noise on a bass usually resides in the frequencies between 2 and 3kHz. Listen to Audio Example 2-35 as I boost at 2kHz, then sweep from 2 to 3 kHz.

Audio Example 2-35
Sweeping the Boost Between 2kHz and 3kHz
CD-1: Track 15

On most bass sounds, the frequencies above 3 or 4kHz don't add much that's usable. Even though the upper frequencies contain important harmonics, they aren't usually boosted because they also contain most of the string and fret noises. The key to getting a great sound is to determine what sound best complements the mix. Always compare the bass sound to the kick drum sound and shape the bass to work with, not against, the kick. If the kick is heavy in one particular low frequency, avoid that frequency on the bass.

Panning

Bass is almost always panned straight down the center of the mix. Bass frequencies are omni-directional, so panning isn't usually very effective from a listening perspective. The upper frequencies of the bass are directional and can indicate placement, but panning the bass track is not good for the stereo level of the mix. If the bass is panned to one side, the mix will read much hotter on that side because of the low-frequency energy in the bass. The bass needs to be centered to distribute the low-frequency energy equally to the left and right sides of the mix and to provide a solid foundation for the rest of the arrangement.

In Audio Example 2-36, I'll pan the bass from left to right, then to 12 o'clock. (When we speak of pan positions, we often indicate pan placements in relation to clock times [Illustration 2-9].) Notice the difference in the sound of the mix. If you're listening on a system that has meters on the playback of this CD, watch the meter change as I pan the bass track.

Audio Example 2-36 Panning the Bass
CD-1: Track 16

Reverb

It's usually best to keep the bass clean and dry. You can set up a bass sound that's incredible by itself with delays, reverb, chorus and even distortion, but as soon as the bass is combined with the drums, guitars and keys, the interest of the bass effects are buried and the bass loses definition and punch. The best approach when recording bass is to keep it simple. I'll give you a couple of tricks that I use to make the bass sound bigger without losing clarity in the mix, but even these should be used sparingly and with caution. If you put effects on the bass, you might end up with a mix that's thin or unpredictable. If you use a clean, simple, dry bass track, you'll have a good foundation for the rest of the arrangement.

Reverb is usually inappropriate for bass. In the context of a rhythm section, there's generally too much going on with the other instruments to be able to appreciate or hear the sound of the reverberation on the bass. Adding reverb to the bass can cause your mix to sound distant or muddy. In the mix in Audio Example 2-37, I'll add reverb to the bass track. Notice the difference in the clarity of the overall sound.

Audio Example 2-37 Adding Reverb to the Bass
CD-1: Track 17

As with other solo instruments, if you're recording a solo bass track, reverb can add rich, full sound. A smooth, rich-sounding hall reverb can add interest to most solo bass sounds. Listen to Audio Example 2-38 as I add hall reverb to the solo bass part.

Illustration 2-10
Splitting the Bass

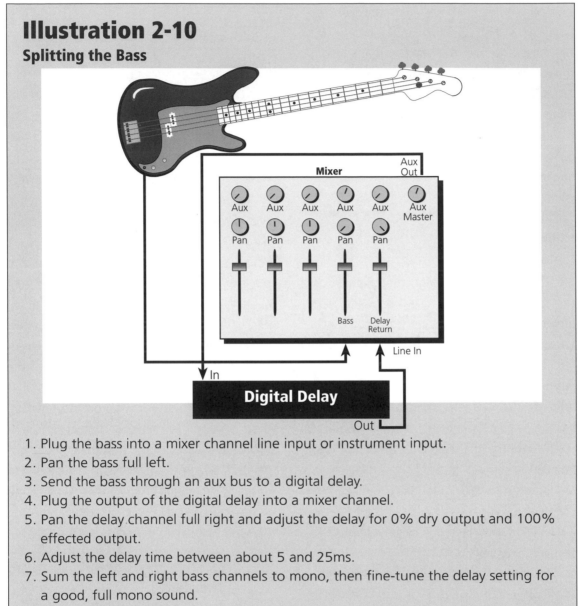

1. Plug the bass into a mixer channel line input or instrument input.
2. Pan the bass full left.
3. Send the bass through an aux bus to a digital delay.
4. Plug the output of the digital delay into a mixer channel.
5. Pan the delay channel full right and adjust the delay for 0% dry output and 100% effected output.
6. Adjust the delay time between about 5 and 25ms.
7. Sum the left and right bass channels to mono, then fine-tune the delay setting for a good, full mono sound.
8. Switch back to stereo.

Audio Example 2-38 Solo Bass With Reverb
CD-1: Track 17

Even though it's best to keep the bass sound simple and clean, here's one technique that works very well, especially on stereo mixes.

Use a digital delay to create a stereo bass sound. First, set up a short delay time, between about 5 and 23ms. Be sure that there's no regeneration. This effect involves panning the original bass to one side, then panning a short delay of the bass to the other side. This creates enough difference in the sound of the left and right channels to make the bass seem to come separately from the left and the right instead of from the center. It sounds stereo! Adjust the levels so that left and right read the same on the VU meter when the bass plays alone. Refer to Illustration 2-10 for a detailed description of how to set up this technique.

Listen to the solo bass track in Audio Example 2-39. It starts with the original bass panned to the center position. Next, the original track pans to the left, then the delay is turned up and panned right.

Audio Example 2-39 The Stereo Bass Sound
CD-1: Track 18

This technique opens up the center of the mix to make room for lead vocals, solos and other instruments that need to occupy that space. The exact delay time is dependent on the sound of the bass track, but it should generally be below about 23ms. If you try this technique, always check the sound in mono *and* stereo. This technique can sound very good in stereo, but when the same part is played back in mono it can sound very bad. The delay of the bass combined with the original bass in mono can result in the canceling and summing of certain frequencies. The delay time determines which frequencies will cancel and sum.

The best way to set up this sound is to listen in mono while you adjust the delay time. Changing the time as little as a fraction of a millisecond can drastically change the sound of the bass in mono, even though the bass still sounds the same in stereo.

Once you have the sound that you need in mono, you can feel confident that this stereo

bass technique will work well for your song. The bass in Audio Example 2-40 starts out stereo. Listen as I combine left and right to mono and then adjust the delay time in one millisecond increments. You can hear how extreme the change can be. Once I've found a sound that's full in mono, I switch back to stereo.

Audio Example 2-40
Adjusting Bass Delay for Mono Compatibility
CD-1: Track 18

This technique can also work well using a chorus, flanger or phase shifter. Pan the original dry bass to one side and the 100 percent wet-effected bass to the other side. These effects are even more important to monitor in mono than the simple delay because the oscillator that varies the delay time can cause the bass to constantly change from very thin to very boomy in mono, even though the sound might be great in stereo. Listen to Audio Example 2-41. The dry bass is panned left and the chorus is panned right. Notice the difference in sound as I switch between stereo and mono.

Audio Example 2-41 The Bass With Chorus
CD-1: Track 19

These bass effects are best left until mixdown. If you don't check the sound in mono, printing a double, chorus, flanger, phase shifter or reverb to the multitrack could result in a great bass part that's not usable in the mix. If at all possible, record a clean and simple bass track to the multitrack.

Synth Bass

When recording a synthesized bass, there's a good chance that the sound is pretty good coming directly out of the keyboard or sound module. If the keyboard has a stereo output, use both left and right if you have enough tracks. The stereo bass sounds on keyboards are usually created in the same way we made the electric bass stereo. A short delay or chorus-type effect is used to widen the stereo image. Using the stereo outputs lets you pan the bass away from the center position while maintaining a full and balanced sound. Audio Example 2-42 demonstrates a stereo bass sound from a sound module. It starts in stereo then switches to mono then switches back. Even though the levels stay the same on the left and right meters, there's a big difference in the sound.

Audio Example 2-42 Stereo Synth Bass
CD-1: Track 20

Using the stereo outs from a keyboard presents the same dangers that we had when we delayed or chorused the electric bass guitar. The bass might sound great in stereo but thin and wimpy in mono. If you really want the stereo bass sound, listen to the bass in mono and adjust the delay settings till the bass sounds good. If you don't have access to the delay settings on your sampled sound and if the bass sound is unacceptable in mono, use one side of the bass sample for a mono sound. You can always create your own stereo bass sound that is mono-compatible using an outboard delay, phase shifter or chorus.

Plugging the Synth Bass In

Most of the time the keyboard outputs work best running directly into the line inputs of the mixer. If you're plugging into the line input of a mixer that operates at -10dBV, you'll almost always have plenty of gain from the keyboard to get sufficient level to tape with the mixer settings at their normal levels. (Refer to Volume 1, Chapter 1 of the *AudioPro Home Recording Course* if you're unfamiliar with the difference between +4dBm and -10dBV.)

If you're plugging into the line input of a mixer that operates at +4dBm, your keyboard or sound module will seem to have a weaker signal. Sometimes you'll barely have enough signal to get sufficient level to tape—even when the input fader, output fader and keyboard volume are at maximum. This will result in more noise being included with your signal. If you're plugging into the line input of a +4dBm mixer and the level from your keyboard is too low, plug the keyboard into a direct box, then plug the XLR output of the direct box into a mic input of the mixer. This'll give you plenty of gain *and* you'll be able to use the mic preamp to optimize the levels at each point of the signal path.

The simplest approach to recording keyboard is simply plugging into the line inputs. If the levels are sufficient, this is usually the purest approach since it includes the least amount of circuitry. Also, it's less expensive since you don't need a direct box for every keyboard or sound module output. Home recording equipment often operates at -10dBV. Professional recording equipment operates at +4dBm. A lot of the newer keyboards have higher output levels, which increases their compatibility with mixers operating at +4dBm. I use a few keyboards regularly that have plenty of output to run into any mixer.

To maintain a better signal-to-noise ratio, always turn the keyboard volume control up as far as possible without overdriving the mixer input. Most of the time you'll be able to set the keyboard at maximum gain.

If you need to use a DI, sometimes the keyboard output will be too hot for the direct box input. There might be a pad on the direct box to help optimize this initial gain setting. It's important that the pad be adjusted properly to maintain a good signal-to-noise ratio without distortion. There might be a one- or two-position pad that will attenuate the input by 10-40dB.

Listen to the keyboard sound without attenuation. If there's distortion, pad the signal with the attenuator on the direct box. If there's still distortion, use more pad (10–20dB of attenuation is usually enough to clean up the sound at this initial gain point).

Miking the Synth Bass

The normal procedure for recording synth bass is plugging direct into the recording console. There's usually enough control over the sound within the keyboard to get the sound you need going direct into the mixer. That's not to say that

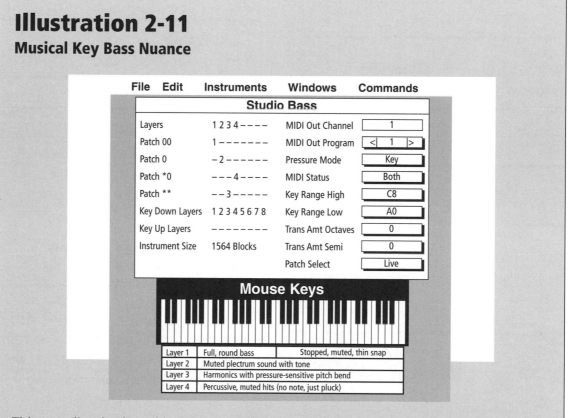

Illustration 2-11
Musical Key Bass Nuance

File	Edit	Instruments	Windows	Commands

Studio Bass

Layers	1 2 3 4 – – – –	MIDI Out Channel	1
Patch 00	1 – – – – – – –	MIDI Out Program	< 1 >
Patch 0	– 2 – – – – – –	Pressure Mode	Key
Patch *0	– – – 4 – – – –	MIDI Status	Both
Patch **	– – 3 – – – – –	Key Range High	C8
Key Down Layers	1 2 3 4 5 6 7 8	Key Range Low	A0
Key Up Layers	– – – – – – – –	Trans Amt Octaves	0
Instrument Size	1564 Blocks	Trans Amt Semi	0
		Patch Select	Live

Mouse Keys

Layer 1	Full, round bass	Stopped, muted, thin snap
Layer 2	Muted plectrum sound with tone	
Layer 3	Harmonics with pressure-sensitive pitch bend	
Layer 4	Percussive, muted hits (no note, just pluck)	

This sampling keyboard has several different types of sounds available at once. Using two buttons by the mod wheel and pitch bend lets you shift the entire keyboard through four different layers. Adding these interesting sounds that a bassist naturally incorporates into a musical part helps the bass part sound very alive and believable.

you shouldn't try miking the bass speaker cabinet if you're in search of a different sound. Some very high quality recordings are made with a synth run into an amplifier, then miked. This approach has the potential of adding acoustic interest to your sounds that differentiate them from the stock sounds coming straight out of the synth. Listen to the differences between Audio Examples 2-43 through 2-45.

Audio Example 2-43 demonstrates a good, solid sampled bass sound recorded directly into the line input of the mixer.

Audio Example 2-43 Synth Bass Direct In
CD-1: Track 21

Audio Example 2-44 demonstrates the same part played into a bass amp and miked with a moving-coil mic from a distance of about two feet.

Audio Example 2-44 Synth Bass Miked
CD-1: Track 21

Notice in Audio Example 2-45 the blending of the direct synth bass sound and the miked synth bass sound.

Audio Example 2-45
Blending Direct and Miked Synth Bass
CD-1: Track 21

Performance of the Synth Bass Part

One very important part of the keyboard bass sound is the musical performance. Nuances char-

acteristic of a real bassist are the foundation of any good bass part. Muted notes, harmonics, string squeaks and snaps are used tastefully by any good bassist. A set of bass samples containing some of these musical sounds can help make your bass parts believable, interesting and authentic. A raw bass sound on its own isn't always enough to create a believable part.

Listen to the sampled bass in Audio Example 2-46. With all of the different bass sounds available at once on the keyboard, a strong, musically supportive bass part can be crafted by any player familiar with bass guitar idiomatics (Illustration 2-11).

Audio Example 2-46 Sampled Bass Nuance
CD-1: Track 22

Now listen to a bass track using these different sounds. Audio Example 2-47 definitely has more interest and spark than it would without the characteristic bass subtleties.

Audio Example 2-47
Using the Sampled Bass Nuance
CD-1: Track 22

Another tool that can help put more interest into your bass parts is a guitar MIDI controller. For a real bass sound, natural bends and slides are a lot easier to achieve with a guitar controller than with a keyboard, especially for a guitarist.

The keyboard bass in Audio Example 2-48 is being played with a guitar MIDI controller.

Audio Example 2-48
Key Bass Played by Guitar MIDI Controller
CD-1: Track 23

Audio Example 2-49 demonstrates a musical part similar to the one in Audio Example 2-48, this time played on the keyboard. Notice the difference in how this track feels.

Audio Example 2-49
Bass Part Played on the Keyboard
CD-1: Track 24

The bass part in Audio Example 2-50 is played on a guitar MIDI controller. Notice how the color added by the guitar-like nuance enhances the feel of the rhythm section.

Audio Example 2-50
Guitar-Controlled Key Bass in a Rhythm Section
CD-1: Track 25

Bass Range and EQ

Using keyboard bass has become such a common technique that the range of acceptable bass sounds has increased greatly. The usable range of the instrument has even been affected. Most musicians in the earlier days of synthesized bass sounds tried to stay within the natural range of a four-string bass. It was thought that using any notes below low E on the bass guitar would result in a part that wasn't believable or natural-sounding.

It didn't take too long to break that barrier because the full, rich sound of the low synthesized bass notes sounded *and* felt good. Now it's not uncommon to hear a bass part that goes as low as the C or even the B below low E on a four-string bass guitar. In fact, five-string and six-string bass guitars have become commonplace as real bass players try to match the full sound of the synthesized bass.

When recording these low bass notes, always listen to the bass parts on small speakers before you commit to any EQ settings. On large, far-field monitors, the low bass notes can sound great. They might be warm and full on the big speakers if you boost the bass or sub-bass, but when the mix is played back on a boom box the bass part could be inaudible. A small stereo might not even reproduce frequencies below 100Hz or so. If you've recorded a part with lots of low notes and boosted the very low frequencies, you'll be dissatisfied with the sound you hear from a small set of speakers.

Consider that low E, the lowest note on a four-string bass guitar, has a frequency of 41.20Hz. If you're using bass notes lower than low E, it becomes increasingly important to EQ for smaller speakers. The fundamental frequencies of the common notes below E are 36.71Hz for low D and 32.7Hz for low C. The only way to make these notes discernible on small systems is to boost the harmonics rather than the fundamental frequencies. The way to get a fuller sound from that note *and* be assured that the note will be heard on any setup is to boost a harmonic of that note. If you boost 30–40Hz, you'll be raising the overall level of the mix with a frequency that won't be heard on most systems, but if you boost a harmonic the note will sound stronger on more systems. The first harmonic above 40Hz (low E) is 80Hz, so boosting between 60 and 80Hz is a good choice for a song that contains a lot of lower bass notes.

The notes in the bass part in Audio Example 2-51 go down to low C. I've boosted a one-octave-wide band centered at 40Hz, essentially boosting fundamental frequencies between about 30 and 60Hz. This sounds very warm and powerful on the far-field monitors in my studio, but it is less than impressive on most systems.

Audio Example 2-51 Bass Boosted at 40Hz
CD-1: Track 26

In Audio Example 2-52, I've equalized the bass to sound good on smaller speakers by boosting at 80Hz rather than 40Hz. The bass still sounds good on larger monitors and also sounds good on smaller near-field monitors.

Audio Example 2-52 Bass Boosted at 80Hz
CD-1: Track 26

In Audio Example 2-53, I've boosted at 160Hz. This helps the part come alive more on small speakers, but we're losing a little punch on the large far-field monitors.

Audio Example 2-53 Bass Boosted at 160Hz
CD-1: Track 26

Now listen to the previous three examples in a row. You'll hear eight bars with 40Hz boosted, eight bars with 80Hz boosted, then eight bars with 160Hz boosted. Play these examples on a few different systems to hear the real difference.

Audio Example 2-54
The Previous Three Audio Examples
CD-1: Track 26

Compressing the Synth Bass

Low notes from a keyboard are almost always pretty even in output, so compressing the synth bass part isn't common. Using the compressor to accentuate the attack of a note might be a good plan if it weren't for the fact that the envelope of the sound is usually controllable within the keyboard. If you need more attack from a note, the place to get it is from the keyboard. Even sampled bass sounds are typically pretty even in volume and compressing isn't needed.

Recording Level for the Synth Bass

Recording level for the synth bass depends on the tonal character of the sound. For most full but not boomy bass sounds, the VU meter can read up to +1 or +2VU at the hottest part of the track. If the sound is thin in the low end with lots of attack, recording levels should be more conservative, around -3VU.

Audio Example 2-55 demonstrates a bass sound that can be recorded at 0VU.

Audio Example 2-55
Bass Sound Recorded at 0VU
CD-1: Track 27

Audio Example 2-56 demonstrates a bass sound that should be recorded at about -3VU.

Audio Example 2-56
Bass Sound Recorded at -3VU
CD-1: Track 27

Panning Synth Bass

Keyboard bass, like the electric bass, should be panned to the center in order to distribute the low-frequency information evenly between the left and right channels. If the keyboard has stereo outputs, it's usually okay to pan the bass hard right and hard left, but always be sure to

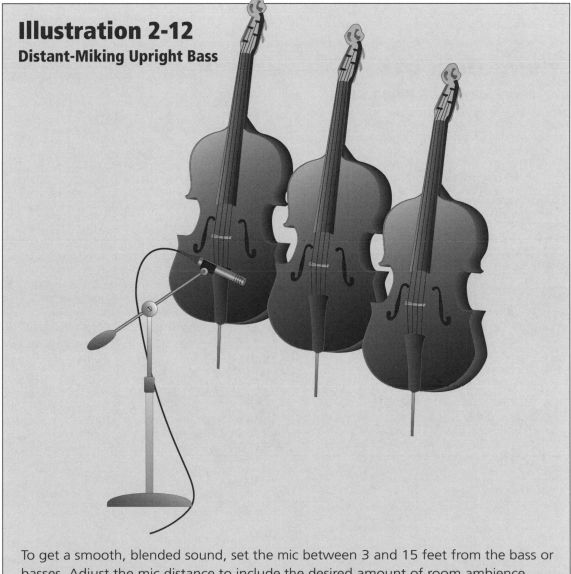

Illustration 2-12
Distant-Miking Upright Bass

To get a smooth, blended sound, set the mic between 3 and 15 feet from the bass or basses. Adjust the mic distance to include the desired amount of room ambience. This technique is good for an orchestral sound but isn't typical for a jazz or pop rhythm section sound.

check the bass sound in mono. Most stereo synth bass sounds work well in stereo and mono, but never assume; always check.

When tracks are panned hard left and right, they'll often be easy to hear in a stereo mix but will get buried in a mono mix. This is especially true if there aren't other instruments hard-panned. As we get more into mixing, we'll see that giving an instrument its own space in a stereo mix will isolate that instrument and help it to be easily heard.

If your bass track is very audible in stereo but buried in mono, try soft panning the stereo bass. Listen to the stereo key bass sound in Audio Example 2-57. First it's hard-panned apart, then you'll hear it summed to mono. Notice how the level of the bass seems to change when I switch to mono.

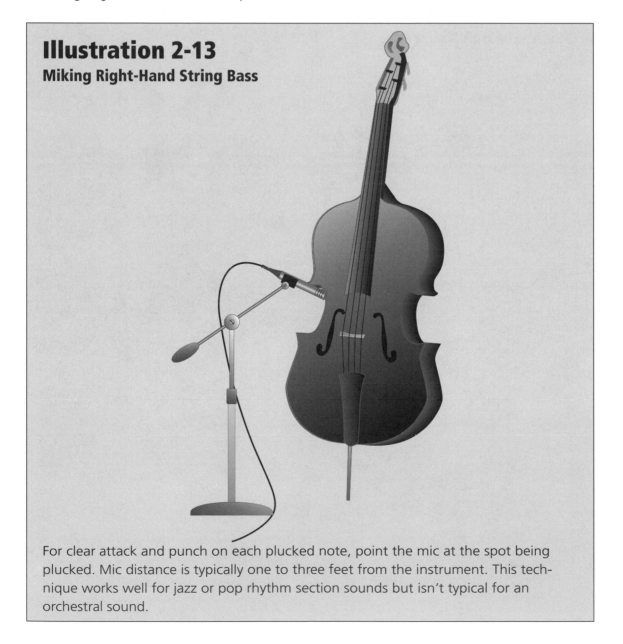

Illustration 2-13
Miking Right-Hand String Bass

For clear attack and punch on each plucked note, point the mic at the spot being plucked. Mic distance is typically one to three feet from the instrument. This technique works well for jazz or pop rhythm section sounds but isn't typical for an orchestral sound.

Audio Example 2-57
Switching Between Stereo and Mono
CD-1: Track 28

Audio Example 2-58 demonstrates the same bass sound used in Audio Example 2-57, this time panned to about 9:00 and 3:00. Notice that the bass still sounds stereo, but when I switch to mono the apparent volume of the bass stays more constant than the previous example.

Audio Example 2-58
Bass Panned at 9:00 and 3:00
CD-1: Track 29

Effects and the Synth Bass

Approach reverberation on key bass the same way you approach electric bass. Reverb isn't usually appropriate except on flowing ballads where you need the bass to blend into a smooth pad.

The same delay and chorus techniques that work well on the electric bass sound good on key bass. In fact, most of the stock stereo key bass sounds from the manufacturer use these techniques. Again, check the sounds in mono before you commit them to tape.

Acoustic Bass

The acoustic bass, also called the stand-up bass, string bass or (more traditionally) the double bass, is an instrument that's uncommon in most commercial, pop, country and rock recording situations. Unless you're regularly recording sym-

phony orchestras or full-blown film scores, you don't encounter acoustic bass very often.

In addition to symphonic settings, string bass will sometimes show up in a jazz group, either small ensemble or big band. Occasionally the bassist in a '50s rock and roll band will use stand-up to give the band a different edge and drive, but it's generally a novelty in commercial rock.

There are two approaches for recording this instrument, symphonic and pop, including rock, jazz, country, blues, etc. When recording string bass for a traditional symphonic setting, the key considerations are:

1. The ambience
2. Blending between basses if there's more than one
3. Blending with the rest of the string section
4. Blending with the rest of the orchestra
5. Separation

Essentially, we're looking for a bass sound that's smooth, blended and supportive of the rest of the orchestra. If the strings are plucked (pizzicato), we're looking for a smooth, blending sound. If the bass is being played with a bow (arco), we're trying to capture the smooth, supportive sound of the bass, not the scraping sound of the bow pulling across the strings.

First of all, find a good sounding hall or room. If you're recording a symphony, you're probably already in a pretty sizable studio or concert hall, but if you have an option, find the best sounding room to record in. Orchestras have been known to go to great extremes to record in just the right concert hall for a particular piece of music.

In any recording situation where the goal is to capture the instrument and the room sound, mic placement is a critical factor. Use a con-

Illustration 2-14
Mic at the F Hole

For more lows and low mids, point the mic at the f hole from a distance of between one and three feet. This technique works well for a jazz or pop rhythm section sound but isn't typical for an orchestral sound. However, if you have a bad sounding room and a good sounding reverb, you can usually simulate an orchestral sound by adding a little hall or chamber reverb to the sound you get when miking the f hole.

denser mic with flat frequency response and place it in the spot that gives you the balance that you need between the instrument and the ambience. The distance from the sound source will usually be between about three feet and fifteen feet (Illustration 2-12).

The determining factor in mic placement is the room. Sound will react differently in different sized rooms, different shaped rooms and rooms constructed with hard or soft materials. Trust your ears to help you find the sound you

need. If the mic is too close to the bass, the sound won't blend with an orchestral texture. Pizzicato will feel too close and arco will have too much of a grind.

If you cannot record in a room that sounds good naturally, try adding hall reverb to the bass sound. This reverberation should blend the sound with the rest of the mix and give the bass a warm, smooth sound.

When you're recording a string bass for a commercial rock, pop or jazz song, the key considerations are:

1. Capturing a close, tight sound
2. Capturing good punch from each note
3. Capturing good attack to each plucked note
4. Capturing a sound that fits with and complements the rest of the rhythm section

Miking the string bass with these goals in mind demands an entirely different approach than miking the string bass for an orchestral setting.

Close-Miking the String Bass

It's best to use a condenser mic with a good full range. Mike the bass from a distance of one to three feet, depending on just how close you want the sound to be. If you place the mic so it's pointing at the area where the strings are plucked, the sound will be tighter and each note will have more attack (Illustration 2-13).

If you place the mic so that it's pointing at the f hole, the sound will be fuller in the lows and low mids, but the attack might not be as clear (Illustration 2-14).

For a natural orchestral sound, it's best to avoid compression on string bass. Sometimes on pop styles, if the bassist is inconsistent in his or her playing attack, it's necessary to compress the upright bass in the same way you do the electric bass. This helps keep the part even in level and supportive, both harmonically and rhythmically.

Equalization of acoustic bass should be applied to compensate for any booming frequencies that might be present as a result of the instrument's individual character.

Conclusion

We've covered a lot of very useful points that'll help you get more out of your bass parts. Each instrument and player is unique, so the variables are always a factor. In recording, all we can do is build a bag of tricks to draw from. The more you learn, the more accurately you'll be able to guess the outcome of each different recording situation.

3 Harmonics/Overtones/Partials

Harmonics, Overtones and Partials

Harmonics are the parts of the instrument sound that add unique character. Without the harmonic content, each instrument would pretty much sound the same, like a simple sine wave. The only real difference would be in the characteristic attack, decay, sustain and release of the individual instrument.

Since harmonics and overtones are so important to sonic character (vocal or instrumental), it's important to understand some basics about harmonics. As your experience level increases, this understanding will help you grasp many other aspects of music and recording.

When you hear middle C on a piano, you're hearing many different notes simultaneously that together form the sound of a piano. These different notes are called harmonics. Harmonics and overtones are a result of, among other considerations, vibration of the instrument; size of the instrument; acoustics; the type of material the instrument is made of; the vibration of the string, membrane, reed, etc. Several factors add to the harmonic content, but it's a law of physics that harmonics combine with the fundamental wave to make a unique sound that is represented by one waveform. That waveform is a result of the combination of energies included in the *fundamental* frequency and all of the harmonics.

The fundamental is the wave that defines the pitch of the sound wave.

The frequencies of the harmonics are simple to calculate. Harmonics are whole number multiples of the fundamental frequency. In other words, if the fundamental has a frequency of 220Hz (A below middle C), calculate the harmonics by multiplying 220 by 1, 2, 3, 4, 5, 6 and so on.

- 220 x 1 = the fundamental, the frequency that gives the note its name, the first harmonic
- 220 x 2 = 440Hz, the second harmonic
- 220 x 3 = 660Hz, the third harmonic
- 220 x 4 = 880Hz, the fourth harmonic
- 220 x 5 = 1100Hz, the fifth harmonic
- 220 x 6 = 1320Hz, the sixth harmonic

It's traditional to primarily consider the sonic implications of the harmonics up to about 20kHz, since that is the typical limitation of our ears and equipment. There is a controversy regarding the importance of the upper harmonics above 20kHz. Engineers involved in archiving music and sounds for future reference carry on spirited debates about this. High quality archival of important recordings is a big topic in the digital realm. Although digital storage seems very well suited to archiving because of its durability and long-lasting construction, the fact that CD quality audio (at 44.1kHz sample rate) cuts off all frequencies above 20kHz sheds a questionable light on its long-term viability for important audio archiving. Digital sample rates of 100kHz or higher make more sense when considering the future of audio storage.

As the harmonics combine with the fundamental, summing and canceling occurs between the fundamental and its harmonics. This summing and canceling interaction is what shapes a new and different sounding waveform each time a new harmonic is added (Illustration 3-1).

Illustration 3-1
Harmonic Interactions

This is the fundamental sine wave. Its frequency determines the note name and pitch for the waveform that's built from it.

This is the second harmonic in relation to the fundamental above. Its frequency is two times the fundamental, so it completes its cycle twice in the same time period that the fundamental completes one cycle.

This is the result of combining the fundamental and the second harmonic. This new waveform has its own unique wave shape and sound. When waves combine, our ears no longer detect separate sound waves, they merely react to the one new wave that is influenced by all simultaneously occurring sounds.

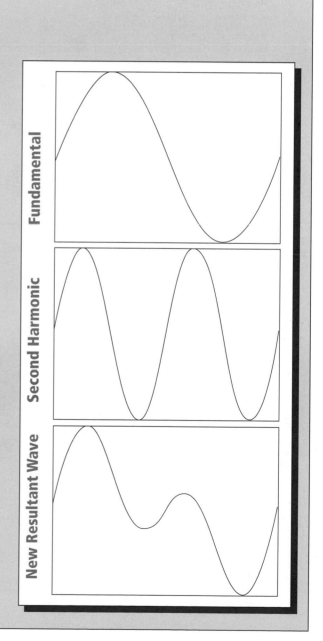

Fundamental

Second Harmonic

New Resultant Wave

Illustration 3-2
Wave Shapes

This is the third harmonic of the sine wave in Illustration 3-1. Notice that each harmonic is also a sine wave, but when they're combined with the fundamental and the other harmonics, an entirely new and unique waveform is created.

This is a sawtooth waveform. It's created by combining all harmonics in proper proportion. The sawtooth and triangle waveforms have a bright, edgy sound. Waveforms are given descriptive names based on the shape of their sound wave.

This is a square wave. It's created by combining the odd harmonics (1, 3, 5, 7, 9, etc.) in the proper proportion. A square wave sounds much like a clarinet.

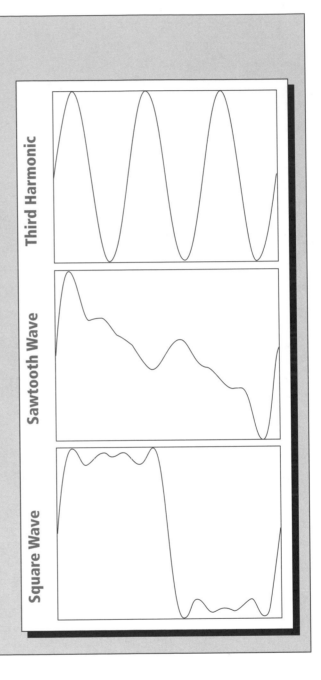

The Difference Between Harmonics, Overtones and Partials

The terms harmonic and *overtone* are often used synonymously, but there is a difference. Whereas the harmonics are always calculated mathematically, as whole number multiples of the fundamental, overtones are referenced to intervals and don't always precisely fit the harmonic formula. In the case of the piano, for example, the overtones are very close to the mathematical harmonics, but some are slightly off.

Some percussion sounds contain a relative of harmonics and overtones called *partials*. Like overtones, partials aren't mathematically

Illustration 3-3
The Piano Waveform

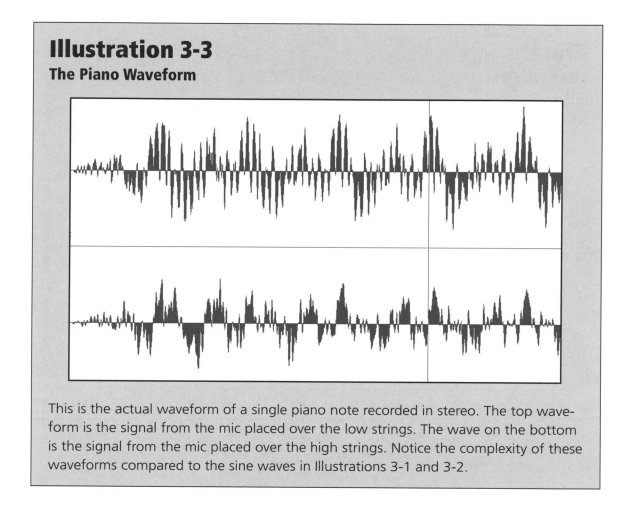

This is the actual waveform of a single piano note recorded in stereo. The top waveform is the signal from the mic placed over the low strings. The wave on the bottom is the signal from the mic placed over the high strings. Notice the complexity of these waveforms compared to the sine waves in Illustrations 3-1 and 3-2.

related to the fundamental in the same simple formula as harmonics, and the effect that these sounds have can be very dramatic and interesting. Some bell-type sounds contain partials that are very far removed from the true harmonics (sometimes they even sound out of tune), but the overall sound still has a defined pitch with a unique tonal character. Partials can also be below the fundamental, whereas harmonics and overtones are considered to be above the fundamental. On bells, there's generally a strong partial at about half the frequency of the fundamental called the hum tone.

These harmonics, overtones and partials can occur far beyond the high-frequency limita-

tions of our ears. When we hear the lowest piano note, we're really hearing the fundamental plus several harmonics working together to complete the piano sound. If we only consider that the piano contains fundamental pitches from 27.50 to 4186.01Hz, it might not seem important to have a microphone that hears above 4186.01Hz. However, if we understand that for each fundamental there are several harmonics, overtones or partials sounding simultaneously that go up to or above 20kHz, we realize the importance of using equipment (mics, mixers, effects and recorders) that accurately reproduces all of the frequencies in and/or above our hearing range. Also, if we see that the combination

Illustration 3-4
The Sine Waveform vs. the Piano Waveform

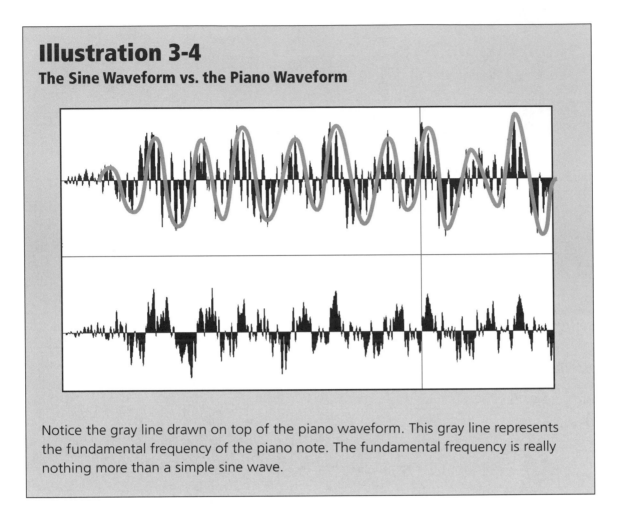

Notice the gray line drawn on top of the piano waveform. This gray line represents the fundamental frequency of the piano note. The fundamental frequency is really nothing more than a simple sine wave.

of these fundamentals and overtones is what shapes the individual waveform, it becomes evident that if we want to accurately record a particular waveform, we should use a microphone that hears all frequencies equally. If the mic adds to or subtracts from the frequency content of a sound, then the mic is really changing the shape of the waveform.

There are some traditional wave shapes that we refer to when describing sounds. Sine, sawtooth, square and triangle waves each have distinct characteristic sounds (Illustration 3-2). The sine wave has the simplest shape. The fundamental is a sine wave, and each of the harmonics and overtones are also sine waves. It's

important to realize that when we hear the fundamental and its harmonics, overtones or partials, we don't hear any of the individual sine waves. Instead, we hear the result of the combination of all waves as one unique and distinct waveform.

Sawtooth, square and triangle waves get their names from the overall shape of their unique wave. Sawtooth and triangle waves are edgy sounding and have more of a brass and bright string-type sound. A square wave sounds like a clarinet.

The complexity of the piano waveform in Illustration 3-3 is the result of a rich harmonic content. Piano is an instrument full of interesting harmonics. Listen carefully to a low note on the piano and notice the complexity of the sound of a single note. If you listen closely, you can isolate and hear several pitches occurring with the fundamental. We perceive the harmonic content, along with the fundamental, as one sound. In actuality the single piano note is constructed of many sine waves combining to give the impression of a single note with a unique timbre.

Illustration 3-4 has the fundamental wave drawn on top of the piano sound wave. This fundamental wave is very simple, yet the sound of the piano is very complex.

Conclusion

If you understand the theory of harmonics, you're well on your way to understanding the theory of sound. You'll also approach music and sound with a little more respect, finesse and insight.

4 Vocals

Recording Vocals

This chapter demonstrates some proven techniques for recording vocals and gives you pointers on getting good, commercially competitive lead and backing vocal sounds.

The art of vocal recording is very involved. It's amazing how sensitive, both mentally and physically, the vocal instrument is. Singing is an interesting blend of technical ability, physical talent and emotional interpretation. There must be a good balance between these factors. The same singer with the same ability can perform in totally different ways depending on the recording environment, the mood we create during the session, the singer's physical and emotional well-being, the mix we set up in the headphones and the kind of vocal sound he or she hears while recording. Awareness and understanding of these factors will help you bring out the best in the singers you record.

Vocals are the focal point of almost all commercial songs. If the vocals sound good, the song will probably sound good. If they sound bad, the song will probably sound bad. The vocal tracks typically contain the most apparent emotional content and impact of the song. Most listeners focus on the vocals first (consciously at least).

The vocal tracks must capture the appropriate emotional and musical feel for the song. For most styles, it's important that they're understandable and in tune and that the lyrics are sung in a way that gives the song meaning. Conveying the meaning of the lyrics usually takes precedence over other factors. Small flaws in technical presentation can be justified by an authentic, emotional, heartfelt performance.

Vocal recording techniques are very subjective. Approach the audio examples in this chapter with that fact in mind. Some of these techniques will jump out at you and you'll easily hear a difference between the before and after. Other examples will be more subtle and you'll need to replay the CD and really focus on the sounds. If you can't hear the difference on a technique that I've presented, try harder. Make a list of everything you hear in each sound, then compare lists. Include the subjective *feeling* each example evokes. Note the high-, mid-, and low-frequency content. Describe the sounds with words like thick, thin, meaty or chunky. Try to hear everything that you can about these sounds. Listen on different systems, at different listening levels and on a good set of headphones.

Some of the scenarios I've set up, like the wind screen comparisons, are very subtle. Whether or not you use a foam wind screen or nylon stocking on an embroidery hoop isn't going to make or break your recording, but attending to this kind of subtle detail throughout the recording process will make a very big difference in the sound of your recordings. I repeat: Listen closely!

Let's start by looking at some techniques that'll help you record a good sound. Commit this information to memory and practice the techniques until they're practically instinctive. Concentrate on recording an excellent vocal *take* rather than simply an excellent vocal sound. An excellent take includes style, emotion, inspiration *and* a good sound. A good sound by itself doesn't do much to make a song appeal to anyone.

Mic Techniques

Placement

Placement of the microphone in relation to the singer is a key variable. Not only does it matter where the mic is, but the best placement changes depending on the type of mic you're using, the vocal timbre, musical style and personal taste.

Condenser microphones are usually the first choice for studio vocal applications. Commercial vocal sounds vary, but most professionally recorded hit vocals are recorded with a good

Illustration 4-1
Vocal Acoustic Interaction

The singer's voice not only reaches the mic through a direct path—it also reflects off the surrounding surfaces. This illustration shows a few of the possible reflections of the walls at each end of the room, floor and ceiling. Even though the sound waves lose energy with each reflection, it's amazing how much they influence vocal sound quality and timbre.

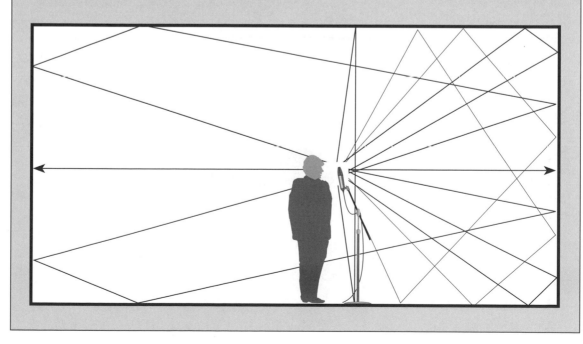

condenser mic set on cardioid pickup pattern, from a distance of 6 to 12 inches. A vocal that's recorded at this distance sounds full and warm on most condenser mics. Recording at this proximity provides the recordist with the option of including the inherent sound of the acoustical environment in varying degrees. Most lead vocals blend better in the mix when recorded with the microphone about a foot or so from the vocalist. Close-mike technique (from a distance of one to three inches) typically provides a sound that is a little too thick and cumbersome, especially when using a condenser mic.

If you're using a moving-coil mic, vocals sound thin and tinny from distances greater than six to eight inches. If you only have a moving-coil mic, you'll get the best results when close-miking solo vocals. When miking group vocals with a moving-coil mic, some fairly extreme addition of low-end EQ or subtraction of the appropriate high-frequency might be necessary to fill out the sound.

Distance

Let's look closer at what's happening with the vocal sound as we mike at one distance or another.

With any instrument, including vocals, the sound of the instrument or voice reflecting off the walls and other hard surfaces can be either

Illustration 4-2
Side Wall Reflections

The vocal sound reflects off each surface in the room. The side walls often play an important role in the combination between direct and reflected sound. Not only does the sound combine at the mic in a varying phase relationship as it reflects off the walls, but reflections off any hard surface in the room influence the recorded vocal sound.

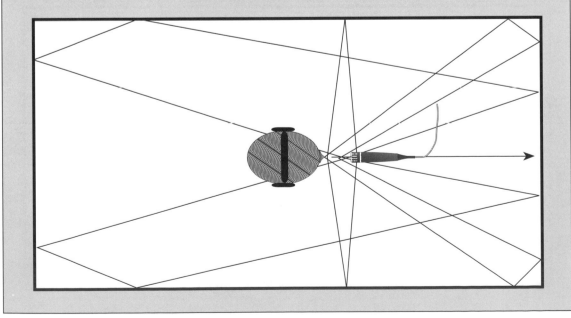

Illustration 4-3
Combinations of Reflections

Each reflection combines with the original sound wave, resulting in a completely new sound wave. The summing and canceling process that occurs when sound waves combine becomes very complex when all the possible reflections are considered.

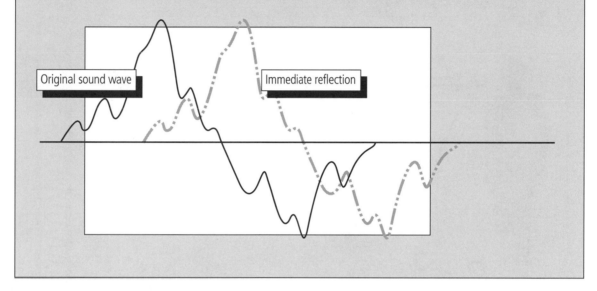

Original sound wave

Immediate reflection

very beneficial or very harmful to the recorded sound. See Illustrations 4-1, 4-2 and 4-3 for graphic examples of what happens with a single vocalist in a room.

The vocalist's sound reaches the mic very quickly as it comes from the singer's mouth. When the sound travels from the mouth, reflects off a room surface, then comes back to the mic, the reflection arrives at the mic in phase or (in varying degrees) out of phase. We've already seen some of the results of undesirable phase interaction in previous chapters, and it's important to understand that any time you use a microphone to record a track there is phase interaction between the direct and reflected sound. This phase interaction is the reason that a room adds its own signature to a sound.

Let's simplify in order to make it easier to

understand. In Audio Example 4-1, I'll hand-hold a mic and walk slowly toward a hard surface (Illustration 4-4).

Audio Example 4-1 Immediate Reflections
CD-1: Track 30

Imagine how complex this scenario becomes when the direct sound combines with every reflection in a room.

Small Room vs. Large Room

If the reflections change the sound quality at the microphone, then we should also realize that, since the size and shape of the room determine the reflections, a singer can sound different when recorded in different rooms. Listen to

Illustration 4-4
The Single Reflection

The sound of the direct voice and the single reflection combine to create a different vocal texture. Moving closer to, or farther from, a hard surface like a wall can affect the sound quality dramatically.

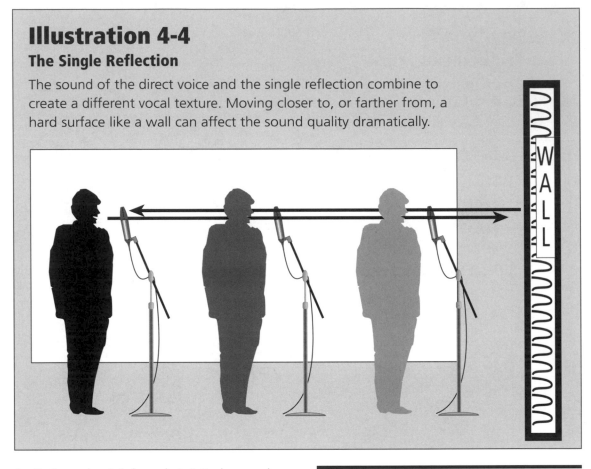

Audio Examples 4-2 through 4-4. Each example demonstrates the effect of different rooms on my vocal sound. On each example, I'm holding the microphone about one foot from my mouth. Aside from the sound change, listen to the difference in natural room ambience. By room ambience I mean the sounds that just happen to be in the particular acoustical environment. Contributors to the ambient sound are things like furnaces, automobile sounds, office equipment, aircraft noise overhead or electrical appliance noise.

Audio Example 4-2 Voice in Medium-sized Room
CD-1: Track 31

Audio Example 4-3 Voice in Small Coat Closet
CD-1: Track 31

Audio Example 4-4 Voice in Large Room
CD-1: Track 31

Based on the previous audio examples, it's clear that the room and mic distance play an important part in the sound of the vocal. We need a good set of rules about recording vocals to help provide a starting point for our choice of recording technique. Don't feel bound by these rules—many great vocal sounds have been recorded by using techniques that break the rules—but use them as a foundation for your

choices. Let's consider mics in two categories:
1. Moving-coil and ribbon
2. Condenser

Moving-Coil/Ribbon

Moving-coil and ribbon mics are almost always designed for close-miking applications and don't typically provide a full sound when the singer is more than six to eight inches from the mic. To get a full, natural sound from these mics, it's best to record the singer from a distance of two to six inches. Moving-coil mics and ribbon mics are the standard choice for live sound reinforcement applications because they work best at close range. In addition, moving-coil microphones are well-suited to live sound reinforcement use because they are the most durable of all the common mic types. Ribbon mics aren't very durable but they provide a good sound when close-miking vocals.

The vocal in Audio Example 4-5 was recorded with a moving-coil mic about three inches from the singer.

Audio Example 4-5
Moving-Coil Mic From Three Inches
CD-1: Track 32

Audio Example 4-6 demonstrates the same set used in Audio Example 4-5 with the mic 12 inches from the singer. Notice the difference in fullness.

Audio Example 4-6
Moving-Coil Mic From 12 Inches
CD-1: Track 32

Audio Example 4-7 demonstrates the same vocal part, this time recorded through a ribbon microphone from a distance of about three inches.

Audio Example 4-7
Ribbon Mic From Three Inches
CD-1: Track 33

The ribbon mic in Audio Example 4-8 is 12 inches from the singer.

Audio Example 4-8 Ribbon Mic From 12 Inches
CD-1: Track 33

Condenser

When recording vocals in a recording studio, condenser microphones are almost always the best choice. The condenser mic operating principle is best suited to accurately capture a singer's natural sound because they color the sound less than other mic types. They also respond more accurately to transients, therefore producing a vocal sound that's very natural and understandable.

Unlike moving-coil and ribbon mics, condenser microphones sound full from a distance of one or two feet. The singer can stand back from the mic a bit and you can still record a full, present sound while retaining the option to include more or less of the room's acoustical character. Miking vocals from one or two feet away often produces a unique and transparent sound. Sometimes when vocals are close-miked, especially with condenser microphones, they sound boomy and thick and don't blend well with the rest of the mix. The vocal line in Audio Example 4-9 was recorded with a condenser mic from about six inches.

Audio Example 4-9
Vocal Melody From Six Inches (Condenser)
CD-1: Track 34

Audio Example 4-10 demonstrates the same vocal line as Audio Example 4-9, this time recorded from a distance of about 12 inches. Notice that the line still sounds full.

Audio Example 4-10
Vocal Melody From 12 Inches (Condenser)
CD-1: Track 34

The condenser mic capsule doesn't respond well to moisture. If the singer is too close, the mic might suddenly quit working and remain inoperable until the capsule dries out. When the capsule dries off sufficiently the mic will work again, but it's frustrating when this happens. If you want the close-miked sound from a condenser mic, use a foam wind screen to diffuse as much air and moisture as possible.

Effects

Most commercial vocal sounds end up in the final mix with reverb and delay added to simulate the interesting and rich sound of a large acoustical environment, such as a concert hall or stadium.

As demonstrated by Audio Examples 4-2 through 4-4, the room plays a key role in the overall recorded sound. Use of reverb and delay effects compound the importance of your control and understanding of natural room ambience. The acoustical space where the vocal tracks are recorded influences the miked sound and the sound created by any electronic additions or manipulations.

Stylistic Considerations

Usually in commercial popular music it's best to record vocals in a room that's acoustically neutral (doesn't have a long reverberation time) and mike the vocalist from a distance of 6 to 12 inches. This approach provides the most flexibility during mixdown. You maintain the freedom to use reverberation and other effects to artificially place the vocal in the space that best suits the emotion of the music.

For classically oriented vocal recordings, it's often the technique of choice to find a great-sounding room or concert hall, then mike the singer from a distance that includes the desired amount of room sound. The room sound is all-important to this vocal-recording approach, and it's common for the best classical singers to travel anywhere in the world to sing a piece of music in the concert hall that they feel is best for the music.

Even for commercial pop styles, you should be willing to experiment with different uses of ambience. Mainly, take care that you don't include so much ambience that the vocal loses the close intimacy that sounds good on a lot of popular music.

Wind Screen

A wind screen is used in the studio to keep abundant air, caused by hard enunciation, from creating loud pops as the microphone capsule is overworked. In an outdoor application, the wind screen is also used to shield the capsule from wind (Illustration 4-5).

Most vocal recordings require the use of a wind screen, also called a pop filter. When a singer pronounces words containing hard consonants, like "p" and "b," there is a lot of air hitting the mic capsule at once. When the air from these hard consonants, called plosives, hits the mic capsule, it can actually bottom out the capsule diaphragm. In other words, this "pop" can be the physical sound of the microphone diaphragm actually hitting the end of its normal travel range. On our recorder, we hear this as a loud and obvious pop. Audio Example 4-11 demonstrates the sound of a problem plosive. This pop is usually difficult to get rid of in the mix so it's best to find a way to not record it.

Audio Example 4-11 The Problem Plosive
CD-1: Track 35

A wind screen can diffuse the air from the singer before it gets to the mic capsule, therefore eliminating the problem plosive. Wind screens come in many different forms. Moving-

Illustration 4-5
The Wind Screen

There are many different types and shapes of foam wind screens. They work very well when used in the proper context but can adversely affect sound quality. When placed over a mic capsule, the sound arriving at the capsule through the foam wind screen is affected mostly by the type of foam material rather than physical shape.

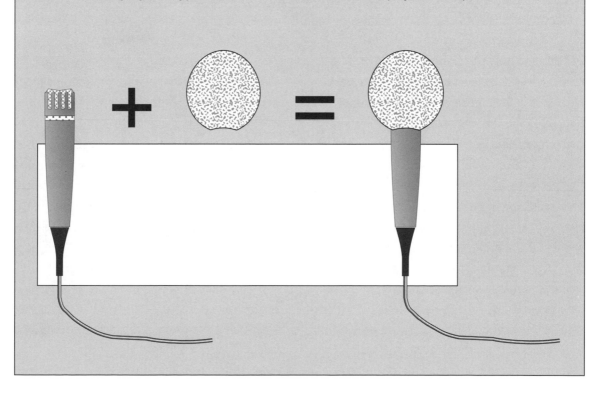

Illustration 4-6
Embroidery Hoop Wind Screen

This wind screen uses a piece of a nylon stocking stretched over an embroidery hoop and attached to the bottom part of a standard mic clip. Most embroidery hoops fit very nicely in the mic clip that comes with a Shure SM57 or SM58. Mount this device on a separate mic stand and place it in front of the mic between the singer and the microphone diaphragm.

This design alters the vocal sound less than most other wind screen designs. An added bonus to this screen is its flexibility in positioning. If the sound you need requires the vocalist to stand one foot (or any other specified distance) from the microphone, simply position the wind screen one foot from the mic capsule. The singer is then given a visual reference to gauge distance from the mic and a barrier to keep from moving too close.

coil and ribbon mics often have the wind screen built in. Most condenser mics don't have the wind screen built in. Since the condenser microphones sound full from a distance, we can have the singer stand back far enough that plosives aren't much of a problem, and we'll still get a full, natural sound. Depending on the singer and the sound you want, you might not be able to keep the mic far enough away to avoid plosives while still achieving the sound you want.

If a singer has hard enunciation, if you're trying to get a close sound or if you're outside on a breezy day, try a foam wind screen. They come in different shapes, sizes and colors, but they're all made from molded porous foam. Their purpose is to diffuse the air before it reaches

the mic capsule. Foam wind screens are the typical choice for outdoor applications because they surround the mic capsule completely and offer the most complete wind diffusion. Purists often reject foam wind screens for any use other than outdoor applications because they muffle the sound and attenuate the high frequencies more than the other designs (Illustration 4-5).

Another type of wind screen can be constructed from a piece of an old nylon stocking, an embroidery hoop and a mic clip (Illustrations 4-6 and 4-7). This design works very well, is inexpensive and typically sounds much better than foam. The nylon, stretched over the hoop and placed between the singer's mouth and the microphone, usually diffuses the air enough to

Illustration 4-7
Attaching the Wind Screen to the Mic Stand

The embroidery hoop screen can be attached to a regular mic stand with a special clamp normally used in live applications to hold a guitar mic on the same mic stand as the singer/guitarist's vocal mic.

Mounting the hoop on a long gooseneck lets you easily position the screen while eliminating the need for a separate mic stand.

avoid plosives and muffles the sound less than a foam wind screen.

Try taping a pencil to the mic so it goes across the front of the mic capsule. If the pencil is directly in front of the center of the mic capsule, it will diffuse the air enough to eliminate the pops. This technique works best on large capsule mics (Illustration 4-8).

Each of these wind screens can have a different effect on the overall sound quality of the vocal track. These differences might be very noticeable or subtly different. Some listeners might have difficulty hearing the difference in sound quality when comparing one wind screen to the next, especially if they're listening on a marginal monitoring system. However, even if the sonic differences are subtle, we should always strive to record the best sound possible

because the final product will benefit.

Listen to Audio Examples 4-12 through 4-15. These four different examples use the same vocalist through the same setup. The only thing that changes is the wind screen.

Audio Example 4-12 uses no wind screen.

Audio Example 4-12 No Wind Screen
CD-1: Track 35

Audio Example 4-13 demonstrates the use of a foam wind screen over the mic. Listen for a difference in the high-frequency content.

Audio Example 4-13 Foam Wind Screen
CD-1: Track 35

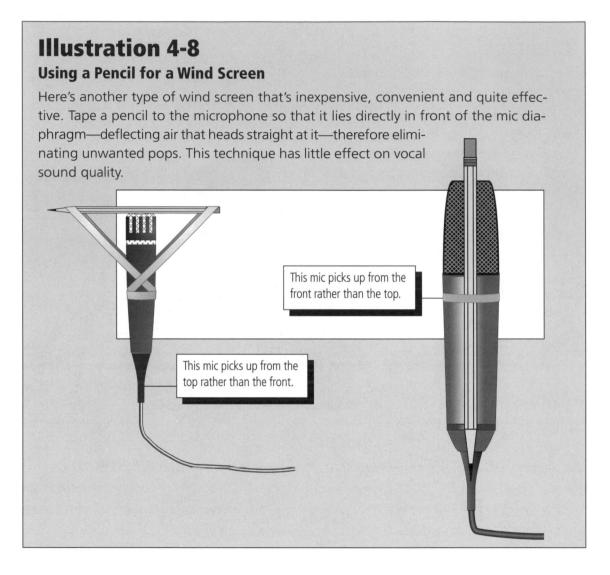

Illustration 4-8
Using a Pencil for a Wind Screen

Here's another type of wind screen that's inexpensive, convenient and quite effective. Tape a pencil to the microphone so that it lies directly in front of the mic diaphragm—deflecting air that heads straight at it—therefore eliminating unwanted pops. This technique has little effect on vocal sound quality.

This mic picks up from the front rather than the top.

This mic picks up from the top rather than the front.

Audio Example 4-14 was recorded using an embroidery hoop with nylon stretched over it. This wind screen has a different and subtle effect on the vocal sound.

Audio Example 4-14
Nylon Over an Embroidery Hoop
CD-1: Track 35

The vocal in Audio Example 4-15 was recorded with a pencil taped to the mic so that it runs across the center of the mic diaphragm.

Audio Example 4-15
Pencil Across the Diaphragm
CD-1: Track 35

Repairing a Problem Plosive

Sometimes even using a good wind screen won't eliminate all pops—or you might have opted to keep a take for musical reasons, in spite of a plosive problem. Try the following three techniques along with, or instead of, a wind screen:

1. Move the mic slightly above or below the singer's mouth. This'll get the air moving past the diaphragm instead of moving directly at it. There might be a slight sound difference, which could be either detrimental or beneficial, but this is typically a good way to avoid pops.

2. Point the mic at an angle to the vocalist. This position, like the previous suggestion, allows the air to move past the capsule instead of at it.

3. Move the mic very close to the vocalist (closer than two inches). The movement of air doesn't reach its peak energy until it's gone more than an inch or so from the singer's mouth so you might be able to position the mic at a point before the air achieves maximum flow, therefore avoiding pops. Positioning the vocalist close to the microphone works best on moving-coil microphones. Condenser mics suffer from close proximity to the singer because the moisture from the vocalist has an adverse effect on the sound and operational status of the mic.

Sometimes, if you've tracked the vocals with the bass or drums turned up artificially high in the monitor mix, a plosive problem can go unnoticed until mixdown, when you begin isolating parts. It might be possible to bring the original vocalist back into the studio to repair the track, but you might not get the same sound or emotional impact that you got on the original take.

One simple solution is equalization. The pop that happens as a result of the strong plosive is heavy in bass frequencies, usually below 100Hz. If you're quick with the EQ controls, you can often turn down the lows at the precise word or part of a word where the problem exists. This technique is very effective and especially useful when you only have one or two problem spots to focus on.

Electronic Plosive Repair

Sometimes simply turning down the lows at the problem spot makes the vocals sound thin and unnatural. Or maybe there are too many complex spots to fix. If you're having big problems like these, electronic plosive repair is definitely worth a try. (This technique will also get you used to using processors creatively and efficiently.)

This kind of repair requires the use of an equalizer and a compressor/limiter with external triggering capability. Follow this procedure:

1. Plug the output of the problem vocal track into a mult in the patch bay or use a simple Y cord to split the output of the track.

2. Patch one output of the mult, or one side of the Y cord, into the input of the compressor/limiter; then patch the output of the compressor/limiter into a line input of your mixer's channel line in, fader in, etc.

3. Patch another output of the mult, or the other side of the Y, into the equalizer input. Outboard graphic or parametric equalizers work best for this technique since they typically have the greatest ability to zero in on a problem frequency (Illustration 4-9).

4. Plug the output of the equalizer into the input of the compressor labeled external input, external, key input or key. We already have the vocal track patched through the main ins and outs of the compressor. In normal operation, the compressor/limiter turns up and down in response to the audio signal coming into the main input. We're setting the

compressor up so that it will turn up and down in response to the signal that comes into the external input. When the internal/external switch is on internal, the processor works normally, responding to the signal coming into the main input. When the internal/external switch is on external, the processor responds to whatever signal is coming into the external or key input.

5. Set the equalizer so that the bass frequen-

cies are boosted. If you can listen to the output of the equalizer, adjust the EQ so the plosives are as obnoxious as they can be.

6. Set the internal/external switch to external or push the key button. By pressing the external or key button, we're telling the processor to respond to the signal we've patched into the external or key input, instead of the signal that's actually running through the main ins and outs. Since the equalized signal

Illustration 4-9
Using a Mult or Y Adapter

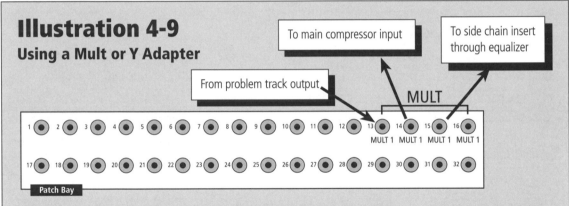

A mult (short for *multiplier*) in a patch bay is, in reality, a simple, convenient Y. Jacks labeled "mult" and grouped together in a patch bay, are joined together internally. Plug the output of the problem track into any one of the mult patch points. The remaining jacks in the mult can then be patched to inputs on other devices.

Note: Feed only one output into a mult.

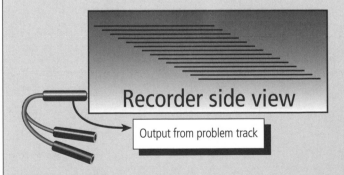

A simple Y adapter works well for splitting an output. These accessories are inexpensive and readily available. It's most convenient to use a Y that has one male end (plug this into the output of the problem track) and two female ends. Connect a patch cord from one of the female ends to the main compressor input; then from the other female end, patch into the input of an equalizer.

Note: Y cables work very well for splitting outputs for multiple sends; however, Y adapters are not good tools for combining multiple outputs to one input.

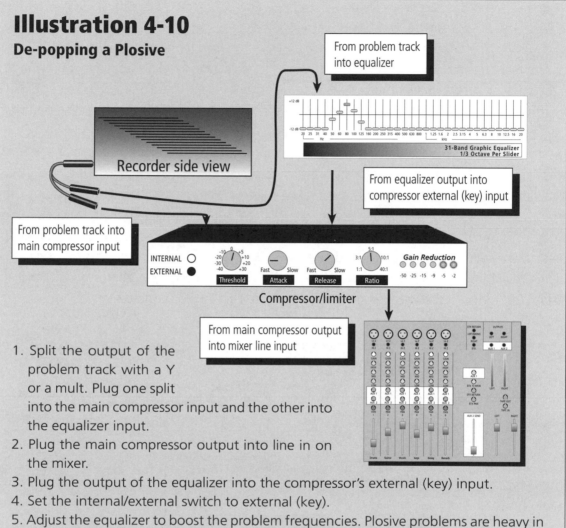

Illustration 4-10
De-popping a Plosive

From problem track into equalizer

+12 dB
-12 dB
20 25 31 40 50 60 80 100 125 160 200 250 315 400 500 630 800 1.25 1.6 2 2.5 3.15 4 5 6.3 8 10 12.5 16 20
Hz
kHz
31-Band Graphic Equalizer
1/3 Octave Per Slider

Recorder side view

From equalizer output into compressor external (key) input

From problem track into main compressor input

INTERNAL ○
EXTERNAL ●

-10 0 +5
-20 +10
-30 +20
-40 +30
Threshold

Fast Slow
Attack

Fast Slow
Release

5:1
3:1 10:1
1:1 40:1
Ratio

Gain Reduction
-50 -25 -15 -9 -5 -2

Compressor/limiter

From main compressor output into mixer line input

1. Split the output of the problem track with a Y or a mult. Plug one split into the main compressor input and the other into the equalizer input.
2. Plug the main compressor output into line in on the mixer.
3. Plug the output of the equalizer into the compressor's external (key) input.
4. Set the internal/external switch to external (key).
5. Adjust the equalizer to boost the problem frequencies. Plosive problems are heavy in low frequencies.
6. Adjust the compressor to show gain reduction only when the plosives occur.
7. Fine-tune the compressor until the plosives are gone and the track sounds natural.

has accentuated the plosive problems, we can adjust the processor controls so that the VCA (voltage controlled amplifier) only turns down when the plosives occur. This gives us an automatic depopper.

7. Set the ratio control to about 7:1.
8. Set the attack time to fast.
9. Set the release time to medium-fast.

Play the section of the tune that contains the problem plosive and adjust the threshold control so that gain reduction is indicated on the gain reduction LEDs every time the plosive occurs. We want gain reduction to occur only when the problem plosives happen. This might take some fine adjusting of the threshold, but since the trigger is responding to the external input that contains the equalized version of the track and the equalized version of the track has highly exaggerated plosive problems, it's almost always possible to successfully repair problem plosives with this technique (Illustration 4-10).

If there's a problem, readjust the EQ. Turn more bass up, turn a different bass frequency up or turn the highs and mids way down. You can get the compressor set so that the only time the gain reduction LEDs show gain reduction is when the plosives occur. When you adjust the equalizer that is patched into the external input, you're not affecting the tone quality of the track. The main input and output of the compressor are not being equalized by this technique. You're just sending an exaggerated EQ to the VCA to trick the unit into responding when

you want it to instead of when it would normally.

Once these adjustments are completed, the compressor should automatically turn the track down every time a problem plosive occurs. The rest of the track should be left unaffected by the processor.

If you own a compressor that has a side chain insert (sends and returns, or ins and outs, other than the main inputs and outputs), you can de-pop a vocal track with fewer steps. You only need to have an equalizer; it's not necessary to use a mult or a Y chord. The side chain output is a separate send of the signal that's coming into the compressor.

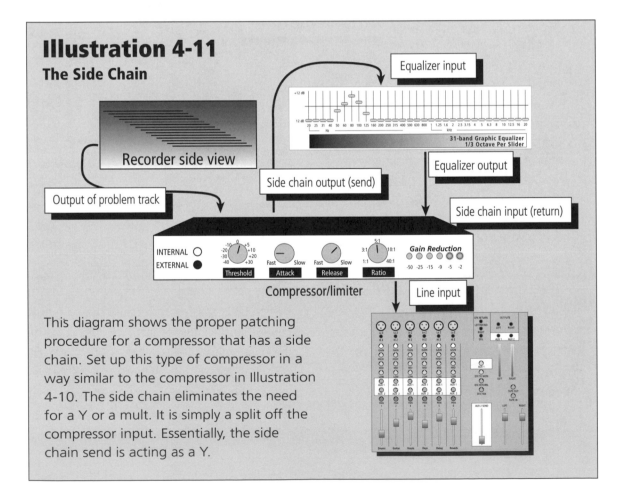

Illustration 4-11
The Side Chain

Equalizer input

Recorder side view

31-band Graphic Equalizer
1/3 Octave Per Slider

Equalizer output

Side chain output (send)

Output of problem track

Side chain input (return)

INTERNAL
EXTERNAL
Threshold Attack Release Ratio

Gain Reduction
-50 -25 -15 -9 -5 -2

Compressor/limiter

Line input

This diagram shows the proper patching procedure for a compressor that has a side chain. Set up this type of compressor in a way similar to the compressor in Illustration 4-10. The side chain eliminates the need for a Y or a mult. It is simply a split off the compressor input. Essentially, the side chain send is acting as a Y.

Illustration 4-12
Bass Roll-off

Most condenser microphones offer a bass roll-off feature. A switch somewhere on the mic body lets you apply the roll-off. Some mic designs even give you a choice between roll-off frequencies and contain a small switch near the bass of the mic housing that is user adjustable. You choose between flat (often labeled *LINEAR, LIN, Flat, or "——"*) and specific roll-off frequencies (possibly 60, 75, 80, 150 or 175).

A bass roll-off doesn't simply cut a band centered on a specific frequency. Instead, it turns everything below a specific frequency down at a rate indicated in dB per octave.

An 80Hz bass roll-off might cut the frequencies below 80Hz at a rate of 12dB per octave. In this case, at 40Hz (one octave below 80Hz) a 12dB decrease in amplitude is realized. At 20Hz (two octaves below 80Hz) a 24dB decrease in amplitude is realized.

Follow this procedure if your compressor/limiter has a side chain.

1. Plug the output of the problem track into the main input of the compressor.
2. Plug the main output of the compressor into a line input of the mixer. (This is the patch for normal compressor use.)
3. Plug the side chain output (send out) into the input of the equalizer.
4. Plug the output of the equalizer into the side chain input (return) of the compressor.
5. Set the external/internal switch to external or key.
6. Adjust the equalizer that's patched into the side chain to boost the problem frequencies.
7. Adjust the ratio, attack time and release time to the desired settings (probably about 7:1 ratio with fast attack and medium-fast release).
8. Adjust the threshold so the gain reduction LEDs only indicate gain reduction when the problem plosives happen (Illustration 4-11).

The Proximity Effect

If you're using a condenser mic to record a vocal sound that's very close and intimate-sounding, you might choose to close-mike the vocalist. You'll need to use a condenser mic that has a bass roll-off switch (Illustration 4-12). The bass roll-off is built into most condenser mics and typically turns down the frequencies below 75 or 80Hz. Any time a singer or narrator moves

Illustration 4-13
Roll-off at 160Hz

The graph below represents the frequency response of a microphone set to roll off the lows below 160Hz. A bass roll-off is also called a high pass filter because it lets the frequencies above a specific point pass through unaffected.

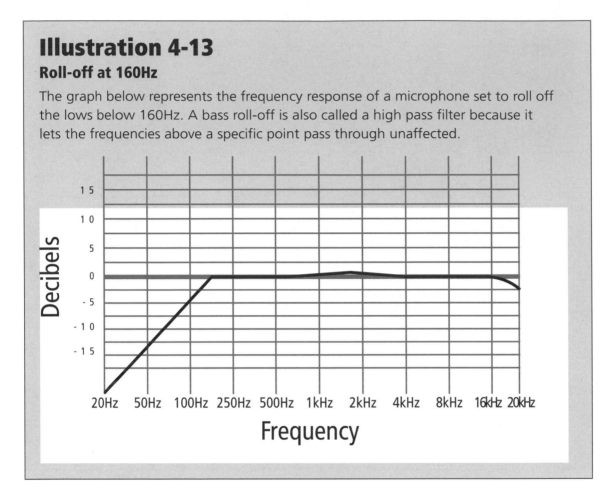

closer to a microphone, the low frequencies get louder in relation to the high frequencies. This can result in a boomy or thick sound, especially if the voice is being recorded through a high quality condenser mic. Low frequencies increasing as the mic distance decreases is called the *proximity effect*. This effect is the most extreme when using a cardioid pickup pattern.

Bass Roll-off

Rolling off the lows lets you get a close sound without getting a thick, boomy sound. Some condenser microphones have variable bass roll-offs that will turn the lows down below a couple of different user-selectable frequencies (Illustration 4-13).

Listen to Audio Examples 4-16, 4-17 and 4-18. Notice how the vocal sound changes with the adjustment of the bass roll-off.

Audio Example 4-16
Two Inches From the Mic With No Bass Roll-off
CD-1: Track 36

Audio Example 4-17
Two Inches From the Mic With 80Hz Bass Roll-off
CD-1: Track 36

Audio Example 4-18
Two Inches From the Mic With 160Hz Bass Roll-off
CD-1: Track 36

Often the lead vocal track doesn't need the frequencies below about 80Hz. In fact, those frequencies can get in the way of the rest of the mix and make things sound muddy. It's common to use the bass roll-off even when miking a vocalist with a high quality condenser mic from a distance of about a foot.

As we've seen with other instruments, the lows contain a lot of energy. If we roll off the bass on the vocal mic, we'll record more of the usable vocal sound and end up with cleaner vocal recordings. Also, our effective record levels will be hotter since the inaudible low frequencies aren't adding to the signal level.

If you're miking the vocal with a moving-coil or ribbon mic, be aware that these mics very typically roll off naturally in the low frequencies. Not many moving-coil or ribbon mics have bass roll-off switches built in because the roll-off is already happening as a result of the mic design. This is not really a disadvantage as long as we operate from an educated perspective. If we use each mic according to its strengths and retain the lessons we learn from our experiences, our recordings will continue to improve.

We can take advantage of the proximity effect to fill out the sound of a moving-coil or ribbon mic by choosing these mics for close-miking applications. Live sound reinforcement is a perfect place for using the moving-coil and ribbon mics to capture a full, warm sound from close proximity, which is what they do best.

A studio recording setting is different than live recording because we don't always need or want to close-mike the instruments and voices. Instead, we often want to capture room ambience along with the intended sound source. Ambience, in the proper proportion, can add individuality and life to an otherwise bland sound.

Listen to the moving-coil mic in Audio Example 4-19 to hear the characteristic sound of one moving-coil mic. This is the moving-coil microphone from two inches.

Audio Example 4-19
Moving-Coil From Two Inches
CD-1: Track 37

Audio Example 4-20 demonstrates the moving-coil mic from about six inches. The sound is rapidly thinning as the mic distance increases from the singer.

Audio Example 4-20 Moving-Coil From Six Inches
CD-1: Track 37

In Audio Example 4-21, the mic is about 15 inches from the singers mouth. This type of texture might be usable in a small sound reinforcement application where a singer has pulled way back from the mic to nail a high note because the acoustic vocal sound would probably be fairly dominant. In the studio, however, this sound is typically far too thin and gutless to be usable.

Audio Example 4-21 Moving-Coil From 15 Inches
CD-1: Track 37

The Pad

Condenser mics produce the strongest signal of all the mic types. Close-miking especially loud singers with these mics might overdrive the electronic circuitry in the mic or, more likely, the signal might overdrive the input to the console.

Almost all condenser mics have a built-in pad, or attenuator, that makes it easy to compensate for this problem. If the sound you're getting is always distorted no matter what you do with the levels on the console, you probably need to apply the pad on the microphone.

The pads usually reduce the signal by 10 or 20dB, and some mics give you the option of -10 or -20. This amount of attenuation is almost always sufficient to avoid overdriving the console input. Be sure to use the least amount of pad necessary; if you attenuate the mic signal further than is necessary, you degrade the signal-to-noise ratio. If you over-attenuate by 10dB, you'll degrade your signal to noise ratio by 10dB.

Different Sounds of Different Pickup Patterns

Some condenser mics have selectable pickup patterns. In other words, one mic can be switched to cardioid, omni, bidirectional and sometimes hypercardioid. These are called the microphone's directional characteristics. If you're not 100 percent sure what each of these phrases mean, refer to Illustrations 4-14 through 4-18. For a more thorough review of microphone characteristics and operating principles, consult Volume 1, Chapter 3 of the *AudioPro Home Recording Course* (Illustrations 4-14 through 4-18).

Each pickup pattern might offer a different sound, and each of these sounds might be useful in different ways. Experiment with variations between pickup patterns and mic distance. Once you find the combination of mic choice,

Illustration 4-14
Cardioid Pattern

A cardioid microphone hears best from the front and actively rejects sounds from behind, producing a heart-shaped pickup pattern. When using a cardioid mic, you can point the mic at the sound you want to record and away from the sound you don't want to record. Rejection of sound from behind the microphone isn't complete, but it's sufficient enough to help minimize unwanted sounds.

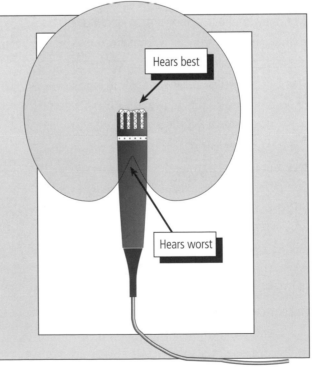

Hears best

Hears worst

Illustration 4-15
Omnidirectional Pattern

A microphone with an omni-directional pickup pattern hears equally from all directions—it doesn't reject sound from any direction.

Most omnidirectional mics use a condenser capsule. Since they don't reject sounds from any direction, omni mics are an excellent choice for capturing room ambience.

Omnidirectional microphones are least susceptible to timbre changes created by variations in the distance of the mic from the sound source.

360° spherical pickup pattern

pattern selection and mic distance that adds life, emotion and superior natural sound quality to a vocal part, you won't turn back. If you spend a little extra time perfecting your mic technique, you'll gain it back several times over as your music comes together with greater ease, inspi-

Illustration 4-16
Bidirectional Pattern

Bidirectional microphones hear equally well from both sides, but they don't pick up sound from the edges (90° off axis). This directional characteristic is also called the figure-eight pattern.

Bidirectional mics work very well when recording two voices or instruments to one track because they induce minimal phase cancelation.

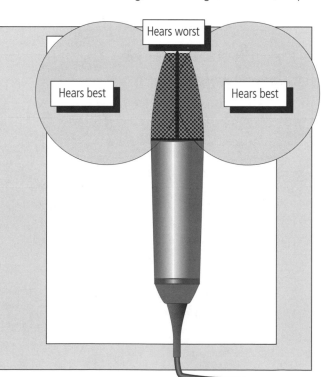

Hears worst

Hears best

Hears best

Illustration 4-17
Hypercardioid Pattern

The hypercardioid directional characteristic is narrower than the traditional cardioid pattern—it doesn't hear as well from the sides as the cardioid mic. In addition, there's an area of sensitivity directly behind the mic (180° off axis) that isn't present in the cardioid mic.

Hypercardioid mics work well when the sound sources are close together (like when you record backing vocals) but you want minimal interaction between the microphones.

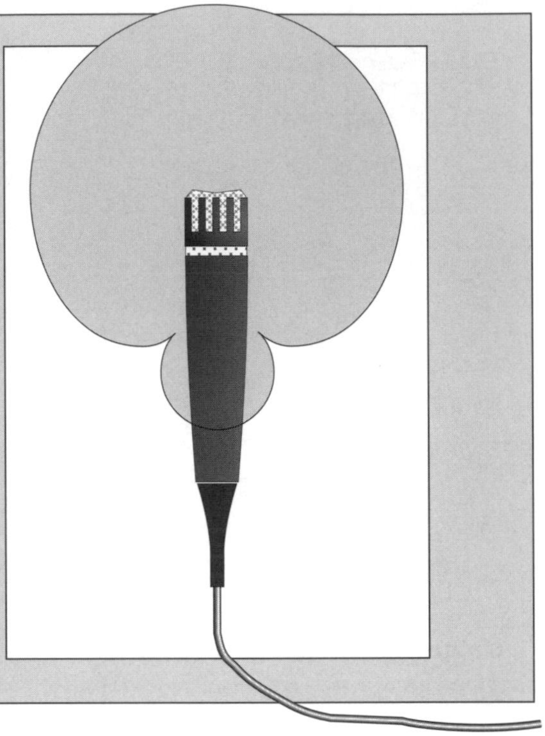

ration and confidence. Good mic technique adds depth to a vocal track that you simply can't get with equalization and other processing.

Cardioid, hypercardioid and supercardioid pickup patterns are the most commonly used when recording vocals. These patterns include

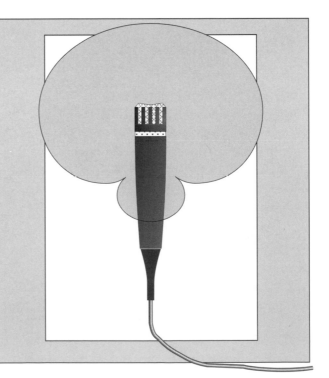

Illustration 4-18
Supercardioid Pattern

The terms supercardioid and hypercardioid are often used interchangeably. In reality, the supercardioid pattern is wider than the hypercardioid pattern—it hears better from the sides.

Hypercardioid and supercardioid mics both work well when you'd like to include room ambience in a controlled amount. They provide less ambience than an omnidirectional mic, but more than a cardioid mic.

the least amount of acoustic room sound while achieving the closest, warmest sound from a fairly close proximity. Listen to Audio Example 4-22, the sound of a condenser mic with a cardioid pattern from eight inches, no pad and no bass roll-off.

Audio Example 4-22
Cardioid Condenser Mic From Eight Inches
CD-1: Track 38

Audio Example 4-23 demonstrates the same mic from the same distance as Audio Example 4-22. This time the pickup pattern is hypercardioid. Notice that the sound is a little more open and roomy.

Audio Example 4-23
Hypercardioid Condenser Mic From Eight Inches
CD-1: Track 39

Next, the same mic, again from the same distance, but with the pickup pattern switched to omnidirectional. This pattern isn't nearly as colored by the proximity effect, and the sound, although still close, has a totally different edge.

Audio Example 4-24
Omnidirectional Condenser Mic From Eight Inches
CD-1: Track 40

Finally, the bidirectional pattern. This isn't always the most obvious choice for a solo lead vocal, but I've had some very good results using this technique on some singers in some rooms. Listen to the room sound and the overall sonic clarity of Audio Example 4-25. This approach also provides less coloration from the proximity effect than the cardioid patterns.

Audio Example 4-25
Bidirectional Condenser Mic From Eight Inches
CD-1: Track 41

Positioning the Microphone

Some singers have a good, smooth sound; other singers have a nasal quality when they sing. And others tend to have a thin, edgy sound. Where you place the mic in relation to the singer *will* affect the tonal quality of the vocal sound. If you place the mic directly in front of the singer's mouth (pointing directly at the singer), you'll get a pretty even and natural tonal balance. But if he or she makes much noise while singing, it will come through, loud and clear, on your recorder. These noises typically include lip smacks, nose sniffs, breaths and sometimes even the sound of air leaking through the nose while the performance is happening.

If the sound isn't good directly in front of the singer, try moving the mic up about three or four inches above the singer's mouth and pointing it down at the mouth. This usually eliminates a lot of the lip smacks and other noises, plus it cleans up the nasal sound that some singers have a problem with.

If you position the mic four to six inches below the vocalist's mouth and then aim the mic up at the mouth, you might fill out a thin sounding voice, but you might get more extraneous noises than you care to deal with.

The basic microphone position is a crucial factor. Sometimes a difference of one inch in

Illustration 4-19
Aiming the Mic Directly at the Singer's Mouth

Both of these microphones are pointing directly at the singer. The large diaphragm mics, like the one on the left, pick up from the side rather than the top. This technique might work well on a vocalist, but often the mic receives too much air, causing problems with plosives.

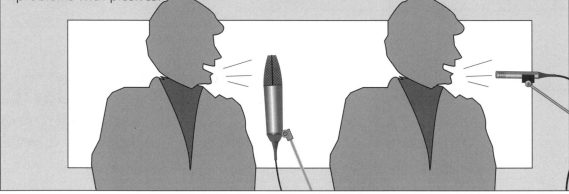

either direction will dramatically affect the quality and impact of the vocal sound. Each singer offers a different set of variables so there are no absolute solutions. Keep up the quest for the best possible sound—you'll know when you've hit the right combination (Illustrations 4-19 through 4-21).

Illustration 4-20
Aiming the Mic Down at the Singer's Mouth

Pointing the microphone down at the singer's mouth produces a sound with minimal nasal quality while de-emphasizing lip smacks, breaths, sniffs, etc.

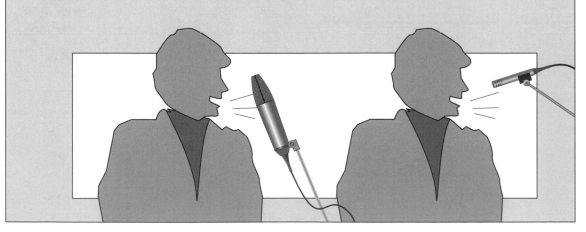

Illustration 4-21
Aiming the Mic Up at the Singer's Mouth

Pointing the mic up at the singer's mouth might fill out an otherwise thin sound. However, this technique accentuates nasal tone quality as well as breaths, lip smacks and snitts.

Compressor/Limiter/Gate/Expander

Vocalists almost always use a wide dynamic range during the course of a song. Often they'll sing very tenderly and quietly during one measure and then emotionally blast you with all the volume and energy they can muster up during the next. Most of the time you need a compressor/limiter to avoid overloading your recorder with signal. If you need to review compressor/limiter features and capabilities, refer to Volume 1, Chapter 2 of the *AudioPro Home Recording Course*.

As the compressor's VCA turns down the signal that passes the threshold, the entire vocal track occupies a narrower dynamic range. When the vocal is in a narrow dynamic range, the loud sounds are easier to record because they aren't out of control, plus the softer sounds can be heard and understood better in the mix.

Dynamic Range

Compression can be the single most important contributor to a vocal recording that's consistently audible and understandable in a mix. Most lead vocals on commercial hit recordings are compressed. So far in this course, we've seen each instrument benefit from compression, and vocals realize much of the same benefit.

Some producers don't like the sound of the compressor's VCA turning up and down so they'll record the vocal tracks without compression. But during mixdown, the engineer still needs to manually ride the vocal level to compensate for the wide vocal dynamic range. The engineer in this case is acting as a manual compressor, substituting for the automatic VCA controlled compressor.

When recording vocal tracks, even with compression, the engineer often rides the record level fader to compensate for the loudest parts of the song. This method works very well if the engineer is familiar with the song and the artist's interpretation, but it also has the potential to cause more problems than it solves. Practice and experience provide the necessary skills to successfully perform this technique.

The benefit of riding the record level fader while recording vocal tracks is the need for less compression. If you can cut 5 or 6dB off the hottest part of the track by riding the fader, you've decreased the amount of leveling required by the compressor. Less action from the compressor almost always results in a clearer, more natural sound (Illustration 4-22).

Even though the most common vocal recording technique utilizes a compressor/limiter, your choice to include a compressor in your vocal recordings should be based on the vocalist, the song, vocal range, dynamic range, emotion and other musical considerations. Avoid ruts. Evaluate each situation separately. There are many times when a compressor is your best

Illustration 4-22
Dynamic Range

These graphs represent vocal energy (the curve) in relation to the rest of the mix (the gray area). The top graph (not compressed) shows the volume of some lyrics sinking into the mix, probably being covered up.

The bottom graph indicates the same performance and lyric after being compressed. This time the lyrics peak at the same level, but notice that after being compressed the softer lyrics are turned up so they can be heard above the rest of the mix. Once the compressor/limiter has decreased the dynamic range and levels have been adjusted to attain the proper peak level, your vocals should be consistently understandable. More emotional nuance will be heard and felt.

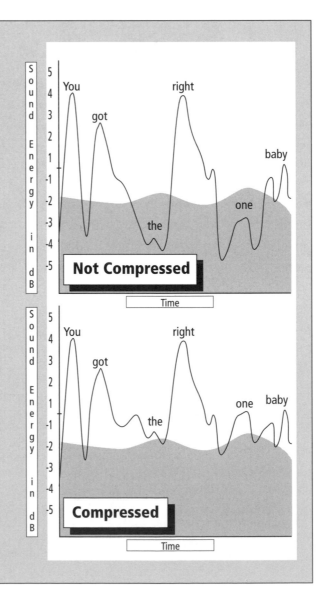

friend when recording vocals. There are also many situations where the compressor sucks the life out of a brilliant performance.

Compression

Vocals are usually compressed using a medium-fast attack time (3 to 5ms), a medium-long release time (from a half second to a second), and a ratio between 3:1 and 7:1 with about 6dB of gain reduction at the loudest part of the track.

A vocalist who is used to recording in the studio can make your job much easier. Less compression is needed on singers who use mic technique to compensate for their changes in level. A seasoned professional will back off a bit on the loud notes and move in a bit on the soft notes. This technique on the vocalist's part will help you record the most controlled, understandable and natural sounding vocal track. If you set the compressor so it indicates no gain reduction most of the time with 2 to 4dB of reduction on the loudest notes, and if the vocal is always understandable and smooth sounding, that's good.

Listen to the vocal track with rhythm accompaniment in Audio Example 4-26. The vocal isn't compressed. Notice how it sometimes disappears in the mix.

Audio Example 4-26 Vocal Without Compression
CD-1: Track 42

Audio Example 4-27 demonstrates the same vocal, compressed using a ratio of 4:1 with up to about 6dB of gain reduction. This time the peak level is the same, but listen for the softer notes. They're easier to hear and understand.

Audio Example 4-27 Vocal With 4:1 Compression
CD-1: Track 42

Sibilance

Avoid overcompressing the vocals. If the attack time isn't instantaneous or at least nearly instantaneous, it's possible to compress most of the words but not the initial sounds. For instance, a word starting with "s" or "t" might have a very fast attack—an attack too fast to be turned down by the compressor. The initial "s" or "t" will sound unnaturally loud and, like other transient sounds, won't register accurately on a VU meter. These exaggerated attacks are called sibilant sounds. When sibilant sounds are recorded too hot, your recordings will have a splatting type of distortion every time sibilance occurs. Sibilance distortion also happens when a sibilant sound occurs in the middle or end of a word (Illustration 4-23).

Each singer has a unique sibilant character. Bone structure, physical alignment of the vocalist's teeth, jaw position and size all play a part in exactly how they produce sibilant sounds. Some vocalists don't produce strong transients; other vocalists produce megatransients. I find that a singer with straight teeth and a perfect bite typically produces a very strong transient on consonants that have a "hiss" sound ("s," "t," "ch," "zh," "sh").

Sibilance problems often slide by when recording to the multitrack (analog or digital), but when cassettes are duplicated you might find a big problem with sibilance distortion. Small tape has less headroom and therefore distorts easier than most multitrack recorders.

Illustration 4-23
Sibilance

These graphs represent the changes in amplitude over time of the word "Sally." The top graph has an average level of about 0VU, but the "S" is about 3dB above the remainder of the word "...ally."

If the compressor's attack time is slow enough that the VCA doesn't begin to act until after the "S" and if the remainder of the word is compressed, exaggeration of the initial sibilant sound results.

The bottom graph represents the result of compressing the word "Sally." Notice the difference in level between the "S" and the remainder of the word. This type of compression technique, when used in moderation (1 to 3dB), can help increase intelligibility and understandability. However, often this scenario leads to overexaggerated sibilance that degrades your music, especially in cassette duplication.

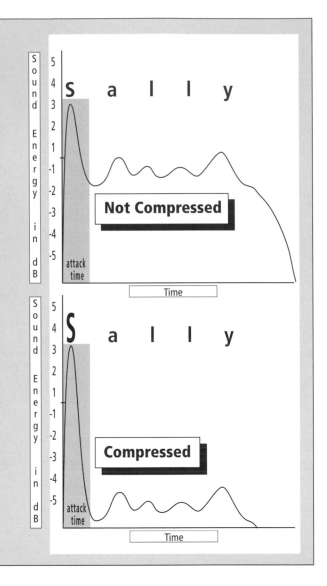

The De-esser

Use a de-esser to help compensate for sibilance problems. A de-esser is a fast acting compressor set to turn down the high frequencies that are present in the sibilant sounds and is often built into a compressor/limiter. If the de-esser is activated, the VCA responds to the highs instead of all frequencies at once, therefore turning down the exaggerated sibilance. De-essers often have a control that sweeps a range of high frequencies, letting the user choose which high frequency will be compressed. The threshold control lets you set the de-esser so it only turns down the high frequencies of the sibilant sounds but leaves the rest of the track alone.

Good compression technique, proper mic choice and positioning are usually the answer to sibilance problems. But these problems have become particularly problematic with the growth of digital recording. Digital metering helps you record the full range of the transient accurately so any transfer to analog mediums, such as cassette tape, provide opportunity for sibilance distortion. Through education and the proper use of compression and de-essing, you can record vocal tracks that are clean and clear and work well within any musical structure.

Listen to the vocal in Audio Example 4-28 as it's overcompressed, exaggerating the sibilance. The compressor in this example is set to a medium-slow attack time, letting the sibilance pass through uncompressed. The ratio is at 7:1 with up to 15dB of gain reduction.

Audio Example 4-28 Exaggerated Sibilance
CD-1: Track 43

Equalization

When tracking vocals to the multitrack, apply equalization only if necessary after positioning the best sounding microphone for the best possible sound. If you print an extremely equalized vocal to the multitrack, you're making EQ decisions that are best reserved for mixdown. Once the final instrumentation and orchestration choices are made, you can make intelligent decisions based on the final textural support. It's better to work with a good raw sound during mixdown than to fight an EQ problem you created in overaggressive tracking. During mixdown it's often necessary to EQ the vocals to help them stand out in the mix. Frequencies that need to be cut or boosted are dependent on the orchestration of the completed arrangement.

If you're using very few tracks or doing a live stereo recording of an entire group, it might be necessary to boost the presence range on the voice (between 3 and 5kHz) to increase the understandability of the part. Also, try cutting the lows (below abut 80Hz) to give the voice a more transparent, clear sound.

Recording Environment

The voice is the most personal of instruments. Most of the magic in a vocal performance comes from the emotional interpretation of the true meaning in a song. We might have all our ducks neatly in a row technically, but if the singer isn't feeling comfortable, secure and confident, there's a good chance that the vocal recording won't be all that spectacular.

The producer and engineer set the emotional tone for the session. If they're uptight and impatient, guess how the session will go? "Not well" would be a good guess. If the producer and engineer are positive and emotionally supportive, they can usually get an artist to perform beyond everyone's expectations.

Only the most experienced and self-confident singers can walk into an emotionally dead, cluttered, poorly lit, uncomfortably cold and clammy room and instantly start performing tender and meaningful lyrics with believability.

It's your job as the engineer or producer to see to it that the vocal room is at a comfortable temperature, that the lighting is soft and flattering, and that there isn't a lot of clutter around. Create a mood in the room. Singing is an emotional art. Get the singer into the right emotional frame of mind.

I've done Christmas albums in the middle of summer and had the full array of decorations all over the place to get into the spirit. I've had vocal groups in the back of my van to capture the feeling of four wild and crazy guys singing goofy songs on the way to a gig. I've turned the studio lights up, down and off. I've used different colored lights. I've had singers standing outside the studio on a city street singing their hearts out and I've had singers wailin' away in the bathroom. I've recorded singers who only felt good singing in the biggest room of the best studio in town, and I've recorded singers that really like the down to earth feel of a great home studio. In other words, do what it takes to get your vocalist in the mood to sing the songs they want to sing.

When the moment of truth is upon you and the singer's in the mood and singing the best parts ever, check to make sure that he or she doesn't have change rattling in a pocket or that there isn't a noisy bracelet, necklace or earring that's audible during the recording. These kind of physical noises can pass by undetected while recording, but when you're boosting highs in the mix for the sake of clarity, these transient sounds might quickly become very apparent. Missing this kind of detail while recording tracks can mean heartache during mixdown and might result in sacrificing the vocal sound or possibly re-recording the vocal. Neither of these options is very fun to deal with.

Physical Aids

Always have plenty of coffee cups, cold water, hot water, coffee, tea, etc. on hand. It's a sure bet that someone will be looking for something to drink or eat. A studio that is well-stocked with food, beverages and condiments can really set a good tone for the feeling of a session. This detail might seem kind of trivial and irrelevant to creating great music, but it's very relevant to making musicians feel at home, relaxed and comfortable. These factors are all very important to a successful session.

What a singer eats and drinks has a definite impact on the working of the voice. You should be aware of appropriate and inappropriate food and drink for a studio vocalist. I'm not suggesting that you boldly dictate the artist's eating and drinking habits in a session. In fact, it's probably best to hang back a little at first. But if the singer's having problems in a session, tuck these suggestions away in your memory bank. These foods are good for the voice and will help the vocalist relax the vocal cords:

- Warm water. This can be warmer than lukewarm but not hot. The warm water relaxes the vocal cords just the right amount for singing. Cold water or other iced beverages tighten the vocal cords and hot water or other hot beverages can actually loosen the vocal cords up too much.

- Bananas. The oil in a banana is soothing to the throat without causing phlegm or other mucus. Have the singer eat the banana slowly to coat the throat.

I see a lot of different singers show up with different things that they like to eat or drink. I'm always on the lookout for another good vocal food aid, but warm water and bananas are the two items that consistently work.

There are some items that might hinder a vocalist's progress. Watch out for these home remedies:

- Hot water. Can make the throat too loose.
- Ice cold beverages. These tighten all of the vocal muscles.
- Alcohol and other drugs. Some musicians assume that alcohol, drugs and the studio go together—they don't—especially if you're engineering or producing. Even if it's just a couple of rounds of beers for the band, the first result is usually that everyone starts to

lose a little accuracy and, after a half hour or so, you've got a lethargic band on your hands. Performance energy decreases, mistakes increase, tempos slow down, tempers can flair, etc.

- Citrus products. Oranges, lemons, etc. tend to do more to irritate a throat than they do to help a voice. If your vocalist is a little thrashed already, citrus fruit usually just makes things worse.
- Caffeine.
- Syrups or other thick liquids that cause mucous secretions.

Intonation

Sometimes during a take it's obvious to everyone that the singer is consistently out of tune. This even happens with singers that always seem to have great intonation. So why do they, all of a sudden, start singing sharp or flat when it comes down to recording?

Some vocalists might never have heard themselves well enough in a live setting to accurately judge intonation. This can be a brutal awakening. Once the singer hears the ends of vocal phrases sliding out of tune or hears inconsistent tonality from note to note, they need inner strength and a strong desire to get it right. The strong will survive. The weak will need to learn to be strong. I've seen some singers make incredible leaps in their vocal accuracy and interpretation quickly once they start the process of recording, hearing, evaluating and revising.

Many young singers simply haven't learned enough about their craft to endure the tedium and scrutiny of the recording world. Even though that fact is brutal, you as the engineer/producer are commissioned with the awesome duty of making the best of the situations you're given.

Enunciation and vocal technique are very important. We need to record the most emotion-filled music possible—that's a fact. And the style of music determines the type of emotion we must capture. There are techniques that will provide endurance and stamina. There are principles of enunciation and diction that, when followed, nearly force good intonation and excellent phrasing. Never underplay the value of quality instruction. Whether you play an instrument or sing, fundamental skills support and lead the way to virtuosity and excellent. Though there are stylists who prefer a raw, unrefined sound and emotion, I've never met any musician who wanted mediocrity from themselves or their recordings. Traditional training can always support your individuality. Grasp of fundamentals always leads to greater longevity, more endurance and better health.

Headphones

Often a singer is out of tune simply because the headphone mix is providing an inaccurate pitch reference or a pitch reference that's hard to pinpoint. Always listen to the headphone mix when you're getting the singer set up. It's even a good idea for you to plug headphones into the same mix they're getting so that you'll know instantly when something's not right.

Sometimes the mix isn't bad but the pitch reference is confusing. If the bass is the only pitched instrument in the mix and you're recording reference vocals, you can have a problem because it's often difficult to tell where the pitch center is on a bass guitar. Singing in tune to bass and drum accompaniment can be very difficult.

For pitch reference, the best instruments to include in the headphone mix are piano and clean guitar. Some of the big keyboard sounds include chorus, reverbs and other effects. These effects tend to obscure the pitch center so they can transform the search for accurate intonation into the impossible quest. A clean, non-effected piano or guitar definitively identifies the tonal center, therefore showing the vocalist exactly where *in tune* is.

Singers demand different amounts of their own voice in the phones. Learn what helps them sing best, then strive to provide that at all times. The headphone mix is a key factor in the vocal recording process. Be aware of the headphone mix throughout all your vocal sessions.

Singers often sing with better intonation when they uncover one of their ears rather than letting the headphones cover both ears. Simply moving one side of the headphones behind the ear lets singers hear themselves more like they would in a live setting. This simple technique has the potential to fix intonation problems instantly!

Singers who prefer to listen through only one side of the headphones often like to cup a hand over their open ear with the open palm of the hand facing forward. The hand acts as a cup to capture the sound of the vocal as it reflects back to the ear. This is a very good way for singers to hear themselves. Singers who hear themselves accurately and have a supportive mix of the background accompaniment rarely sing out of tune. The best singers struggle when they can't hear themselves well and are referencing to a confusing mix.

When the headphones are too loud or when they have fluid-filled earpieces (tightly enclosing the ear), most singers sing flat. Open, foam headphones are good for intonation but bad for headphone leakage. (The sound from the headphone that's picked up by the microphone is called *leakage*.) Most major headphone manufacturers make headphones that offer an excellent compromise between completely open phones and completely sealed ears; these typically work best. Examples of excellent headphones for use in vocal recording are the AKG Model K240M and the Sony MDR-7506.

Singers usually like to hear a little reverb or echo in the phones while they're singing. This usually helps them get in the mood for the song. Like singing in the shower, singing with lots of reverb in the phones can be fun. But sometimes you sound *too* good in the headphones and the reverb in the headphone mix might give the vocalist a false sense of security. Pitch and interpretation often sound fine when recording, but when it's time to mix the dry vocal might sound very marginal. A little reverb is usually okay when tracking, but less reverb in the headphones generally results in more accurate vocal tracks.

Punch In/Punch Out

Punching in is the process of going into record while the track is playing back, keeping the part of the track before you press record, then recording from that point until you punch out. *Punching out* is the process of going out of record while the recorder continues playing back, keeping the part of the track after the part you've punched in. This is a very common technique. If the vocal track is excellent with the exception of a few out of tune notes or awkward interpretations, it doesn't make sense to re-record the whole track. It's common to re-record just the questionable sections or words (Illustration 4-24).

The voice is fairly fragile, and many singers wear out pretty quickly in comparison to instrumentalists. To continually re-record complete takes in order to get the perfect pass isn't practical. Be sure the singers you record understand that punching in is common and that even the best singers use this advantage of multitrack recording. Sometimes inexperienced singers expect to walk into a session, sing the part once, have everyone ooh and ah and start collecting the royalties. But singing in a session is hard work and demands a lot of time to perfect each performance. I'm sure you'd like to feel good about your recordings for the next 30 or 40 years, so spend the time to get it right.

Punching in and out is an art that demands focused concentration on the part of the singer and the engineer. Have the singer sing along, leading up to the punch spot so he or she'll be in the right groove when the punch happens. Also, have the singer keep singing the song while you punch out at the right time. As soon as the singer knows where you're punching out, you have problems. When vocalists don't keep singing past the spot where the engineer intends to punch out, they tend to hold the last note past the spot where the next note in the song starts. This mistake can ruin the note after the punch

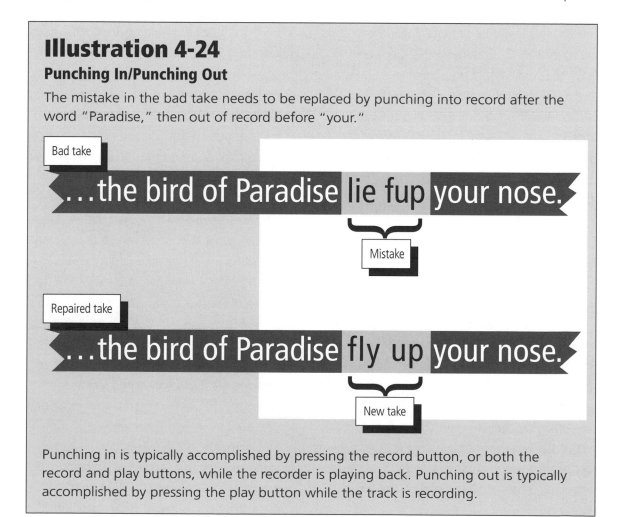

Illustration 4-24
Punching In/Punching Out

The mistake in the bad take needs to be replaced by punching into record after the word "Paradise," then out of record before "your."

Bad take

…the bird of Paradise lie fup your nose.

Mistake

Repaired take

…the bird of Paradise fly up your nose.

New take

Punching in is typically accomplished by pressing the record button, or both the record and play buttons, while the recorder is playing back. Punching out is typically accomplished by pressing the play button while the track is recording.

point, and you'll need to re-record it. This process can get you leapfrogging through most of a song, fast. It's always best to instruct the singer to sing until the recorder stops. This approach also provides you, the engineer, a second chance if you happen to miss your intended punch-out zone.

Sometimes you'll have a very small window for punching in. Good engineers develop the knack for timing the punch-in. A good punch combined with a good performance will be so smooth that no one would ever guess the insert wasn't recorded at the same time as the rest of the track.

Concentrate and focus on the punch-in. As the engineer (and/or producer), you hold the authority to ask all nonessential personnel to leave the studio while you and others essential to the task at hand complete the job. It's easy to be distracted when other people are hanging around, and staying focused is necessary. Nobody has ever expressed anything but appreciation when I've asked people to leave for the good of the recording project.

Perseverance

Even with great singers, you might need to punch in the same exact spot 10 or 20 times. Believe me, it's not fun if you've performed with mechanical precision on the first 19 takes and end up ruining the track on the twentieth take. Somehow the rest of the people around the studio never jump up and happily compliment you on the great job you did on the first 19 takes when that happens. Concentrate and take comfort in the fact that no one has ever spent the rest of their life punching in one word until it was right. Sessions always end at one point or another.

If you have enough tracks, it's a good idea to let the singer sing straight through the song once or twice. Record both takes. Often the first take is the best, especially for inexperienced singers. Once I have the mic and wind screen positioned, the compressor patched in and the headphone mix roughed in, I'll run the tape and have the singer sing the song. I always record this take, even while I'm still tweaking levels and processing. It doesn't hurt anything to record that pass—at worst you've had a pass to get levels set. But if the take is obviously great, you get to hear people say, "You mean you recorded that? Aren't you a swell engineer!" instead of "Boy, I wish we had recorded that one."

If you have a couple of reasonably good takes, the vocalist usually starts to relax a bit because there's a backup. They'll feel free to go for more emotion in the track and to try new and innovative licks. Vocals are mostly mental. If you can provide your singer with a comfortable mental situation, you'll capture better vocal performances.

If you can afford the tracks to keep all vocal takes until mixdown, do it. Often during mixdown you'll hear some unacceptable parts that didn't seem so bad when you recorded them. If you've kept other versions of the lead vocal on other tracks, chances are you'll be able to switch tracks during the mix (if only for a word, a phrase, a verse) repairing the unacceptable passage. Sometimes the first half of one take works great and the second half of another works great. Together they might make up one great take.

Some singers can't deal with punching in and out and having to continually recapture the moment while singing this or that word a little more sharp or flat. If that's the case with the vocalist you're recording, simply print several takes of the complete track. Deal with combining them into one good track during mixdown. Many great recording artists print five to ten full takes and let the producer and engineer piece together an acceptable compilation of the best parts. However, this method requires a lot of tracks and it makes mixdown a lot more involved than if there's simply one good vocal track.

Affordable digital audio workstations have made it possible to perform audio manipulation at home. Until relatively recently, this type of control over pitch and phrasing was performed on very high-cost equipment reserved for only the biggest and best studios. In fact, much of what you can accomplish at home on your Macintosh or PC couldn't be accomplished with respectable quality, at any cost, just a few years ago. The tools available to us are getting better all the time.

In this era, I often find myself capturing the life and fire of the first or second take, then digitally manipulating the pitch or phrasing to suit the artistic expectations of the artist, the band and myself.

Panning

Lead vocals are traditionally panned to the center position. This keeps them the center focal point and, since they're usually very strong in the mix, distributes the vocal energy evenly between the left and right channels. Sometimes certain vocal effects are panned evenly to left and right for a big sound, but no matter what effects we use, the entire lead vocal sound should be evenly balanced between left and right.

Background vocals can be panned left and right depending on how many tracks there are,

but the entire backing track should still be spread out evenly between left and right. When I use multiple backing vocal tracks, I like to spread them across the stereo spectrum, keeping them from the center position. This technique lets you place the lead vocal in the center of the stereo mix with little conflict and competition from the backing vocals.

A duet has, essentially, two lead vocalists. I've had good success panning them both to the center position, and I've also had good results panning them slightly apart. When positioned at 11:30 and 12:30, the two parts separate just enough in stereo to play well off each other, but they're not far enough apart to distract the listener by ping-ponging back and forth across the stereo panorama. A very slight panning to either side of center also translates well to mono.

Common Vocal Effects

Reverb, delay and exciter are commonly used on vocal tracks during mixdown. Sometimes as special effects we use chorus, flanging or phase shifting. Why do we add these effects to vocals anyway? Isn't it better to have true and natural sound?

In recording, it's our goal to produce a sound that's natural, but we need to keep in perspective which acoustical environment we're trying to make it sound natural in. There isn't much that's natural about the sound of a vocalist in a deadened studio singing into one microphone. As engineers, we take that raw sound and, through the use of reverb and other effects, place it in the environment that would make it fun to listen to. For example, in classical recordings, the symphony records in a wonderful concert hall and the recordings include the sound of the hall. A concert hall has several distinct echoes and slapbacks, different types of reverberant sound and, depending on where you're sitting and whether or not you're moving while you listen, chorus type effects and constant EQ changes. Effects simulate the proper acoustical ambience for specific musical styles.

Delay

When you're recording vocals to the multitrack, whether lead or backing, it's always best to record dry. In other words, don't print reverbs, delays, chorus or other effects to the multitrack. The only processing that should be in the signal path between the vocalist and the multitrack is a compressor. If you're doing a live to stereo recording of a band, you obviously need to have all of the effects you want on the vocal while recording, but in a multitrack situation where you'll remix the song later, try hardest to save vocal effects for the mixdown. Let's take a look at some of the effects that work very well in mixdown or on live recordings. If you're not sure how these effects are patched in, refer to Volume 1, Chapters 1 and 2 of the *AudioPro Home Recording Course*.

Reverb is the most commonly heard effect on vocals, but before reverb I'll usually set up a delay or two. A digital delay is a powerful sound shaping tool because it can be used in so many ways. Most new recordists think of delay as having the repeating echo sound like that in Audio Example 4-29. Repeating echoes like this can confuse and clutter an otherwise good mix. Use this effect cautiously.

Audio Example 4-29 Repeating Echo
CD-1: Track 44

Slapback

A slapback is a single repeat of the original signal. The delay time on this single repeat must be longer than 35ms to be categorized as a slapback, with the most common slapback delay times between 120 and 300ms.

The initial delay of the direct sound is what gives the brain its perception of the size of the room the sound is in. The longer the slapback, the larger the room. A slapback can make a vocal sound very big fast, before the addition of reverb. The single delay has a cleaner sound than lots of reverb. Often lead vocals have no reverb, just delay. Listen to the dry vocal track in Audio Example 4-30.

Audio Example 4-30 The Dry Vocal
CD-1: Track 45

Audio Example 4-31 demonstrates the same part with a slapback delay panned center. Notice how much more interesting this simple effect makes the lead vocal.

Audio Example 4-31 The Single Slapback
CD-1: Track 45

The delay in Audio Example 4-31 is in time with the eighth note of this song. Most delays work best if they relate in some way to the tempo of the song. Refer to Volume 1, Chapter 2 of the *AudioPro Home Recording Course* to find out how to calculate delays in relation to tempo.

Another delay effect that's common involves the use of a short slapback as a thickener. This technique utilizes a delay time between about 35 and 75ms. This procedure involves the main lead vocal panned to the center position supported by a thickening delay (also panned center). Bring the level of the delay up behind the main vocal until the combination sounds fuller and larger than just the original—but not so far that the vocal sounds unnatural. Listen to the vocal in Audio Example 4-32. I'll start with just the dry vocal, then turn the 60ms delay up past the point where it sounds natural. Then I'll turn the delay back down to a more realistic, natural-sounding level. Toward the end of the example, I'll switch the delay on and off. Notice when the delay's gone the sound loses some interest, but when the delay's there the sound is still natural.

Audio Example 4-32 60ms Slapback
CD-1: Track 45

Delays blur variations in intonation and generally give the vocal a rich and interesting sound. As the delay combines with the dry sound, we end up with an interaction between the delay and the original that can simulate chorus-type effects. Even a long sustained vocal note benefits from simple delays. The pitch and time differences between the original and effected sounds work together to form a very interesting and smooth combination.

Most current effects processors can produce two delays simultaneously making it easy to combine a long and short slapback. Listen to the lead vocal in Audio Example 4-33. I'll start

dry, add a 60ms delay to thicken the sound, then add a 240ms slapback to give the perception of a large acoustic environment.

Audio Example 4-33
60ms Slapback Combined With 240ms Slapback
CD-1: Track 45

The Electronic Double

Doubling combines the vocal with a delay that's less than 35ms. This effect works very well on backing vocals and sometimes on lead vocals. Typically, the original is panned to one side and the delay is panned to the other side. This gives a wide stereo effect and can provide a great sound in stereo. Caution! Always check these doubling effects in mono. As we've discovered in previous chapters, combining short delays to a mono mix can result in total or partial cancelation of the track. This is never a good thing to do to your lead vocal track. Listen to the mix in mono and adjust the delay time until the sound is full and natural sounding. This'll assure you that the track will sound good in mono and stereo.

In Audio Example 4-34, you'll hear the dry vocal panned center. Then I'll turn up the 19ms delayed vocal on the right as I pan the dry vocal left.

Audio Example 4-34 The Electronic Double
CD-1: Track 46

A double produces a very big sound that's fun to listen to as long as you've cross-checked to mono. In Audio Example 4-35, I'll sum the stereo mix to mono and adjust the delay time in 1ms increments. Notice the extreme differences on some of the changes.

Audio Example 4-35 Delay Changes in Mono
CD-1: Track 46

The Electronic Triple

If your effects processor can produce two separate simultaneous delays, try expanding the double to a triple. Use two delays shorter than 35ms—try 13ms and 29ms. Pan the two delays apart and keep the original in the center. If you don't turn the delays up too far, this technique adds a very full, broad dimension to any sound while maintaining a natural character. As with the double, always be sure to check the sounds in mono. While listening in mono, adjust the delays in 1ms increments until the sound is full and natural. Don't forget that prime numbered delay times generally sound most natural when summing a mix to mono. On the vocal in Audio Example 4-36, I'll add the two delays, left and right, around the original track that is panned center.

Audio Example 4-36 The Electronic Triple
CD-1: Track 47

Regeneration

If you've used a slapback but want a little fuller sound, try regenerating the delay. This makes the delay repeat more times. When I'm regenerating, I'll usually set the delay up to repeat four or five times and typically set the delay time

between 200 and 300ms. If you overuse regeneration, your mix might lose clarity. Too many echoes typically result in a mushy sounding mix. Used in moderation, though, regeneration is capable of smoothing out the rough edges of a vocal in a very pleasing way. Listen to the mix in Audio Example 4-37 as I add regenerating delay to the lead vocal after the first few measures.

Audio Example 4-37 Regenerating Delay
CD-1: Track 48

Although these delay techniques can be used on lead vocals and background vocals, their use is totally dependent on the style and artistic vision for the song. Doubling, tripling and thickening delays are most common on backing vocals because of the enlarging effect that they have while still keeping a tight rhythmic feel. Longer slapback and regenerated delays above 100ms and thickening delays between 50 and 100ms are most common on lead vocals because of the full and flattering sound they add.

Reverb

The most common effect on vocals is reverberation. Even a marginal vocal track can sound pretty good all by itself if you pour enough reverb on it. Excessive reverberation can put a haze over the sound of your mix and give your music an amateur sound. Most current reverberation devices let you control reverb times, predelays, pre-echoes, EQ and most any parameter you can imagine controlling. This flexibility actually puts more responsibility on the engineer to achieve a specific sound that fits a song. Refer to Volume 1, Chapter 2 of the *AudioPro Home Recording Course* if you are unclear about the controls and common features available on a reverberation or multi-effects device.

Ballads in most styles sound good with long reverb times, between two and four seconds on the lead vocal. The decaying reverberation blends the space that exists between the beats of a slow tempo ballad. Hall and chamber reverb sounds fill a song the best, in most cases, because of their dark, rich sound. The ballad in Audio Example 4-38 uses hall reverb with a delay time of 2.6 seconds and a predelay of 60ms.

Audio Example 4-38 Hall Reverb on a Ballad
CD-1: Track 49

The sound of hall and chamber reverberation tends to get covered up on faster songs that contain a lot of different rhythmic and harmonic parts. There has to be so much reverb to actually hear the effect that the mix sounds very muddy. Bright reverb works better on fast songs; plates, some room sounds and bright chamber sounds work best. You can hear the effect without drowning the mix in reverb. Listen to the plate reverb sound on the lead vocal in Audio Example 4-39.

Audio Example 4-39
Plate Reverb on the Lead Vocal
CD-1: Track 50

Predelay

The predelay setting can simulate the sound of slapback delay with reverberation occurring only after the slapback. This feature is very useful. Like the slapback, it lets the original sound happen dry and uneffected, then the delay fills in the holes and adds interest. Predelay replaces the simple slapback echo with the delayed, 100 percent wet reverberation. We keep the clean effect of the slapback while adding the filling effect of reverb. Every vocal note is heard clean and dry for the first instant, only to be followed and filled out by smooth reverberation. Using short decay times (between .5 and 1 second) and long predelays (between 100 and 250ms) produces vocal sounds that are very big and impressive while maintaining a tight sounding mix. The vocal in Audio Example 4-40 has a predelay of 120ms and a decay time of .7 seconds.

Audio Example 4-40
120ms Predelay With .7 Second Decay
CD-1: Track 51

If you're in the market for a reverb, buy at least 16-bit technology; anything less lacks clarity and transparency. Reverb effects are essential to all but a few styles of recorded music. Don't be afraid to try different brands and types of effects. Even some of the seemingly less sophisticated equipment works very well in the appropriate musical context.

Classic equipment offers unique character and usually a very musical sound, and the sound is what counts. As long as you aren't adding unacceptable amounts of noise to your recordings, use the tool that best supports the emotional impact of the song. Putting a personal touch on your recordings is good. Many of the classic microphones and signal processors are unrivaled by modern technology. I recommend that you test any gear you can get your hands on.

Exciter

An exciter can add an edge to a lead or backing vocal that can make them stand out in the mix without actually adding EQ. The exciter adds presence and an airy quality that differs from the sound created by simply boosting the high frequencies. If you want more presence in your vocal sound, try either boosting between 3 and 5kHz and cutting the lows below 80Hz or adding an exciter.

Most exciters operate on the premise that boosting harmonics produces a cleaner, more natural presence than simply boosting highs. Therefore, the exciters alter the incoming waveform by adding to the upper harmonic content. Most exciters let you control which harmonics are boosted and in this way act much like equalizers. Some exciters let you excite the low end as well as the high end. No matter how they work, exciters offer a different sound than simple equalization. I find plenty of uses for them, but I also find plenty of situations when they aren't musically appropriate.

The exciter patches in like any other effects processor. As with other effects, it's best to keep the original vocal clean while blending the excited sound in through a return channel. Listen to the lead vocal in Audio Example 4-41. After the first few measures I'll start adding the return from the exciter. This effect is often subtle, but listen to the change in lead vocal clarity as I turn up the exciter.

Audio Example 4-41 The Exciter
CD-1: Track 52

In Audio Example 4-42, instead of using the exciter to add clarity to the vocal, I'll boost high frequencies at 4kHz and roll off the lows below 80Hz.

Audio Example 4-42
Boosting 4kHz and Rolling Off the
Lows Below 80Hz
CD-1: Track 53

Both the exciter and equalization increase vocal clarity and presence, but they each have a different feeling and sound.

Chorus/Flanger/Phase Shifter

Chorus, flanger and phase shifting effects are used mostly as special effects on lead vocals. In stereo they can produce an interesting sound at first, but they tend to make a lead vocal sound unnatural. When overused, these modulating effects get old fast. When used as a special effect just on the chorus or verse, these effects can help break up an otherwise bland arrangement. Keep these techniques in mind, but try not to overuse them.

Chorus effects often sound very good on a backing vocal group. If you have two or three backing vocal tracks, try panning them across the spectrum at 3:00 and 9:00 or possibly 10:00, 12:00 and 2:00. This by itself usually produces an impressively full sound. Using an aux bus, send these vocal tracks to a stereo effects unit set to chorus. Bring the returns back into the mixer on two separate channels and pan them hard right and hard left. Blend the chorus in to fill out the backing vocal sound. Listen to Audio Example 4-43 as I use this technique to fill out the backing vocals.

Audio Example 4-43
Chorusing the Backing Vocals
CD-1: Track 54

Doubling and tripling also work very well on backing vocals. To double, try panning all the backing vocals left, then send them to a delay using an aux bus. Bring the return from the delay back into the mixer on a separate channel and pan the delay hard right. Use a delay time between about 7 and 23ms. This technique produces a very wide and impressive backing vocal sound. Remember, with all these techniques that use short delays, cross-check your mixes in mono. The backing vocal in Audio Example 4-44 has been panned left, then combined with a short delay panned right.

Audio Example 4-44 Doubling the Backing Vocals
CD-1: Track 54

Tripling is set up the same way as the chorus in Audio Example 4-44. The backing vocal tracks in Audio Example 4-45 are panned across the stereo spectrum and then combined with two separate short delays panned hard right and hard left.

Audio Example 4-45 Tripling the Backing Vocals
CD-1: Track 54

If you're having problems getting these full vocal sounds to transfer well to mono, try panning just short of hard right and hard left, rather than full left and right—try 9:00 and 3:00 or 8:00 and 4:00.

Backing Vocals

When recording background vocals, there are several considerations to keep in mind: Do you want a natural, live sound? Do you want a textured, layered sound? Do you have one singer to do one part? Are you trying to make one background singer sound like several? If you have a group of singers, how good are they at singing parts together? The list of considerations goes on and on. I'd like to present some guidelines that'll help you through some basic backing vocal recording situations.

First of all, use as few mics as possible to get the job done. If you have four singers in one room, the temptation is to set up four separate mics to get a good controlled blend at the mixer. With this type of setup, there's typically so much phase interaction between the four mics that the overall sound of the vocals takes a nose dive and won't sound full and clean, especially when you're recording in a small room.

Try using one good microphone, in omni- or bidirectional setting. Move the singers around the mic until you find the blend you need. Once you get a good performance recorded, try recording it again on another track. This live doubling technique produces very big, full-sounding backing vocals. Have the singers change places on the doubled take to capture a little different blend, adding to the dimension of the live double.

If you want ultimate control of the vocal blend during mixdown, record the singers at the same time but isolate each singer in separate rooms, using separate mics. Or, record them one at a time to different tracks. This technique eats up tracks fast but allows you flexibility in the mixdown, plus it gives you the ability to get each part just right, one at a time, instead of trying to get the entire group to sing it right simultaneously.

If your multitrack has a variable speed control, record two or three tracks of the same part. Each time you record a new track, change the speed of the recorder, slightly—this change doesn't need to be drastic. Changes measured in hundredths of a half step or tenths of a cent are typically effective. If you alter the speed of the multitrack between 1 and 7 cents during record mode, then play back at normal speed, you've effectively changed the harmonic content of the vocal track. If you record a few different takes, all at different speeds, the backing vocal sound will be much larger as a result. Often the slight timbre changes produced by this technique give your backing vocals an airy, ringing texture very difficult to achieve in any other way. Since the timbre changes are constant between the tracks, the resulting group sound takes on the sound of a double occurring an octave above the recorded parts. With a digital audio workstation you can achieve this effect by adjusting the pitch of the different tracks, slightly altering the pitch until you find the texture that best suits the music.

Use these tips as guidelines to achieve the sound you want, but let the needs of the song rule the procedures you take. Maybe the only way the vocal group can perform their task of emotionally interpretating musical thoughts is to record in one small room, using separate microphones on each singer. If that's the case, you need to make sure everything works out well for the project. But at least, if you're aware of the potential damage caused by combining multiple mics in a small room, you'll do your best to isolate the vocalists as much as possible; constantly reference the group vocal sound in mono to verify the sonic integrity of each song.

Conclusion

Recording vocals, more than any other instrument, involves people skills as much as technical skills. Relations between the artist and the engineer or producer are usually key in getting a good take. A great take consists of an excellent recording of an especially emotional interpretation of a song. A good technical recording of a bad lyrical interpretation won't get anyone anywhere in the music business.

Practice these techniques. The more vocalists you record, the better. They'll each have a different set of technical and emotional demands for you. Rise to the occasion. Be accommodating but be diligent. Do your best to get the vocalist to do his or her best, and you can both expect a vocal take that far exceeds the norm.

Master the principles I've presented in this chapter, then use them while you expand on them. I'm always trying new techniques. It doesn't usually take that long to set something up if you already have the visual picture in your mind. Experiment!

All vocals were written and performed by Antowaine Richardson from Seattle, WA. Antowaine's a cappella vocal group, The Main Attraction, started singing on the streets of the Pike Place Market area in Seattle. Now they have a heavy concert performance schedule in and out of the country and their albums are distributed nationally, as well as in Europe and Japan. These guys are the real thing, and Antowaine is an incredible vocal talent. Thanks, "Twon!"

5 Acoustic Piano and Rhodes

Piano is popular in almost all commercial styles. Since practically speaking, it contains all usable musical pitches and often dominates the musical texture of a song, it's especially important that we study recording techniques for this instrument.

Acoustic piano and the Rhodes-type electric piano typically fulfill the same musical function, but there are differences in the way the sounds are recorded and in the effects that are appropriate for each.

Before you start miking any piano, see that it's in tune and has been serviced to eliminate buzzes, clicks and thumps. If there are physical noises that occur spontaneously while the piano plays, your job is suddenly much more difficult than it should be. The piano must sound good by itself so that it will meet the high standards you should be setting for your recordings.

Grand Piano

The Basics

Whether recording a nine-foot grand piano, a spinet piano, an old-time upright piano or a sampled piano, it's understood that we're trying to achieve the full, rich sound that only an acoustic piano can provide. A great piano, miked and recorded well, has life, transparency and openness that's hard to beat.

For the purpose of this chapter, we're going to study the grand piano first because this is really the instrument that provides the right sound in the right place. Most people don't have a full-sized grand piano living in their personal studio, but if there's a respectably decent console or spinet piano around, there are some techniques we can pull out of a hat to simulate the sound of a grand piano. Or, if you have a sampler with some really good piano samples, you're in luck.

In Audio Example 5-1, listen to a grand piano miked with a couple of good condenser mics for a wide, impressive solo piano sound.

Audio Example 5-1 Stereo Grand Piano
CD-1: Track 55

We'll compare the other acoustic piano sounds to the grand, so listen closely to each example. Take notes on the differences in sound. Also, note the subjective differences that you perceive in the "feel" of these different sounds. Some sounds might seem more open or airy while others might seem blocky, chunky or thick. Use your own terms. Keeping track of these sometimes intangible impressions is valuable, especially when you need to communicate with other people you're recording with. Often our choice of one sound over another is based largely—or totally—on the impression the

Illustration 5-1
Basic Piano Miking

Two condenser mics are aimed at the strings from above the piano with the lid open on the long or short stick.

Mic 1 is centered over the treble strings, 6–18" above the strings and 6–18" behind the hammers.

Mic 2 is centered over the bass strings, 6–18" from the strings and 2–4' from the end of the piano, depending on the size of the piano and the desired sound.

Condenser microphones are the best to use on piano because of their typically excellent frequency response curve and their accurate transient response.

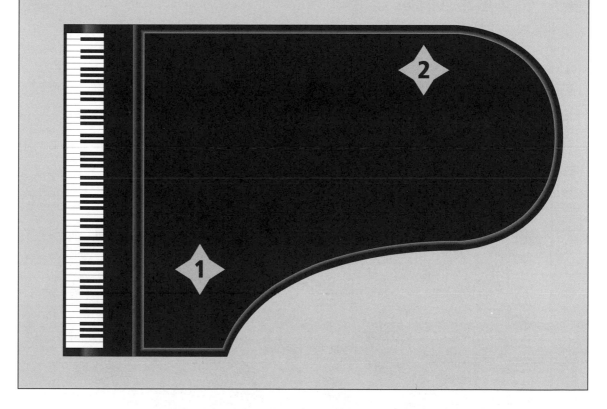

sound gives us, rather than the technical perfection of the recording.

The method of choice for most engineers when recording grand piano is two good condenser mics aimed at the strings (Illustration 5-1). One mic is placed over the high strings, and the other is placed over the low strings. When these mics are panned across the stereo spectrum, the piano has a very big sound and provides good support for most vocal or instrumental solos. How far apart you pan the highs and lows is dependent on the musical context: If the two mics can be printed to separate tracks of the multitrack, save these decisions for mixdown.

In order to get a good transition from lows to highs and a good recording of most of the piano range, it's necessary to keep the mics about a foot or more from the strings. If they are placed much closer, the mid notes might get lost in the blend. This can sometimes be at the expense of the very highs and the very lows, but that's OK if you're getting the sound that supports the music or the piano part doesn't use the extreme highs and lows of the keyboard (Illustration 5-2).

Always experiment with the exact mic placement for two specific reasons:

- Different musical parts have different musical ranges for the left and/or the right hand. Musical style and consideration dictate the microphone placement.

- Again, the phase interaction between the two

Illustration 5-2
Mics Close to the Strings and Each Other

If mics 1 and 2 are close to the strings, they need to be close to each other to fill in the mid notes. This decreases the punch of the very high and very low notes, but it produces a close sound that's quite good—as long as the musical part doesn't emphasize the extreme highs and lows.

Phase interaction between the mics can be detrimental to a mono track, especially as the mics move closer together. Be sure you check the sound of the two mics summed to mono before you record the piano track.

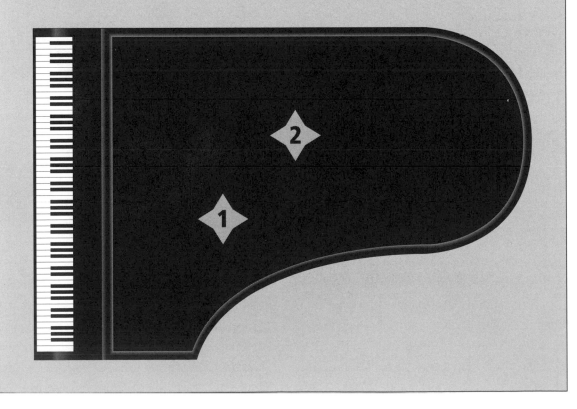

microphones is critical. If the distance between the mics changes a few inches, the sound of the piano changes drastically when heard in mono.

There are quite a few variables involved with piano so let's look at some of the differ-ences in sound that we can bring about with the various techniques we apply.

Condenser mics are the best choice for achieving the most accurate and natural-sounding recording of any piano because it's technically a percussion instrument. The felt

Illustration 5-3
Miking the Piano With One Condenser Centered
With the lid wide open, place one condenser mic centered at the opening of the lid.

hammers hitting the strings produce a transient attack to each note, and as we've found with drums and percussion, condenser mics respond better to transients than other mics.

The intensity of the transient is dependent upon the condition of the felt hammers and the brilliance of the strings. The felt hammers on any piano can be conditioned to produce a sharper attack with a brighter tone or a duller attack with a mellower tone. If you have the felt hammers on your piano conditioned, keep in mind that a brighter sound with more attack stands out in a rhythm section mix very well; on the other hand, solo pianists often prefer a darker, mellower tone. This conditioning is called *voicing* the piano.

The grand piano in Audio Example 5-2 is miked with one condenser mic inside the wide open lid, from a distance of about three feet. It's necessary to keep the mic back a little to get an even balance between the low notes and the high notes (Illustration 5-3).

Audio Example 5-2
One Condenser Mic From Three Feet
CD-1: Track 56

Mic Choice and Technique

Each condenser microphone provides a unique sound on piano. Even though two mics might have identical specifications, the sounds they produce might be very different. Here are some mics that I've used on grand piano and some of my observations on them. Keep in mind that each room and each piano is a little different. These are just a few of the combinations I've tried; you might find great result with other mics.

- AKG 451, AKG 460, Neumann KM84. I've found these mics and those similar in style and price to be the most accurate mics on piano. They capture a sound that's very true to the natural sound of the instrument. These mics have become my first choice for grand piano.

- AKG 414. This is also a great mic and the first choice piano mic for many engineers. It has a more present high end and low end than the mics in the AKG 451 category, and in some mixes, the added highs and lows might get in the way of the other instruments.

- Neumann U87. This mic is very warm in the lows and mids, but for my taste is a little lacking in presence. Many engineers prefer this mic for piano.

- Neumann TLM170. In the right musical context, this is a fabulous mic and sounds good on vocals as well as piano.

- Cheaper condenser mics, like the Sony ECM22P, often sound fine on piano. Check the sound of several different mics on your piano; each situation is a little different.

Most of us have a limited number of choices when it comes to mic selection. If all you own is a moving-coil mic like the SM57, then that's what you'll need to use. But as your engineering skills and opportunities increase, try some of these mics—along with anything else you can get your hands on.

If you mike the piano with a moving-coil mic, you usually get a sound with a little more edge and less accuracy in the transient. The piano in Audio Example 5-3 is miked with one moving-coil microphone from about three inches. Listen closely to the attack of each note and notice whether the sound is full or thin.

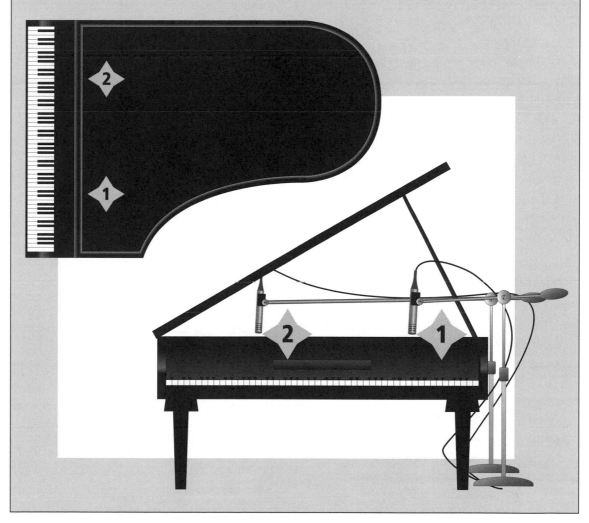

Illustration 5-4
Both Mics by the Hammers

Place both mics 6–12" behind the hammers, aiming them at the strings from a distance of 6–18". Center mic 1 over the treble strings and center mic 2 over the bass strings.

Audio Example 5-3 One Mic From Three Inches
CD-1: Track 57

Moving farther away from the piano provides an interesting texture, depending on the room where the piano is being recorded. It's usually best to mike the grand piano from within four feet of the sound board. Close-mike technique gives us an intimate sound that we can add space to with reverb if it's needed in the mix.

Room sound is easy to add with a good controllable reverb, but if the piano on tape has too much room sound, it's difficult or impossible to get rid of. The piano in Audio Example 5-4 is miked with a condenser microphone about six feet from the open piano lid. Notice the room sound.

Audio Example 5-4
One Mic, Six Feet From the Open Piano Lid
CD-1: Track 58

When miking the piano with two mics, move in closer to the strings still enabling balance control between the treble and bass strings. With two mics, we can get as close as six inches from the strings. A distance of eight to twelve inches is usually the best distance for miking the grand piano with two mics.

Listen to the piano in Audio Example 5-5 miked with two condenser mics. First I solo the mic for the bass strings, then I solo the mic for the treble strings. Listen as I blend the two mics for a good even mono sound, then pan the two mics slowly apart for a wider stereo image.

Audio Example 5-5
Two Condenser Mics From About Eight Inches
CD-1: Track 59

There are several options for mic placement when miking the grand piano. The mics can either both be placed by the hammers (Illustration 5-1) or they can be positioned with one mic over the treble strings by the hammers and the other over the bass strings, about halfway toward the far end of the piano (Illustration 5-4).

In Audio Example 5-6, the piano is miked

with two condenser mics a few inches behind the hammers: one aimed toward the high notes and one aimed toward the low notes. The mics are about a foot apart and about eight inches from the strings.

Audio Example 5-6
Two Condenser Mics by the Hammers
CD-1: Track 60

To get a wider stereo image, or to gain better control of the lows in relation to the highs, move the mics further apart. Compare Audio Example 5-7 to the previous example. Notice the difference in treble to bass balance with the mics further apart in example 5-7.

Audio Example 5-7
Two Condenser Mics Further Apart
CD-1: Track 60

Try miking the grand piano with the same kind of coincident stereo miking techniques we've used on other instruments in this course. Set up a coincident stereo X-Y mic configuration with the piano lid up and the mics facing the strings (Illustration 5-5). Audio Example 5-8 demonstrates the sound of a grand piano with two cardioid condenser mics placed at the edge of the open piano facing in and positioned in an X-Y configuration.

Audio Example 5-8 X-Y Configuration
CD-1: Track 61

Be sure your mic cables are wired in proper

Illustration 5-5
Coincident Stereo Miking

Mics 1 and 2 are in a traditional X-Y configuration, facing into the piano at the edge with the lid open. This technique produces a full stereo sound with minimal problematic phase cancelation in mono, although there isn't much control over the bass and treble ranges of the instrument.

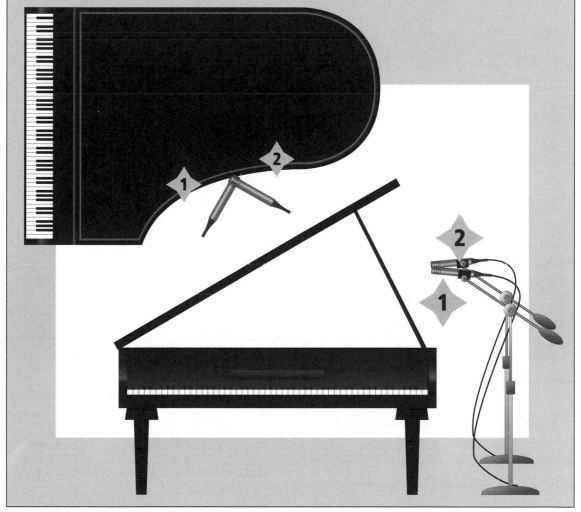

phase; always check the piano in mono. If the left mic and right mic are 180° out of phase, your mix might be in for big trouble if anyone listens to it in mono. Audio Example 5-9 demonstrates the stereo sound of a piano with the two mics 180° out of phase.

Audio Example 5-9
Stereo Sound With Two Mics 180° Out of Phase
CD-1: Track 62

While Audio Example 5-9 sounds fine in stereo, Audio Example 5-10 demonstrates the exact same take, this time combined to mono.

Audio Example 5-10
Mono Sound With Two Mics 180° Out of Phase
CD-1: Track 62

From the previous two Audio Examples, you can hear how crucial it is to test piano in mono, just in case the mono monster is lurking around the stereo corner.

There'll probably not be many times when mic placement alone results in two piano mics being exactly 180° out of phase, but there will often be times when the mics are in a phase relationship that ends up sounding thin and weak when summed to mono.

Listen to the three recordings of a piano in Audio Examples 5-11 through 5-13. The mics, the piano and the player are all the same. On all takes, the mics are in the same general position—only slight position changes are made. You'll hear each track in stereo first, then in mono. Notice the sound change in mono.

Audio Example 5-11
Configuration 1 in Stereo, Then Mono
CD-1: Track 63

Audio Example 5-12
Configuration 2 in Stereo, Then Mono
CD-1: Track 63

Audio Example 5-13
Configuration 3 in Stereo, Then Mono
CD-1: Track 63

From these examples, it's clear that checking the piano in mono is an important part of getting a good, usable track.

Stereo or Mono

Even when the piano is miked with two mics, it's not always best to keep the piano stereo in the mix. If the stereo tracks are hard-panned, the sound might be unnatural, with the highs and lows spread far apart in the stereo image. Often the two mics—or tracks—are simply used to get a good balance between the treble, mid and bass strings. A mono track might sound very natural, and if the sound needs to spread apart in the stereo spectrum, we can use the same kind of delay effect we've used on other instruments to create a stereo sound. Again, be sure to check these delay effects in mono to verify that you have commercially usable tracks.

Audio Example 5-14 demonstrates a piano track recorded with two mics blended to a mono track.

Audio Example 5-14 Two Mics Blended to Mono
CD-1: Track 64

Audio Example 5-15 is the mono track from Audio Example 5-14 panned left with a doubling delay of about 11ms panned right.

Audio Example 5-15
Mono Track Panned Left With an 11ms
Delay Panned Right
CD-1: Track 65

Chorus, phase shifter and flanging effects don't produce a natural sound on the acoustic piano and are rarely used. Audio Example 5-16 demonstrates an acoustic piano through a flanger. This unnatural piano sound is used only for special effects.

Audio Example 5-16 Flanged Piano
CD-1: Track 66

If the piano remains stereo, the mics might be soft-panned at about 10:00 and 2:00. If the piano is in the same rhythm section with a guitar, the stereo piano tracks often lean to one side—say at about 11:00 and 4:00—and the guitar track or tracks are positioned across the panorama to offset the piano.

Instrument Maintenance

Even if you do everything technically perfect, don't overlook the importance of keeping the piano in tune and properly serviced. Without good conditioning and intonation, there's not much chance of recording an acceptable piano track.

It's sometimes tempting to try tuning or voicing a piano yourself. This is a difficult task that is best left to professionals. It's not uncommon for would-be piano technicians to attempt to brighten the piano sound by putting shellac, fingernail polish or tacks on the felt hammers. While these techniques might provide some good and interesting piano sounds, they can also cause a lot of problems if done incorrectly—problems that can cost a substantial amount of money to repair. Be careful! Have the pros service your piano.

Setting the Mood

Creating a comfortable, pleasant atmosphere for the pianist is an important part of a good recording, especially when recording a very emotional solo piece. The room temperature should be comfortable, and your attitude should be positive and supportive.

If these seem like unimportant factors to you, you're wrong. Recording music is an emotional experience for the artist and the engineer. A negative attitude can destroy the emotion of a session and therefore destroy the interpretation of the music. Too many engineers, producers and musicians get so into the technical aspects of the recording process that they inhibit the artistic flow of the music. Somewhere between perfected details and totally free interpretation, there's a balance where the technical and emotional sides of the music are as good as they can cumulatively be for a particular moment in time.

Processing Piano Sounds

No Two Pianos Sound Identical

No two pianos sound the same. When you're trying to get the best sound from any instrument, remember to use mic choice and technique before equalizing the sound. Fine-tune the sound quality by changing the mic distance and placement over the strings. Adjust the mic placement for the least problematic phase interaction between the mics.

Listen to the sound changes resulting from these different mic placement combinations. Each Audio Example (5-17 through 5-22) uses the same two condenser mics, panned hard left

Illustration 5-6
Piano Miking Variation
Mics 1 and 2 are aimed at the strings from a distance of about 6".

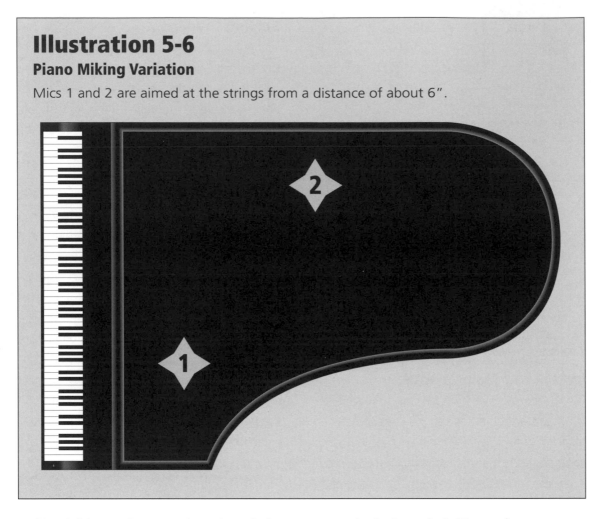

and hard right, on the same piano through the same console.

Audio Example 5-17 demonstrates a stereo piano mic setup with one mic four inches behind the hammers centered over the treble strings and one mic three to four feet behind the hammers centered over the bass strings. Each mic is about six inches from the strings (Illustration 5-6).

Audio Example 5-17
One Mic Over the Treble Strings and
One Mic Over the Bass Strings
CD-1: Track 67

Audio Example 5-18 uses the exact same configuration as the previous example, except the mics are about 18 inches from the strings (Illustration 5-7).

Audio Example 5-18
Mics 18 Inches From the Strings
CD-1: Track 68

In Audio Example 5-19, both mics are about six inches behind the hammers and about a foot from the strings. One mic is centered over the treble strings, and the other mic is centered over the bass strings (Illustration 5-8).

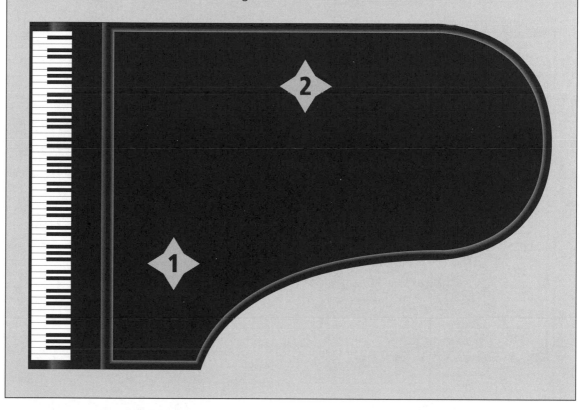

Illustration 5-7
Piano Miking Variation

Mics 1 and 2 are aimed at the strings from a distance of about 18".

Audio Example 5-19
Both Mics Six Inches Behind the Hammers
CD-1: Track 69

Audio Example 5-20
Mics Over the Hammers, But Further Apart
CD-1: Track 70

Audio Example 5-20 is the same as the previous example, except the mics are further apart. The treble mic is aimed at a point about ten inches in from the highest string, and the low mic is aimed at a point about ten inches in from the lowest string (Illustration 5-9).

In Audio Example 5-21, there's a stereo pair of mics in an X-Y configuration facing into the piano about one foot inside the piano with the lid up in its highest position (Illustration 5-10).

Audio Example 5-21
Stereo X-Y Configuration Aiming Into the Piano
CD-1: Track 71

Illustration 5-8
Piano Miking Variation

Both mics are about 6" behind the hammers and about 12" from the strings.

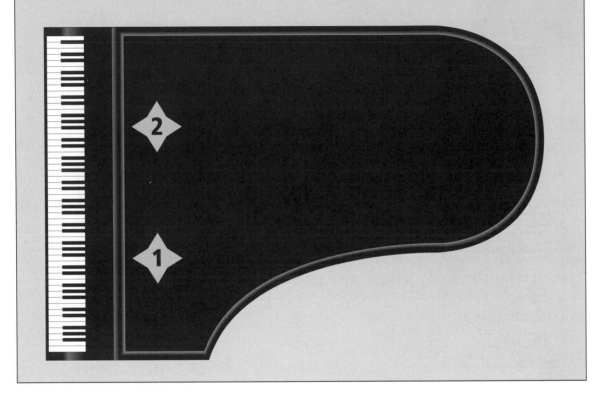

Audio Example 5-22 demonstrates the same configuration as 5-21 but with the piano lid in its lowest position and a packing blanket covering the opening. This is one of the techniques we might use to help acoustically isolate the piano tracks (Illustration 5-11).

Audio Example 5-22
X-Y With the Lid Lower and a
Blanket Over the Opening
CD-1: Track 71

Listen closely to Audio Examples 5-17 through 5-22. Use the chart provided in Illus-tration 5-12 to list your opinions about the char-acteristic sound qualities in each example. These are valuable comparisons that will help your opinions about sound mature to new levels. We can learn as much by noting configuration changes that don't noticeably change the sound quality as we do by noting configuration changes that do make significant sound changes.

Recording Levels

Suggested recording levels vary from piano to piano, depending on the low-frequency content of the piano sound and the sharpness of each note's attack.

The piano is a percussion instrument—

Illustration 5-9
Piano Miking Variation

Both mics are at the extreme ends of the keyboard, aimed at the strings from a distance of approximately 12". This technique produces a very wide stereo image, but it can leave the mid notes softer than the highs or lows.

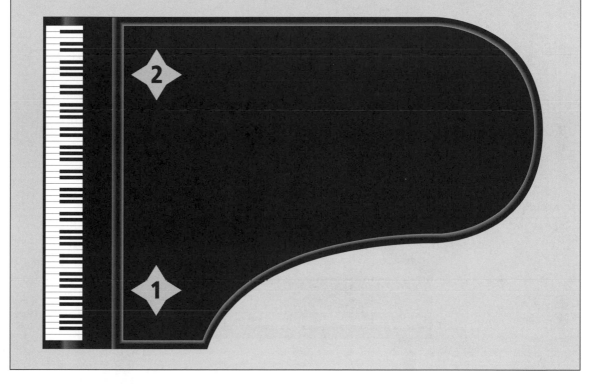

because the hammers hit the strings—and there are transients in the attack of each note. We can only estimate optimum recording levels based on judgment, experience and knowledge. Our goal is to record at levels that accurately capture the transients while still maintaining hot enough levels to stay away from the noise floor—or, in digital recording, to fully use the digital audio resolution.

As I mentioned earlier in this chapter, pianos are voiced bright and aggressive or warm and smooth to suit the performer's taste. If the sound is bright and aggressive, we must record at lower levels—in the range of -7 to -3VU—at the hottest part of the track. As a rule of thumb, record at colder levels when the sound contains less low-frequency information.

If the sound is warm and smooth—in other words, it contains more low-frequency information and has a softer attack—you are typically safe to record at hotter levels. Recording levels of about 0VU at the hottest part of the track should work fine.

These suggested levels refer, primarily, to analog recording. If you're recording directly to DAT, ADAT or any other digital storage medium, the primary concern is to avoid recording at levels hotter than zero on the machine's

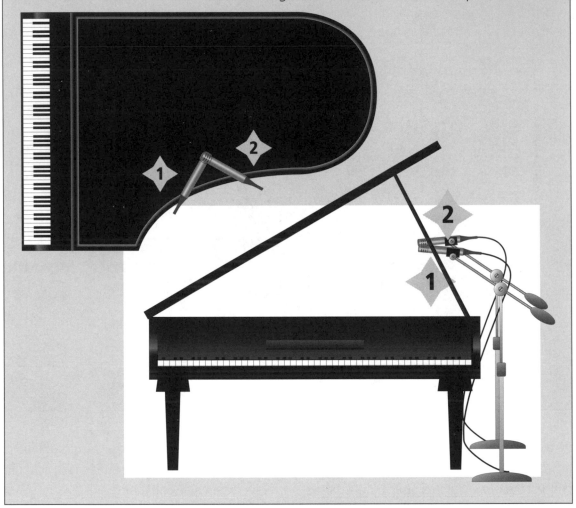

Illustration 5-10
Piano Miking Variation

Mics 1 and 2 are in a traditional X-Y configuration about 1' inside the open lid.

meter. In digital recording, it's best to have the strongest part of the track react zero on the meter. If there isn't one portion of the musical take that reaches zero, you're not using the complete resolution of your digital system. If you record at low levels on a digital system you probably won't have a noise problem, but you probably *will* have a clarity problem.

If you record piano too hot to analog tape, the first thing you'll lose is definition of the tran-

sient attack, and then you'll hear distortion as the levels increase. If you record too cold to analog tape, there'll be an unacceptable amount of noise in relation to the piano signal (i.e., an unacceptable signal-to-noise ratio).

Practice recording the piano at different levels. Record the same piano part peaking at different levels: -9VU, -7VU, -3VU, 0VU, +3VU, +5VU and +7VU. Write down what you notice about the changes in each sound. Notice the

Illustration 5-11
Piano Miking Variation

Place a stereo pair of mics at the opening of the lid, then use a packing blanket over the top for acoustic isolation and separation.

The packing blanket can do a good job of isolating most grand piano recording techniques, but it can also hinder the acoustic life of the piano sound.

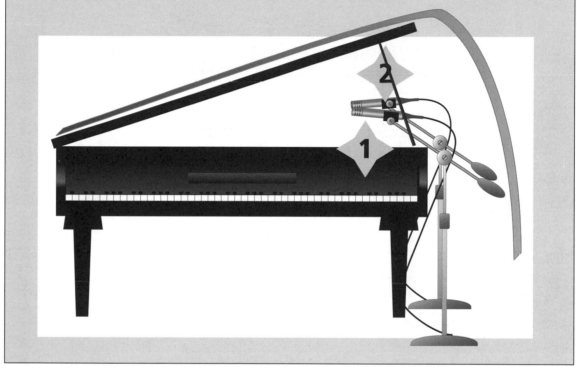

variation in clarity of attack, the amount of audible distortion and the difference in audible noise. This exercise will help you better understand the recording procedure for acoustic piano.

Equalizing the Piano

Most of the time, it's best to print the piano track or tracks to the multitrack without EQ. Using a pair of good condenser mics, placed for the best sound and the least detrimental phase interaction, should produce tracks that sound good. If EQ is necessary, it'll usually be fairly subtle—

and best if left for mixdown.

If you're recording live to 2-track master or if you're recording and mixing a band live, you might need to EQ the piano while recording.

As I mentioned before, there's a difference between the sound that works best for solo piano and the sound that works best for piano within a complex orchestration. Solo piano should be full and even in the low end, mids and highs. Essentially, you need to cover the entire frequency spectrum evenly. Audio Example 5-23 is an example of a good, full solo piano sound.

Illustration 5-12
Piano Sound Chart

Listen to Audio Examples 5-17 through 5-22 and rate each category 1–10. "1" is the best and "10" is the worst. The "Subjective appeal" and "Emotional feel" categories are included simply to get your gut level response to the sounds. This exercise will help you develop discernment regarding different piano recording techniques.

Audio Examples	High end clarity	Low end clarity	Sustain	Low mid punch	Subjective appeal	Emotional feel
Audio Ex. 5-17						
Audio Ex. 5-18						
Audio Ex. 5-19						
Audio Ex. 5-20						
Audio Ex. 5-21						
Audio Ex. 5-22						

Audio Example 5-23 Solo Piano Sound
CD-1: Track 72

Musically, a piano part that works well in a rhythm section is usually percussive. A more aggressive approach to equalization combined with a more percussive musical part, usually results in a part that can be heard well in the mix without being in the way of other instruments or voices.

Acoustic piano within the context of a full band orchestration should be somewhat thin in the low end. The kick drum and bass guitar cover the low frequencies quite well; to include an abundance of lows in the piano sound could result in a muddy-sounding mix that's confusing in the low frequencies.

To thin out the lows, try cutting in the range of 60Hz to about 150Hz. This is very noticeable to the solo sound, but in the context of a rhythm section won't be noticed. This will prevent the low frequencies of the piano from conflicting as much with the low frequencies of the bass guitar or kick. Listen to Audio Example 5-24 as I cut 60Hz, then sweep from 60Hz up to about 150Hz.

Audio Example 5-24
Cutting the Lows From 60Hz to 150Hz
CD-1: Track 73

To give the piano more clarity and an aggressive edge, boost slightly between 3kHz and 5kHz. Be careful! Dramatic equalization might sound fine on one monitor system and terrible on another. In Audio Example 5-25, I'll start with the EQ flat, then I'll boost the 4kHz range slowly until I reach a 7dB boost.

Audio Example 5-25 Boosting 4kHz
CD-1: Track 74

Compressing the Piano

The dynamic range of the piano can be very wide, depending on the musical part. Most solo pieces contain some very soft passages and some very loud passages. If you're recording to a digital format that will end up being released on CD or other digital format, it's nice to have that wide dynamic range recorded the way it happened from the instrument. If you're recording a piece that'll be listened to on a standard cassette or within the context of a rhythm section, your recording might be easier to listen to if you compress the signal.

Try a ratio of about 3:1 with a medium-fast attack time and a medium-slow release time. Adjust the threshold for 3 or 4dB of gain reduction at the hottest part of the track. This approach will give you natural-sounding compression while letting you record 3 or 4dB hotter to tape on everything but the peaks. The piano track in Audio Example 5-26 was recorded using this technique.

Audio Example 5-26 Compressing the Piano
CD-1: Track 75

Exciting the Piano

An exciter can add clarity to the piano's high end without using normal equalization. Exciters work by boosting specific harmonics rather than simply boosting a range of frequencies. Equalizing and exciting produce similar results, but an exciter often sounds cleaner, which gives the piano a more transparent edge than equalization. Be cautious. Overusing an exciter or equalizer could cause problems if your recording is heard on many different systems. Listen to the piano in Audio Example 5-27. I'll add the exciter after the first few measures.

Audio Example 5-27 Exciting the Piano
CD-1: Track 76

Reverberation

If at all possible, save the addition of reverberation for mixdown.

Reverberation is very appropriate for acoustic piano in the proper musical context, especially on ballads and solo pieces. A solo piano in a concert hall has a very rich, reverberant sound; a live ensemble performance in a concert hall has the same kind of sound. Ballads, with open spaces in the orchestration, give the listener the opportunity to hear the sound of the hall. Using a smooth, warm hall reverb, with a medium to long predelay and a decay time of two to three seconds, usually produces an interesting and very usable piano track. If you don't know what some of these terms mean, refer to Volume 1 of the *AudioPro Home Recording Course*.

The solo piano in Audio Example 5-28 uses hall reverberation with a 75ms predelay and a 2.5 second decay time.

Audio Example 5-28
Hall Reverb, 75ms Predelay and
2.5 Second Decay Time
CD-1: Track 77

On faster songs with busier arrangements, the hall reverb tends to add clutter and can make the mix sound muddy. If you want your mix to sound close, tight and punchy, a good piano sound with no reverberation works great.

If you want the piano to blend into the mix without sounding like it's at the other end of the hall, try adding a little plate reverb with a short predelay (between 0 and 50ms) and a short decay time (between .5 seconds and 1 second). This effect adds an interesting ambience while maintaining a feel of closeness. The piano in Audio Example 5-29 has a plate reverb with a 35ms predelay and a decay time of .6 seconds.

The track starts dry, then I slowly add the reverberation.

Audio Example 5-29
Plate Reverb With 35ms Predelay and
.6 Second Decay Time
CD-1: Track 77

Another reverberation effect that fills out the piano sound and helps it blend with the rest of the mix is room reverb. This type of reverberation is designed to give the listener the perception that the sound is being heard in a specific-sized room—typically smaller than a concert hall, gymnasium or theater. Adding a fairly tight-sounding room to the piano often results in a subtle change that makes the instrument sound more interesting. This sound-shaping technique gives your recordings an interesting edge that is difficult for the listener to consciously hear, but without it there would be a very noticeable loss of character in the sound. The piano in Audio Example 5-30 starts dry, then I add room reverberation.

Audio Example 5-30 Room Reverberation
CD-1: Track 77

Using digital delay on piano isn't common, especially from the purist's perspective, but it can produce an interesting effect on some styles in some settings. A floating, emotional, freestyle solo piano might sound great with the right type of delay. Longer delay times that match the tempo of the quarter note or eighth note usually work best. Short delay times, below about 100ms, usually give an artificial flavor to the acoustic piano sound. The piano track in Audio Example 5-31 has a delay time of 300ms; the regeneration is set for three or four repeats.

Audio Example 5-31 300ms Delay
CD-1: Track 78

Miking the Vertical Piano

Having a nine-foot grand piano at your disposal is ideal. The first part of this chapter is dedicated to understanding the sound of the grand as a point of reference—a benchmark. But hardly anyone has a nine-foot grand piano in their home studio. Most home recordists are fortunate to have a spinet, console, studio or upright piano to work with; these all fall under the

Illustration 5-13
Miking the Vertical Piano

Remove the top and front panels to gain access to the strings.

Use one or two condenser mics on the console, spinet or upright piano. If you use one mic, point the mic at the front of the piano. Position the mic around middle C, 12–18" from the strings.

If you use two mics, center one over the bass strings and one over the treble strings. Point the mic at the strings from a distance of 6–12".

To widen the stereo image, point the mics slightly away from each other.

Illustration 5-14
Miking the Vertical Piano

Angle mics up to 90° in relation to each other. Angles up to 90° increase the stereo image; angles greater than 90° create negative phase interaction as the mics approach 180° out of phase.

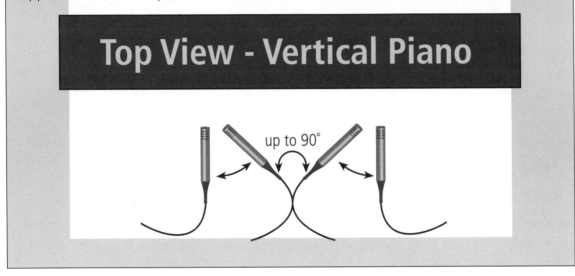

Top View - Vertical Piano

up to 90°

category of pianos called vertical pianos.

Realizing that not everyone has a grand piano—or even a decent vertical piano—we need to use what we know about the grand piano as a guideline to help us get the most from any piano. There are a few techniques that can help us get a very usable sound from a vertical piano.

One of the primary and most obvious differences between a high-quality grand piano and a marginal-quality home console piano is the sound of the low notes. A good grand has great richness and depth on all of the low notes. An average console piano loses any resemblance to a full sound about an octave or two above the lowest A on the keyboard.

Try putting a separate mic on the lowest notes; experiment with boosting lows and cutting certain lower mids to try to get the console

piano to approach the rich sound of the grand.

To get the best sound out of a vertical piano, use two condenser mics placed about six to twelve inches from the strings, pointing at the strings, and three or four inches above the hammers. Center one mic over the treble strings and one mic over the bass strings (Illustration 5-13). Pointing the mics away from each other at a 90° angle to each other enhances the stereo image (Illustration 5-14).

If you have a console piano and want to record parts that sound good and musically enhance the texture of your music, start by devising a musical part that uses the strong range and avoids the weak range of the console piano. In other words, leave the bass range of your orchestration to instruments like the bass guitar and kick drum. Devise a piano part that doesn't go much more than an octave or so below

Illustration 5-15
Miking the Vertical Piano

Try an X-Y configuration aimed at the strings from a distance of about 12″. Adjust the mic position toward the bass or treble strings, depending on the musical part. If the highest range on the instrument isn't being used, move the stereo pair of mics toward the bass end of the piano and vice versa.

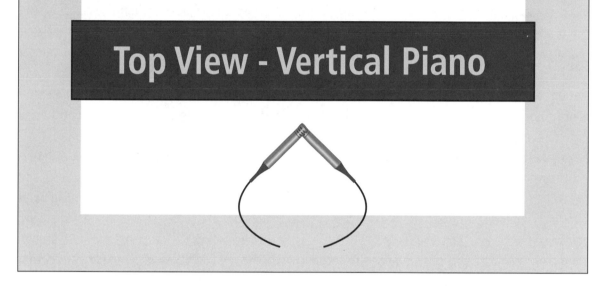

Top View - Vertical Piano

middle C and stays out of the upper octave. The difference in sound quality between the grand and vertical piano can be minimized with the right musical part played within a rhythm section and mixed properly.

If your musical arrangement does not include the low notes or the very high notes, center a pair of mics over middle C and use a coincident miking technique, like the standard X-Y. This'll give your recording a good stereo image, along with clarity in the range of notes that sound good on the vertical piano (Illustration 5-15).

If you're trying to make the vertical piano sound good as a solo instrument, patch both channels through separate parametric equalizers.

Adjust the mid band to cut at 200 to 300Hz. Adjust the bandwidth between .5

octaves and 1.5 octaves. Each piano is amazingly different so you'll really need to focus your listening. This one adjustment should clean up the mids enough to be able to hear the bass and treble ranges better. This is the minimum amount of cut you'll need to clean up the sound, but don't be afraid to use whatever it takes to get the job done; usually a 2 to 6dB cut should be sufficient.

Adjust the low band to boost between 2 and 6dB; set the bandwidth between .5 octave and one octave; sweep the frequency selector from 120Hz to 60Hz to find the sweet spot that produces a strong, solid low end. Give the piano as much punch as possible without creating an obviously boomy sound.

Finally, set up a 2 to 6dB boost in the high band. Set the bandwidth between one and two octaves and sweep the frequency selector between 3.5kHz and 7kHz to achieve clarity and attack in the treble strings.

Once the musical part is composed to enhance the good sounds and avoid the not-so-good sounds, and once the raw sound of the vertical piano is miked for the sound you need, use dynamics and effects processing and adjust the levels in the same way you would for the grand piano.

If your reverb has controls to adjust equalization, boost the low frequencies to get a full, warm solo piano sound.

Sampled Piano Sounds

If you own or have access to a sampler, you can get some really great piano sounds. The advantage of a sampled piano is that, in most cases, you reap the benefit of someone else's work. Somebody records a very good piano with very good microphones through very good preamps in a studio that sounds good, and you get to use it in your recordings—what a deal!

The disadvantage to a sampled piano is that you don't always get the full benefit of the natural harmonics that occur on every string in the piano. The real acoustic piano might have a smoother, more natural sound throughout the range of the instrument than the sampled piano. On the other hand, many piano parts in many songs don't require the full benefit of a real acoustic piano so the subtle differences between the real and sampled piano might be totally insignificant.

These differences in quality between the real and sampled grand piano live in the gray zone that isn't always noticeable or obvious; the practical differences are totally dependent on the musical context.

The method of choice for recording sampled piano or any other electronic keyboard is direct into the console, either through a direct box or plugged into line in.

There are some really good samples available that give the player access to some incredible instruments that only the best players or studios have. For most home recordists, the question usually comes down to this: Is it better to get the best possible recording of a vertical piano to keep the pure harmonics present in the instrument or to use a sample of an incredible instrument that's been recorded in a world-class studio?

I've had the opportunity to work with several great sounding nine-foot grand pianos, and it's tough to beat a good stereo recording of an instrument like that—period. There will always be a difference, but at least the margin is shrinking.

If you don't have access to a grand piano, try the sampled pianos that are available to you. For a fairly reasonable cost—often less than a good vertical piano—a good 16–20 bit sampler gives you access not only to great piano sounds but to any other acoustic or synthesized sound you can imagine.

Listen to this sample of a Steinway Grand in Audio Example 5-32. This kind of sound isn't achievable in the vast majority of home studios without the use of a sampler.

Audio Example 5-32
Sampled Steinway Grand Piano
CD-1: Track 79

Aside from the fact that you're able to use samples of a piano you might not be able to afford—or even gain access to—a sampler gives you choices between different great pianos. Not too many of us are fortunate enough to be able to choose whether to mike and record the Steinway or the Bösendorfer Grand on a particular day at home in the studio.

The sample of a full sized Bösendorfer Grand in Audio Example 5-33 has a much more aggressive edge than the Steinway.

Audio Example 5-33 Sampled Bösendorfer Grand
CD-1: Track 79

Many samplers have effects available within the unit. This extra effects processor alone can enlarge the flexibility of your setup. Audio Example 5-34 demonstrates the Bösendorfer again, this time with reverb that's built into the sampler.

Audio Example 5-34
Bösendorfer Grand With Reverb
CD-1: Track 80

Recording levels from the sampler should be adjusted using the same considerations you use when miking the acoustic piano. A thinner sound that has a more aggressive attack should be recorded colder, around -3 to -7VU at the peaks. A warmer, full-sounding piano can usually be recorded with the peaks reading about 0VU with no problem. If you're recording to DAT or some other digital storage medium, the primary concern is to set the record level so the meter never reads above zero.

Be patient and diligent with your sampler. Search out different pianos around town, and build your own custom library of piano samples.

Some studios, churches, schools or theaters are willing to let you sit at their instrument for a while with your sampler and microphone. Even if you end up with a substantial list of favors that you need to pay back one day, a good library of great piano samples is a valuable tool.

Another big advantage to sampled pianos is that they're simple to layer with other keyboard sounds. You can add strings, electric pianos, guitars or virtually any other sound to your piano part. Live layering to an acoustic piano recording can be tedious, to say the least, if you're trying to match an emotional interpretation perfectly. But with a sampler that allows layering, this process is painless, effective and instantaneous. Audio Example 5-35 demonstrates the Bösendorfer layered with a simple string sound. In the correct musical context, this technique can add fullness and depth that's hard to duplicate with an acoustic piano alone.

Audio Example 5-35
The Bösendorfer Layered With Strings
CD-1: Track 81

Connecting the sampler to other MIDI keyboards expands your musical network. I've worked with acoustic grands that can send MIDI data to a sequencer and that does add flexibility to it. But with a sampler, the MIDI data can also be changed, fixed or transposed and then sent back to the sampler for playback during another take. For those of us who aren't really piano players but can come up with decent musical parts if we can play them slowly into a sequencer (overdubbing parts and then speeding the sequencer up to the correct tempo for playback), a sampler can be our only chance to record the piano parts we need without hiring a good player.

Treat the sampled piano with the same processing and effects that you'd use on an acoustic piano to get a believable and natural sound. Avoid pitch bend, modulation, chorus and the other MIDI keyboard functions that don't exist on a real piano.

Rhodes-type Sounds

The musical function of the piano part is almost always to provide a predominant harmonic and rhythmic bed for the rest of the orchestration, and this role is very important to the feel of a song. That's why it's important to learn as much as possible about recording a good piano track and then practicing until the piano sounds you're getting are comparable to pianos you hear on other recordings.

Actively compare your piano recordings to recordings you hear on your favorite CDs or tapes. At this you should be capable of listening critically and analyzing a sound with respect to its overall quality.

The other instrument that fulfills the same function as the acoustic piano is the Rhodes or electric piano. The Fender Rhodes piano came on strong, especially in the early '70s because it was portable, stayed in tune when moved and had a rich full sound quality. Like the grand piano, it provides an interesting musical texture to lay the rest of an arrangement over. Although the Rhodes itself isn't as common now as it was in the '70s, its sound has been cloned, copied, modified and sampled into almost every keyboard available today.

The original Suitcase Rhodes had stereo outputs that plugged into the speaker cabinet it sat on. The stereo effect was an autopan back and forth between the 12-inch speakers in the cabinet. When these first came out, this was the epitome of high-tech, leading-edge, fun listening—technology has come quite a way since the introduction of the Fender Rhodes.

The Rhodes is texturally different from the acoustic piano, even though its musical function is the same. The method of choice for recording electric piano, or any other electronic keyboard, is direct into the console, either through a direct box or plugged into line in.

Rhodes Effects

To get a simulation of the original suitcase Rhodes stereo-panning sound, use an auto panner; many current multi-effects processors have auto panners built in. This effect simply takes the input signal and pans it from left to right according to how you set the processor. Of course, the output from the processor needs to be stereo, but you probably won't need the piano to pan hard left and right in the mix; the extreme panning sounds unnatural and might be distracting to the rest of the arrangement. Adjust the speed of the panner to work with the tempo of the song.

The original stock Rhodes sound was fairly mellow. Listen to the Rhodes sound in Audio Example 5-36. It is similar to the original sound. After a few measures I'll include the auto panner.

Audio Example 5-36
The Rhodes and the Auto Panner
CD-1: Track 82

If you're not sure how to patch an effect

like this into your system, refer to Volume 1, Chapters 1 and 2 of the *AudioPro Home Recording Course*.

The ideal recording level for Rhodes electric piano sounds is 0VU. All the effects that sound good on acoustic piano also sound good on Rhodes. Reverbs, delay and compression are common on this instrument.

The Rhodes piano sound in Audio Example 5-37 has hall reverb with a 2.5 second decay time and a 125ms predelay.

Audio Example 5-37 Rhodes With Hall Reverb
CD-1: Track 83

As the Rhodes grew in popularity and players experimented with the different types of sounds that could be found in the instrument, it became popular to include more of the sound of the actual tines in the piano being hit. To us, that translates into boosting the upper harmonics of the sound at the attack of the note.

Audio Example 5-38 demonstrates the original Rhodes sound.

Audio Example 5-38 The Original Rhodes
CD-1: Track 84

Audio Example 5-39 demonstrates the tine sound that became—and still is—very popular.

Audio Example 5-39 The Tine Sound
CD-1: Track 84

The tine sound became popular because the attack clearly defined the sound in a way that didn't interfere with the rest of the musical texture; the upper harmonics made the reverb and other effects sound even better and more interesting than they did without the tine sound.

Chorus, flanging and phase shifting are also very common—and sound great—on electric piano. Since the electric piano is simpler in its harmonic content, the richness and fullness that these effects add enhances rather than clutters the original sound.

It's best if you can keep the original sound clean and dry on the multitrack, or within the sequence, and then fine-tune the exact effect you'll need during mixdown. Chorus sounds can be an integral part of the piano sound; if you must print the chorus effect with the piano because of a lack of tracks or limited outboard equipment for mixdown, it will probably sound all right. Still, try to save the addition of reverberation until the mix.

Listen to the smooth, sweeping sound as I add the phase shifter to the electric piano in Audio Example 5-40.

Audio Example 5-40
Electric Piano With Phase Shifter
CD-1: Track 85

For a little more complex sweep, try adding a flanger like the one in Audio Example 5-41.

Audio Example 5-41 Flanged Electric Piano
CD-1: Track 85

And for less of a sweep sound and a more

interesting blend of changing harmonics and overtones, add a chorus to the electric piano like the one in Audio Example 5-42

Audio Example 5-42 Chorused Electric Piano
CD-1: Track 85

Another possibility, although not common, is the use of distortion on a simple and pure Rhodes sound. In the earlier Rhodes days, players used guitar pedal distortion on Rhodes occasionally to mimic the sound and effect of electric guitar. This technique doesn't totally fill the shoes of a guitar, but it's worth keeping in

your bag of tricks for that one session where this sound is the only right choice.

Audio Example 5-43 is the sound of distorted electric piano. If the musical part is appropriate, this sound has the potential to be very effective.

Audio Example 5-43 Distorted Electric Piano
CD-1: Track 86

Equalizing the Rhodes

Equalize the piano sound according to the needs of the particular musical piece. For solo electric

Illustration 5-16
Harmonizer

Set one harmonizer output to eight cents sharp, and then set the other harmonizer output to eight cents flat. Plug the harmonizer outputs into two line inputs of the mixer. Pan the harmonizer's mix channels hard left and hard right while panning the original electric piano track center.

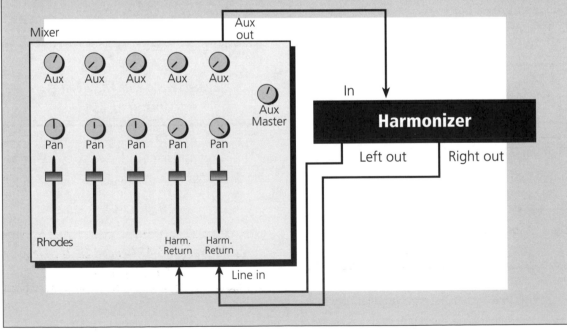

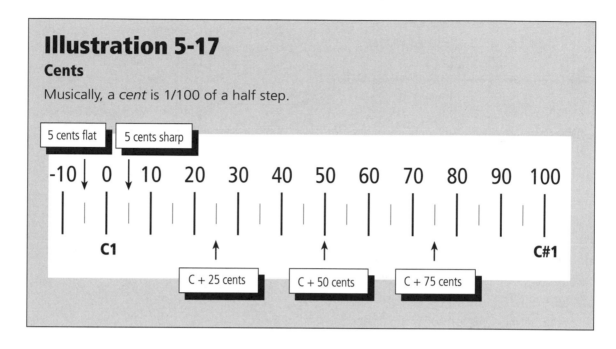

Illustration 5-17
Cents

Musically, a *cent* is 1/100 of a half step.

5 cents flat   5 cents sharp

-10   0   10   20   30   40   50   60   70   80   90   100

C1   C + 25 cents   C + 50 cents   C + 75 cents   C#1

piano, the sound should be full and smooth in the low end. Often no EQ is needed in this case, since the Rhodes sound is typically full and smooth in the lows and low-mids. Audio Example 5-44 demonstrates an electric piano sound that might work well in a solo piece or exposed, open orchestration.

Audio Example 5-44 Solo Rhodes Sound
CD-1: Track 87

If the arrangement is full and contains other active rhythm section instruments like guitars, synthesizers and possibly strings or brass, it's not necessary for the electric piano to fill out the texture in the lows and low-mids. In this case, roll off the lows between about 60 and 120Hz to clean up the low end. Turning the lows down on the piano results in a low end that's easier to understand and conflicts less with the other low-frequency instruments. Also, try boosting between 2.5 and 5kHz to accentuate the

clear edge of the tine sound. Audio Example 5-45 starts flat, then I turn the lows down and sweep between 60 and 120Hz. Next, I boost the highs and sweep between 2.5kHz and 5kHz.

Audio Example 5-45
Cut the Lows, Boost the Highs
CD-1: Track 88

The actual frequencies that you select to boost or cut are totally dependent on the needs of the musical arrangement. If another instrument in the song is accentuated at 2.5kHz, you might need to cut 2.5kHz on the electric piano but boost 5kHz to accentuate the tine sound.

Exciter on the electric piano can accentuate the upper harmonics of the tine sound and help the piano cut through the rest of the orchestration without an abrasive edge to the sound. Listen to the high end in Audio Example 5-46 to hear the effect of the exciter on the Rhodes-type sound.

Audio Example 5-46 Excited Rhodes
CD-1: Track 89

An effect we really haven't covered so far is the harmonizer, which is capable of changing the pitch of the incoming signal. Typically, the pitch can be altered in half-step increments above or below the incoming signal. The pitch is typically adjustable within a range of 12 half steps in either direction, or in one cent increments above or below the incoming signal—usually with a range of 99 cents in either direction (one cent is 1/100 of a half step).

The harmonizer can be used for special effect by setting the pitch change to a certain number of half steps. Many harmonizers can even produce two separate pitch changes simultaneously so you can create a chord from a single note on the keyboard, or any other instrument, as in Audio Example 5-47.

Audio Example 5-47 Harmonizer on the Rhodes
CD-1: Track 90

A much more common use for the harmonizer, in respect to the electric piano, involves using the fine-tune control and adjusting the two pitch shifters almost imperceptibly above and below the incoming signal. Set one pitch change between one and eight cents above the original pitch, and set the other pitch change between one and eight cents below the original pitch. These pitch changes don't really sound out of tune, but the interaction between the original incoming signal and the effected outputs adds harmonic depth and richness to most sounds. Pan the two shifted outputs hard left and hard right, keeping the original panned center for a very full and interesting sound (Illustrations 5-16 and 5-17). This sound can also be used on any other instrument to get a full, wide sound. Try this technique on guitars, voices, synth sounds or even on some brass and string tracks.

Listen to the electric piano in Audio Example 5-48. After the first few bars I'll add the harmonizer, set eight cents sharp on the left and eight cents flat on the right.

Audio Example 5-48
Subtle Harmonizer on the Rhodes
CD-1: Track 90

If you have a harmonizer that only produces one pitch change at a time, try panning the original track hard left and the harmonized output hard right.

On exposed and open musical pieces, it's common to used multiple effects on an instrument like the electric piano. Using delay, reverb, chorus, harmonizer, EQ and compression together can produce a great sound when you use them in the right amounts. The key is that you need to understand what each effect is doing and combine them using a controlled, deliberate approach. Try to hear the sound in your head, then use your equipment efficiently to set it up. Avoid the random-knob-turning syndrome.

Modern technology gives you unbelievable control over effects. Practice each of the processing techniques that we've covered. Be sure you're familiar with all of the controllable parameters. Know your equipment, then start building sounds.

The electric piano sound in Audio Example 5-49 has been equalized to accentuate the tine sound. It has a room reverb, a hall reverb and a slight flange; the harmonizer is six cents sharp on the left and six cents flat on the right. Some of the effects might be very subtle, but each effect works together to build the overall sound.

Audio Example 5-49
The Rhodes With EQ, Room, Hall,
Flange and Harmonizer
CD-1: Track 91

Conclusion

Acoustic piano and electric piano are the framework for many songs. Often the orchestration can sound full even if you strip away all of the instruments but the piano. It's important that we practice recording these instruments and always use processing that enhances the music being made on the instrument. If we go too far out of the boundaries, it can be distracting to the rest of the song; but on that one occasion where it suddenly becomes appropriate to go outside normal limits, you should be prepared to do so.

Practice! Set up normal sounds and set up abnormal sounds. I'm sure you've noticed that it's often easier to recall the essence of a sound you got two or three months ago than it is to recall the way you set it up, so keep a log of how you set different sounds up—including all settings and a verbal description of the sound.

If you don't have immediate access to a piano, check around with friends, schools, churches or the local musicians' union hall until you find a good piano to practice on, and then practice recording it. If you're serious about recording, there'll be a time when the experience of actually trying these techniques on a real piano will pay off.

We're covering a lot of ground in this course. It's important that you continue to review all of the previous chapters. Experiment with each technique in the situation that it's presented in, and then try each technique in other situations that make musical sense to you.

Special thanks to Robbie Ott for his assistance in performing the grand piano examples in this chapter. Robbie is an excellent musician, songwriter and vocalist, and he's involved heavily in the Christian Music Ministry.

Chapter 6 Recording Synthesizers

Recording Synths:
Strings, Pads, Bell-like Sounds,
Brass and Effects

Strings, pads, bell-like sounds, brass and special effects are very important to the emotional impact of most music and are worthy of study and practice.

One quick word about synthesized sounds: Modern technology is making it possible to get incredible sounds at our fingertips. A good sampler gives you the real acoustical instrument sound on the keyboard and, combined with other units that build their sounds around digital samples of real instruments, provides powerful potential. If you want a real string or brass sound, you can have it quickly. The trick lies in knowing how to use those sounds to create musically believable parts. Each instrument has a unique set of performance techniques. If you're not familiar with those techniques, it'll be difficult or impossible to record realistic-sounding string and brass parts.

Phrasing, articulation and interpretation are very important to any musical performance. Make it your goal to learn as much as you can about the instruments you're trying to emulate. There are many resources available that will help you learn specifically how to recreate real string,

brass and woodwind sounds.

As your production proficiency and budgets increase, you'll probably find that when you want a real string or brass sound, it's best to hire a live string section or a live brass section. If you hire musicians, hire the best you can find—pay the price. There are no bargains when it comes to hiring musicians. You'll be thrilled with a good player who, familiar with the studio environment, works fast and efficiently. In the long run, it's cheaper to pay for the best player, especially if you're paying for a studio by the hour.

Even if you can afford to hire great players every day, there'll still be plenty of times when you'll want to work the parts out on your sequencer before you hire musicians to do the real thing. There might even be times when synthesized strings or brass will be the best musical choice for your song.

Line in vs. Mic in Through DI

It's true that keyboards almost always work best when they are run directly into the console, either into line in or through a direct box. As you increase your recording skill level and learn different tricks, begin to be particular about how you record sounds. Is the method you're using to record an instrument or sound the best way or simply an accepted way to record? We've covered several methods to record other instruments; some of those techniques apply to these

Illustration 6-1
Synths to Line Input

This is the most basic patch. Simply plug the keyboard outputs into the line inputs of the mixer. This setup is only a problem when the output level of the keyboard is weak, therefore creating a need to boost the mixer levels to a point where the amount of noise induced by the mixer is unacceptable. Most newer keyboards have ample signal strength to work well when plugged into a line input.

L & R out — Synth — Line in — Mixer — Pan Pan Pan Pan Pan Pan Pan Pan

sounds, some don't. There are even situations where miking an amp produces superior results to running direct in. Begin to open up and try some different approaches; combine some of the ideas from this course or use any of these ideas as a springboard to some new technique. Have fun trying new things!

Refer to Illustration 6-1 through 6-3 for examples of patching configurations for keyboards: direct in, line in and through an amplifier.

Line In

Patching the keys into the line input is really the simplest way to patch into a mixer. There's only a problem with this technique when the keyboard has a weak output level. A weak signal coming from the keyboard forces you to excessively boost the level at the final stages of your mixer's signal path. Remember, it's our job to keep the signal strength as hot as possible at the beginning of the signal path—without causing distortion—so that we don't have to boost the inherent noise from the mixer at the output.

Listen to the keyboard sound in Audio Example 6-1. There's a weak signal coming from the sound module so I've had to boost the mixer's final output levels excessively. Listen for the amount of noise present in relation to the amount of keyboard sound.

Audio Example 6-1 Weak Keyboard Signal
CD-2: Track 1

Now listen to the same sound through the same system in Audio Example 6-2. This time I've gotten more level from the keyboard itself so the final output of the mixer signal path doesn't need to be excessively hot. Listen to the

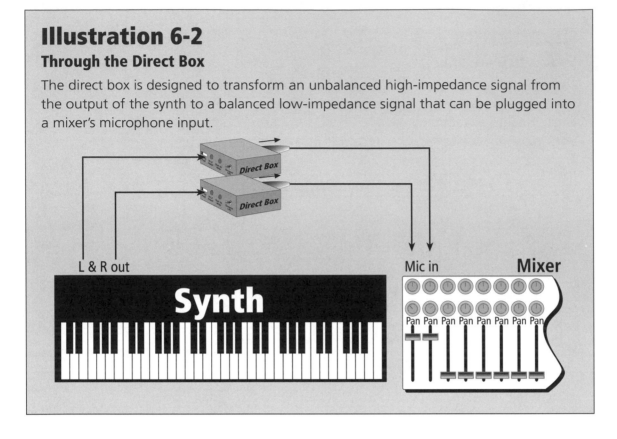

Illustration 6-2
Through the Direct Box

The direct box is designed to transform an unbalanced high-impedance signal from the output of the synth to a balanced low-impedance signal that can be plugged into a mixer's microphone input.

amount of noise in relation to the amount of the keyboard sound.

Audio Example 6-2 Hotter Keyboard Signal
CD-2: Track 1

If the signal coming from the keyboard or sound module is weak, you could be in for a noise problem. It's almost always best to have the output of the keyboard at maximum to help avoid noise.

DI Can Color the Sound Adversely

If your keyboard simply won't put out enough signal for you to get a clean, noise-free recording when you patch into line in, you'll probably need to use a direct box, especially when connecting to a mixer with +4dB operating levels.

Plugging into a direct box lets us use the mixer's input preamp level control to boost the keyboard signal since the DI plugs into a mic input; therefore, we increase the signal level at the beginning of the signal path rather than at the end. For a diagram explaining patching through a direct box refer to Illustration 6-2.

The quality of the direct box you're using is a very important factor when recording any instrument direct in. In Chapter 1, we learned that there's a big difference between the sound of a passive and an active direct box. Active direct boxes typically have a cleaner low end and a more present high end than passive direct boxes. I've also found that, generally, the least

Illustration 6-3
Miking the Speaker Cabinet

Most of the time, it's simplest to run the synth directly into the mixer, but in some cases—especially if you're recording an acoustic sounding instrument—the sound of the amp and the acoustic interaction of the room add realism to an otherwise sterile sound.

Adjust the amount of room you include with the sound by moving the mic toward or away from the speaker.

If you're close-miking the speaker, remember that the penetrating highs come from the center of the speaker and the warmer, smoother lows come from the outer part of the cone.

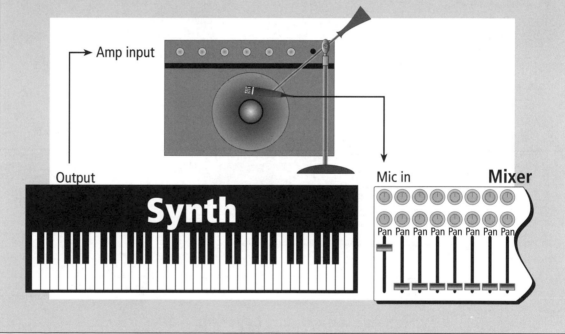

expensive direct boxes don't sound as good as the more expensive direct boxes. If you're using direct boxes frequently, invest in a good, high-quality active direct box from a well-known and respected manufacturer.

Even though the signal going into the direct box from the keyboard is unbalanced high impedance, the signal coming out of the direct box is balanced low impedance. From that point on, your keyboard signal receives all the posi-tive benefits of balanced low impedance: reduced or eliminated electrostatic interference, hums and buzzes.

Strings and Pads

When recording strings and other keyboard pads, it's our goal to create an interesting sound that fits the texture and style of the orchestration.

Illustration 6-4
Combining the Direct and Miked Signals

If you're all set up to mike the speaker cabinet anyway, it's usually best—and fairly convenient—to simultaneously run a direct signal to the mixer. Patch the direct signal into one channel and the miked signal into a separate channel. Assign the channels to different tracks of the multitrack or assign them both to one track and blend for the best sound.

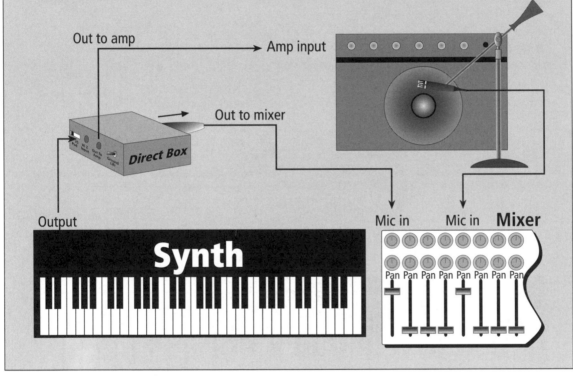

Out to amp → Amp input

Out to mixer

Direct Box

Output

Synth

Mic in   Mic in   **Mixer**

Pan Pan Pan Pan Pan Pan Pan Pan

It's important that you learn to create some very good and usable sounds working from fairly plain and simple original sounds. The keyboard you're recording won't always have a great stereo sound with just the perfect musical feel for the song. In fact, often all you'll have to work with in the studio is an approximation of the sound you really need. Approach each of these recording situations with the intent to learn or devise techniques that create a great sound from a simple, raw source.

Layering

When you hear a string pad that sounds rich, full and very interesting, the appeal isn't always the result of an incredible raw sound. What's been done with the sound is often the most impressive part. One technique that consistently produces good interesting sounds is *layering*. Layering is a common keyboard term that refers to the process of stacking one sound on top of another. Within the keyboard, layering is done by assigning two or more internal sounds to play at once, every time you hit a key. This works well because, as the two basic sounds interact, the harmonics and overtones combine. Rather than continually shaping one sound to achieve just the right sound, find two separate sounds that each contain part of what you need, then play them together.

One of the ways we can create interesting new sounds that no one has heard before is by layering one keyboard with a different keyboard. The chances of someone creating the exact sound that you've found, combining a DX7 with an 01/W, for instance, aren't nearly as likely as

Illustration 6-5
Add the Room Sound

Keep expanding your list of possibilities. There is a lot to be said for keeping it simple, but often it's well worth taking a little time to set up a different and unique approach.

This illustration is like Illustration 6-4 with the addition of room microphones. Blend them into your overall sound or assign them to their own tracks so you can save choices for mixdown.

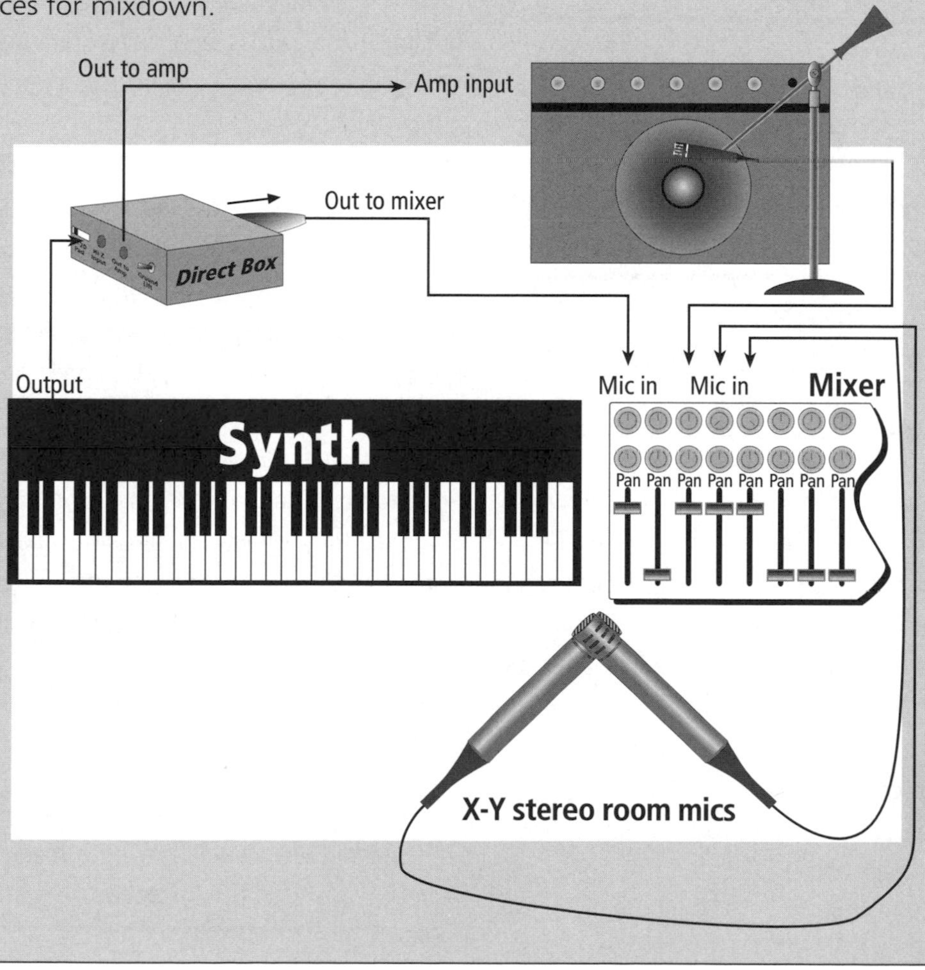

Out to amp

Amp input

Out to mixer

Direct Box

Output

Synth

Mic in   Mic in   **Mixer**

Pan Pan Pan Pan Pan Pan Pan Pan

X-Y stereo room mics

if you'd layered two of the standard internal 01/W sounds. Take advantage of the tools that are available to you. Just because a keyboard isn't the newest piece of technology on the block doesn't mean that it won't sound great with another keyboard or sound module.

Listen to the two fairly plain and simple string sounds in Audio Example 6-3. I'll play the parts separately, then I'll layer them together. Notice how they take on a much more rich and interesting character when they're heard together than when they're heard separately.

Audio Example 6-3 Layering
CD-2: Track 2

If there are enough tracks or channels available, pan the two keyboards slightly apart to simulate a wider "section" sound as in Audio Example 6-4.

Audio Example 6-4
Panning the Layered Sounds Apart
CD-2: Track 2

A common technique when layering sounds is to slightly de-tune the sounds. This accentuates the harmonic interaction between the two sounds, creating a larger overall feel. This is similar to the effect we created with a harmonizer on the Rhodes in Chapter 5, but this technique has the potential to be even more extreme, since we're layering two different sounds rather than simply running one sound through the harmonizer.

In Audio Example 6-5, I'll slightly de-tune the two different string sounds. One keyboard is tuned eight cents sharp and the other is tuned eight cents flat. If your keyboard doesn't have a tuner that indicates tuning by cents, try using a guitar tuner; most guitar tuners show tuning in cents. I'll add these sounds one at a time, pan them apart, then pan them together to center.

Audio Example 6-5 De-tuning Two String Sounds
CD-2: Track 3

The technique of layering can be carried as far as your mixer, tracks and available keyboards will allow. Although you can reach a point where simply adding one more keyboard sound doesn't make much of a difference, it is common to use two, three or even four keyboards playing the identical part to shape an interesting, unique sound.

Use each keyboard or sound module for a specific part of the overall sound you're building. Samplers often help to add realism. If a very intimate sampled string sound—including the sound of the bow scraping across the strings—is combined with a very full lush pad, the result is usually very impressive and full.

In Audio Example 6-6, I'll combine three elements: the bright sampled single-string sound, the large defined string pad and the mellow, filling, smooth string pad. I'll play each sound separately, then combine them; finally, I'll vary their pan placement. Notice how the sum of all these parts sounds much better—and more interesting—than any of the individual pieces.

Audio Example 6-6 Layering Three Sounds
CD-2: Track 4

Illustration 6-6
Equalizing the String Pad

When applying EQ, keep the orchestration in mind. It's not necessary to create a monstrous sound for every ingredient in the mix. It's our job to create sounds that work well together, supporting the musical vision. This illustration supplies a graphic example of two EQ curves that support each other. Together they support the musical goal, though separately they might be less than spectacular.

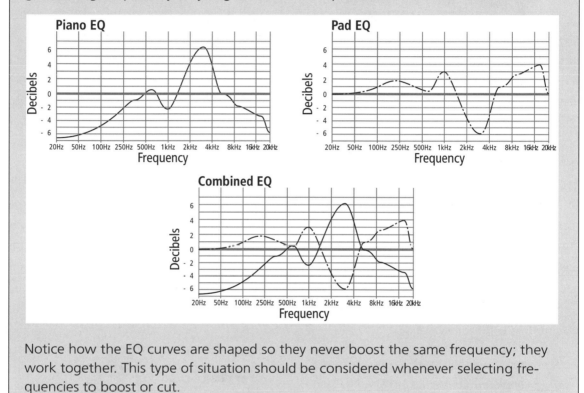

Notice how the EQ curves are shaped so they never boost the same frequency; they work together. This type of situation should be considered whenever selecting frequencies to boost or cut.

Equalizing Pads

Once you've found the sound that complements your music, it's time to combine it with the rest of the orchestration. At this point, the tone might need a slight adjustment. Remember, adjustments are made to help the sound work *with* the rest of the instrumentation not against it.

Equalizing can be accomplished on the mixer or within the keyboard. It's usually best to adjust the sound in the keyboard so that it fits with the music; but sometimes—if you've combined two or more keyboards to get one sound or if you're adjusting the timbre from the multitrack—your only option is to use the mixer EQ or outboard EQ. Practically speaking, either of these methods will work fine as long as you stick within the normal guidelines of applying equalization.

String pads can be boosted or cut at almost any frequency and sound good—that's not the problem. The problem is adjusting the sound around other instruments like piano, keys, guitars or percussion. If the string pad is playing along with a very bright grand piano that has a lot of high-frequency content around 5 or 6kHz, it would only be destructive and confusing to boost the strings anywhere between about 4 and 7kHz.

When playing against a bright grand piano, the string pad might be boosted in the lows or low-mids (between about 150 and 800Hz) to fill out the texture or, possibly, in the very high range (around 8 to 12kHz). If the piano is, indeed, strong in the 5 to 6kHz range, it might be wise to cut the string pad in those frequencies in order to stay out of the way of the piano. The actual frequencies that are boosted or cut totally depend on the musical and textural placement of the other instruments.

Audio Example 6-7 contains piano and a simple string pad. This is a bright piano sound. Once I add the string pad, I'll boost the presence range (around 6kHz). Notice that the strings get in the way of the piano and vice versa.

Audio Example 6-7 Combining Strings and Piano
CD-2: Track 5

Now, with the same piano used in Audio Example 6-7, I'll add the same basic string sound, but I'll boost the lows on the strings to complement and support the piano sound in Audio Example 6-8. I'll also cut the highs where the piano is strong (around 5kHz). Finally, I'll boost the brilliance range (around 12kHz). Note that boosting these lows and very highs supports the piano sound to create an overall improved texture (Illustration 6-6).

Audio Example 6-8
Equalizing Strings and Piano Together
CD-2: Track 5

Dynamic Processing the Synth

The compressor/limiter is rarely used on string pads. Usually the string pad level is so consistent and predictable that compression isn't necessary. Keyboards are very adjustable when determining the dynamic range that's possible for each sound, and adjusting the appropriate MIDI parameters on the keyboard is almost always preferable to including the VCA from a dynamic processor in the signal path.

If you're working with a keyboard that's noisy, it's often very convenient to run the keyboard outputs through a gate/expander to get rid of noise when the string pad isn't sounding. This is almost always best left for the mixdown.

Illustration 6-7
Combining Synths

Consider a simple scenario using two separate keyboards or sound modules. Set one keyboard an octave above the other and play or sequence a single musical part. Typically, the sound will be interesting and powerful.

Reverb

Reverberation is almost always an appropriate effect for string pads. String pads are usually a wash of full string texture, meant to fill in the holes of an orchestration. Since melodic and harmonic movement is typically very smooth, simple and consonant, the sustain and long decay of a full sounding hall reverb makes the strings sound more like a real string section in a real concert hall. With the addition of a warm plate reverb sound, a basic string pad—which sounds a little harsh and edgy by itself—can be shaped into a silky, smooth, appealing texture. Reverberation smoothes out the rough edges of almost any harsh sound.

In Audio Example 6-9, I'll add reverberation to this fairly blatant basic string sound. Notice how the sound smoothes out when, after a few seconds, I add the reverb.

Audio Example 6-9 Reverb on Strings
CD-2: Track 6

If you're layering separate keyboards on a single-note string part, try setting one sound an octave below the other for a very big, full sound (Illustration 6-7). Since you have two different sound sources, experiment with combining different textures on the high and low sounds and try adding reverb to one or the other sounds. Notice that there's a far different effect when you add reverberation to the high part only than when you add reverberation to the low part only. There's also a different feel depending on whether the high or low parts are smooth or edgy (Illustration 6-8).

Combining Textures

If you're adding layers of sound to achieve just the right texture, think about the final sound that you're looking for before you start piling sound upon sound.

When you to need to design a keyboard sound, first jot down a quick list of all the textures you think you'll need. Your list might include these kinds of entries:
1. String pad
2. Smooth and full feeling
3. Interesting, airy texture
4. Sweeping, swooshing sound
5. Big reverb sound
6. Definite high-end string definition

Let's briefly consider each point:
1. String pad. If you're in search of a string pad, you might only need one string sound in your layer specifically to define the texture. Sounds with high-end definition work well to define the texture. A thin single violin or small string group works very well to define the overall sound of a pad. If you're looking for a brass pad, a brass sound with good high-end definition works well.
2. Smooth and full feeling. Fullness in a pad is easy to achieve with mellow brass sounds like French horns, mellow trombones, etc. Some mellow string sounds can add fullness if played in the appropriate musical range and if the high end of the sound is subtle and smooth.
3. Interesting, airy texture. Vocal samples and pads can add an appealing interest to the sound of a large, rich pad. Vocal "ah," "oh" and "oo" sounds each have a different effect on the overall feeling and sound of a pad.

Illustration 6-8
Combining Sounds, Textures and Effects

When layering sounds, adjust each sound individually to add what you want to the texture. Adding reverb to just one part of the texture changes the sound dramatically, depending on which ingredient you choose to reverberate. Try these combinations with your setup:

1. High part - Edgy with no reverberation • Low part - Edgy with no reverberation
2. High part - Edgy with reverberation • Low part - Edgy with no reverberation
3. High part - Smooth with no reverberation • Low part - Edgy with no reverberation
4. High part - Edgy with no reverberation • Low part - Smooth with no reverberation
5. High part - Smooth with reverberation • Low part - Edgy with no reverberation
6. High part - Edgy with no reverberation • Low part - Smooth with reverberation

Use the chart below to record your own results with these and other possible combinations of sounds and reverbs. The possibilities are numerous. Try all the combinations you can come up with. Copy this chart so you can document every combination you try.

	High	Low	Edgy	Smooth	Reverb	Comments
Sound 1	X		X		Hall	Very clear reverb and highs but with a close feel.
Sound 2		X		X	No	
Sound 1						
Sound 2						
Sound 1						
Sound 2						
Sound 1						
Sound 2						
Sound 1						
Sound 2						
Sound 1						
Sound 2						
Sound 1						
Sound 2						
Sound 1						
Sound 2						
Sound 1						
Sound 2						

4. Sweeping, swooshing sound. Use chorus, phase shifter and flanger to increase the harmonic interest. Remember, the chorus generally works best for increasing harmonic depth and interest without causing a sweeping *swoosh* sound. Phase shifters and flangers are very interesting, but they typically have a noticeable sweeping sound that can be distracting.

5. Big reverb sound. Reverberation is almost always a good choice to smooth out the sound of the multilayer pad. Using a long hall

reverb sound in the range of two to three seconds sounds warm and smooth. Depending on the musical context, using shorter reverb times (.5 to 1.5 seconds) might be appropriate. Shorter decay times make it possible to include more reverb without the effect "welling up" and obscuring any melodic or harmonic movement in the pad.

6. Definite high-end string definition. Exciters add clarity and high-end definition that help identify the type of pad you're actually creating (string, brass, vocal, etc.).

As an exercise, build these sounds with your setup. If you don't have all the sound modules necessary, come as close as you can; be resourceful and creative. A resourceful and creative engineer is a good engineer.

Pad One
1. Brass pad
2. Smooth and rich full sound
3. Interesting, sweeping sound

Pad Two
1. Vocal pad
2. Full low end
3. Simple sound

Pad Three
1. Small string sound
2. Very high and airy
3. Large room

Pad Four
1. Big strings
2. Very full
3. Very rich and interesting texture
4. Large room
5. Very well defined

Make up your own list of at least ten more types of pads to construct, from very small and simple to very large and complex.

Exciter

The exciter can be a great tool when you need to add upper presence to a pad. Without using a normal equalizer, the exciter boosts harmonics and increases understandability and high-end definition with less risk of the sound becoming harsh and abrasive than there is when you merely use EQ.

Listen to the string pad in Audio Example 6-10. I'll start without the exciter and add it after the first few measures. Notice the difference in high-end clarity. In the right orchestration, this effect makes the strings much more noticeable without distracting from the rest of the orchestration.

Audio Example 6-10 Exciting the String Pad
CD-2: Track 7

Chorus, Flanger, Phase Shifter

Chorus, flanger and phase shifter are definite options on strings and other pads that need to have a smooth and rich sound, although this type of effect isn't useful when you want a small, intimate, acoustic string group sound unless it's used very sparingly.

Many keyboards that have effects built in include chorus-type effects in their stock patches. The harmonic richness a subtle chorus adds can bring a bland sound to life. Chorus is typically the most natural of these effects because it has the least obvious sweep or swoosh. The harmonic interaction of the chorus with the original sound most closely approximates the natural interaction between multiple instrumentalists or the natural reaction of sound to an active acoustical environment.

Listen to the simple, clean string sound in Audio Example 6-11.

Audio Example 6-11 Simple, Clean String Sound
CD-2: Track 8

Now I'll slowly blend in the chorus until it's overdone and then I'll back off. Notice that the subtle effect adds interest while still sounding very natural.

Audio Example 6-12
Chorus on the Simple, Clean String Sound
CD-2: Track 8

Audio Example 6-13 demonstrates a flanger on the simple, clean string sound. Although this is a very interesting sound, the sweeping sound detracts from the natural sound of the strings.

Audio Example 6-13
Flanging the Simple, Clean String Sound
CD-2: Track 8

In Audio Example 6-14, I add a phase shifter to the same basic string sound we've been using. Like the flanger, the phase shifter doesn't necessarily sound natural, but it's an interesting effect.

Audio Example 6-14
Phase Shifter on the Simple, Clean String Sound
CD-2: Track 8

A very thick, textured string pad might have two or three different basic sounds included, plus chorus, reverberation and an exciter. With each effect used in some moderation, the result of this approach can be a very smooth, full and interesting texture.

Even if you're searching for a string pad, you might only need one violin sound to define the string texture and then combine it with a mellow brass pad for smooth lows and mids with an airy vocal sustained "ah" sound for textural interest. Add a little reverb, chorus and exciter to these sounds, and you'll have a potentially incredible sound. In Audio Example 6-15, I build this sound one ingredient at a time: violin, smooth brass, vocal "ah" sound, reverberation, chorus and, finally, the exciter.

Audio Example 6-15 Building a Big Sound
CD-2: Track 9

Panning

Most contemporary keyboards and effects have stereo outputs, so creating a very wide supportive pad sound is pretty easy. Simply pan all of the left outputs left and all of the right outputs right. This commonly used technique works well when the rest of the orchestration is laid over the top of a very full, broad sustained pad. The stereo part of the individual keyboards or sound modules is typically a result of the addition of stereo chorus, delay or reverberation effects within the instrument. These are the same kind of effects we've been using to add depth, interest and size to guitars, vocals and other keyboard sounds. Audio Example 6-16 demonstrates the full left, full right, multiple-layered keyboard pad, with full stereo reverb and stereo chorus.

Audio Example 6-16 Stereo Sounds
CD-2: Track 10

If you are layering keyboards and want a more unique and wide texture, set two keyboards on a similar—but not identical—pad sound, then pan both outputs of one keyboard to the left and both outputs of the other keyboard to the right. Audio Example 6-17 demonstrates this technique.

Audio Example 6-17
Panning Similar Sounds Apart
CD-2: Track 11

Pan positions don't need to be hard right and hard left. You can even spread them across the spectrum, with the first keyboard set around 8:00 and 10:00, and the second keyboard at 2:00 and 4:00. Experiment in your own musical setting.

When determining the pan settings, always check the mix in stereo. Sometimes sounds that are very wide and full in stereo are hidden and weak in mono.

Delay

Adding a stereo delay to a simple string pad can produce a much wider and more interesting sound. This effect works especially well on single keyboards with a mono output. Audio Example 6-18 demonstrates a very simple mono string sound.

Audio Example 6-18 Simple Mono String Sound
CD-2: Track 12

Audio Example 6-19 combines the simple mono string sound from Audio Example 6-18 with a stereo delay. The delays, hard-panned left and right, are 11ms and 23ms. Notice how much more interesting this sound becomes with this simple delay technique.

Audio Example 6-19 Stereo Delay on Strings
CD-2: Track 13

Delays longer than about 50ms can detract from the smooth pad effect, particularly when the individual delay is obvious. A very soft, long delay in the range of 250-350ms can add depth when it's used in the appropriate context, but more often, reverberation achieves the same kind of effect as the longer delay with a smoother, less intrusive sound.

Bell-like Sounds

Bell-like sounds often contain transients. Some of these sounds are created around a metallic percussion instrument. At this point in the course, you should be capable of evaluating a transient sound with respect to recording level based on the apparent transient content and the amount of low-frequency content.

If the sound is thin with lots of transient

information, recording levels should be colder—between about -7VU and -3VU. If the sound contains plenty of low end and the attack is more of a thunk than a click, the VU meter can read 0VU at the strongest part of the track.

Before we can perform an excellent recording of a bell-like sound, we must have an instrument capable of producing a good bell-like sound. Some synths put out a reasonable facsimile of a bell sound; others produce these sounds with great purity and clarity. Check the local music store to see what's currently available. Roland, Ensoniq, Yamaha and Korg make some incredible instruments that produce world-class sounds. As with all recording situations, everything works best when the sound is excellent at the source. We can work some wonders with mediocre sounds, but when we start with great sounds, we get better results all the way around.

Equalizing the Bell-like Sounds

Equalizing bell sounds can be tricky. If you find a sound that needs more highs for clarity, boosting the highs very drastically can add an unnecessary amount of noise, whether the sound comes directly from the sound module or from the recorder.

If you're recording the bell sounds to analog tape, it's best to print the sound with plenty of high end. If you print too much high-frequency content to tape and need to cut it later during mixdown, the result will be a decreased amount of noise from the track. Listen to the two sounds in Audio Example 6-20. They've both been printed to analog tape, but the first was printed with no EQ and needed to be boosted on playback at about 7kHz for clarity. The second example is the same sound, but 7kHz was

boosted as it was being printed to tape; I was actually able to cut at 7kHz on playback and still have a clear sound. Notice the difference in audible noise.

Audio Example 6-20
Comparing Noise From Analog Tape
CD-2: Track 14

Adjusting the sound at the keyboard so that there's enough high end coming from the keyboard output is the best approach.

Be careful when drastically boosting the highs of a bell-like sound, especially if you only monitor on one set of speakers. A bell sound might be wonderful and clear on one set of speakers and painfully piercing on another.

Boosting between 3kHz and 7kHz increases the clarity of the bell sounds with a cutting edge. Boosting between about 8kHz and 15kHz can add a transparent high end, though possibly at the expense of noise problems, depending on the keyboard, mixer and recorder.

Low-frequency content is generally not necessary on bell sounds, especially in the context of a song. The mids and highs define the sound and are usually all that's needed to fulfill the bell function; cut the frequencies below 150Hz or so. This probably won't affect the sound of the bells but it'll keep any low-frequency content from causing confusion in the mix.

If your mixer has a highpass filter, try using it on bells. Remember, a highpass filter lets only the highs above a specific low frequency pass through unaffected. The lows are extremely cut, ordinarily at a rate of 6 to 12dB per octave. The cutoff point for most highpass filters is usu-

Illustration 6-9
Highpass/Lowpass Filters

A highpass filter lets all frequencies above a certain point pass through unaffected. All frequencies below that point are cut by a specific number of dB per octave—usually 6 or 12. Filtering like this is an excellent choice when you need all frequencies below a specific point cut compared to simply cutting a curve in the frequency spectrum, as in normal equalization.

The opposite of the highpass filter is the lowpass filter, which lets the low frequencies below a specific point, pass through unaffected, cutting all highs above that point—usually by 6 to 12dB per octave

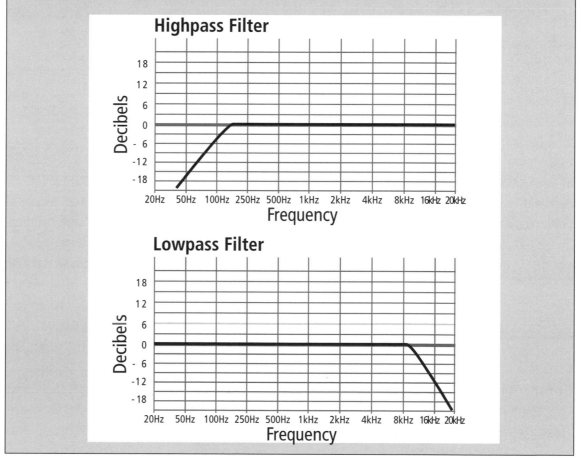

ally between 60 and 150Hz (Illustration 6-9).

Listening to the orchestration, cut as much of the low- and mid-frequency range as you can without detracting from the bell sound. If you cut a wider range of frequencies, still getting the sound you need, your mix will sound cleaner and more transparent. A parametric EQ is an excellent tool for cutting broad bands of low and mid frequencies, since the bandwidth is typically adjustable up to three or four octaves.

Panning Bell-like Sounds

Depending on the musical setting, bell sounds with transient attacks and lots of high end are often panned to one side of the mix, and there's usually some other transient-oriented instrument panned to the opposite side to provide balance for the listener. Listen to the basic mix in Audio Example 6-21. The bells are panned left and the upper percussion is panned right.

Audio Example 6-21 Bell Sound Panned Left
CD-2: Track 15

Some bell sounds with a broad, full range of frequencies are used for a full textural color at a musical section change. A sound like this is usually stereo coming from the sound module; its full sound works well with left and right hard-panned apart for even musical coverage. Listen to Audio Example 6-22. The bells enter at the section change and are a full, even addition to the texture.

Audio Example 6-22 Stereo Bell Sound
CD-2: Track 16

Compression

Most bell sounds don't need compression, especially since the sound coming from the keyboard is very predictable; in fact, compressing a bell-like sound often robs the sound of its clarity.

If you're trying to accentuate the attack of a bell sound, use the same technique that we've used on the guitars and drums. Adjust the attack time to medium-slow, then set the thresh-old for a gain reduction between about 3 and 9dB. This lets the attack pass through the compressor uncompressed, but the body of the sound is compressed.

If you set the release time to a slow setting, the VCA turns the sound back up as the bell sustains, effectively increasing the audible length of the note.

Listen to Audio Example 6-23. The simple bell sound is compressed, with the attack time adjusted to its fastest setting. After the first few seconds, I'll slow down the attack time. Notice the increase in the attack of the bell.

Audio Example 6-23
Accentuating the Attack of the Bell Sound
CD-2: Track 17

Reverb

Often, bell sounds don't require reverberation. The natural decay of a bell-like sound is similar in its harmonic interest to a reverberated sound. If necessary, adding reverb can lengthen the natural decay of the bell-like sound. When your access to sounds is limited, this technique comes in handy. Musically speaking, bell parts are often sparse. Sometimes only one long note at the beginning of a new section works great; if the sound needs to be longer, add plate reverb with four or more seconds of decay time. Plate reverb ordinarily has similar frequencies to most bell sounds; therefore, the increased length added by the plate reverb usually sounds like part of the original sound.

In Audio Example 6-24, you'll first hear the original bell sound with no reverb. Then I'll add plate reverb with a decay time of eight seconds.

Audio Example 6-24 Lengthening the Bell Sound
CD-2: Track 18

Chorus/Flanger/Phase Shifter

Chorus, flanger or phase shifter can make a simple bell sound come alive. Part of what makes a rich, full bell sound is the movement of the bell when hit. The changing phase interaction that accompanies that movement is a naturally occurring equivalent to the chorus-type effects. These are also good effects choices for transforming a mono bell sound into a wide, interesting stereo image.

Listen to the simple bell sound in Audio Example 6-25.

Audio Example 6-25 Simple Bell Sound
CD-2: Track 19

In Audio Example 6-26, I'll add chorus after the first few seconds, then change the chorus to a flanger and, finally, change the flanger to a phase shifter. Notice that, though the character changes, all three effects sound rich and full.

Audio Example 6-26
Adding Chorus, Flange and
Phase Shift to the Bell Sound
CD-2: Track 19

Brass

Mic Technique

Like the other keyboard sounds, brass sounds can be recorded direct in to the mixer with excellent results. Also try running the synth into an amp and using a distant-miking technique to get the kind of natural room ambience that would normally be part of a live brass recording.

Use the best monitor system you can, and crank up the volume so that the room is filled with the brass sound. Set a condenser mic back from the speakers at a distance of roughly three and ten feet. The exact distance depends on the room, the monitors, the brass sound and the needs of the music.

If you're miking speakers, it's usually best to run the keyboard direct into the mixer at the same time so that you can balance the room sound and the direct sound (Illustration 6-4).

Audio Example 6-27 demonstrates a simple brass sound, direct into the mixer.

Audio Example 6-27 Simple Brass, Direct In
CD-2: Track 20

Audio Example 6-28 demonstrates the simple brass sound again, this time played through a set of monitor speakers, then miked from a distance of about eight feet with a good condenser mic.

Audio Example 6-28 Brass Room Sound
CD-2: Track 20

In Audio Example 6-29, I blend the direct and miked sounds from the previous two examples.

Audio Example 6-29
Blending the Direct and Room Sounds
CD-2: Track 20

Levels

Most brass sounds can successfully be recorded with the strongest part of the track at about 0VU.

Brass Samples

If you have a sampler, try the different samples that you have in the context of a song. Many times the brass samples sound thin by themselves but realistic within a song.

If you have an authentic but thin brass sample, try combining that with a full brass sound from another synth. This type of technique will usually provide the best of both worlds: the realism of the sample and the full warmth of a synthesized brass sound.

Audio Example 6-30 demonstrates a sampled trumpet.

Audio Example 6-30 Sampled Trumpet
CD-2: Track 21

Audio Example 6-31 demonstrates a full brass sound from another synth.

Audio Example 6-31 Full Brass Sound
CD-2: Track 22

When these are layered, the result is a full and natural brass sound.

Audio Example 6-32 Layering Brass Sounds
CD-2: Track 23

Brass Equalization

If your brass sound needs more edge, try boosting between 4 and 10kHz. It's common to cut the lows, below 100 or 200Hz, since these frequencies are almost always covered well by other instruments in an orchestration.

I've had the best results when I've optimized the sound from the synth—tweaking the EQ internally first—and saved console equalization until mixdown. Specific EQ changes are dependent on musical needs and are often better left until mixdown.

Panning

Depending on your synth, panning considerations are very dependent on the number of available tracks. If you only have one stereo keyboard, you might be limited to hard or soft panning the left and right outputs of the keyboard or panning the brass left or right with another instrument panned to the opposite side for a balanced mix. If you have multiple keyboards and plenty of tracks, you can open things up a bit.

Try using two separate keyboards. Find similar brass sounds on each keyboard and pan the two keyboards apart. This technique produces a much wider sound; the fact that the sounds on each side are slightly different increases the harmonic interest. To increase interest even more, play the parts separately rather than simply doing an exact MIDI clone of

Illustration 6-10
Brass Section 1

This is the widest approach to panning a brass section with four trumpets and four trombones. The trumpets are panned all the way across the stereo spectrum with the first and second trumpets in the center. The trombones are in a similar arrangement, but they're panned into the holes between the trumpets.

If you're recording a stereo submix to the multitrack, this technique works very well. The brass can be positioned for a very wide spread if the two tracks are panned hard right and hard left, or they can be evenly condensed into a smaller space as you pan both tracks toward the center position.

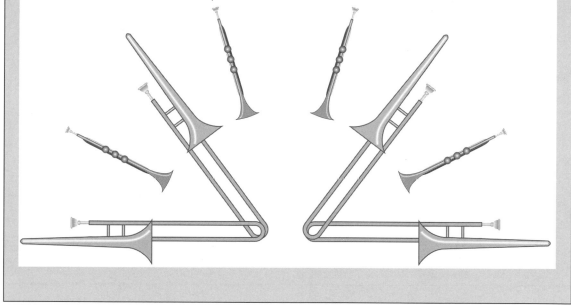

the same part. If the tracks are slightly off rhythmically, the part will sound much more realistic and believable.

The brass part in Audio Example 6-33 comes from one keyboard's stereo output.

Audio Example 6-33 Brass From One Synth
CD-2: Track 24

In Audio Example 6-34, the same part is played simultaneously into two separate keyboards. One keyboard is hard-panned left and the other is hard-panned right.

Audio Example 6-34
Two Synths at Once on the Same Brass Part
CD-2: Track 25

In Audio Example 6-35, I've played the brass part twice rather than simply sending the same MIDI data to the two keyboards.

Illustration 6-11
Brass Section 2

Below is another panning arrangement that works well on brass. It's likely to be a physical arrangement of the brass section at a concert or other live performance.

Depending on the musical arrangement and orchestration, this grouping of brass often sounds very powerful in a mix.

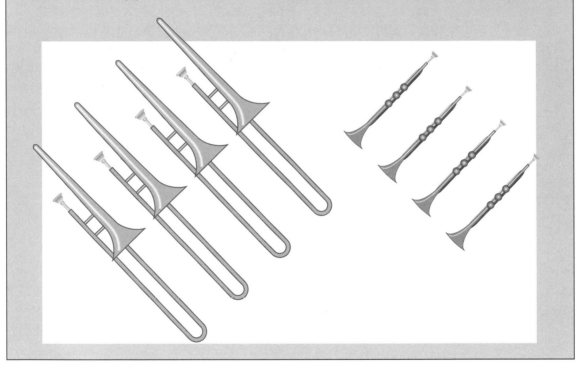

Audio Example 6-35 Playing the Brass Part Twice
CD-2: Track 26

Current MIDI devices and sequencers let you layer and pan multiple instruments even though they're all combining at the same stereo output; therefore you don't necessarily need multiple synthesizers to combine brass parts. But you do need to understand your MIDI system!

If you have lots of available sounds or tracks and you're recording four-part trumpet and trombone section parts, try spreading the parts out across the spectrum. Play each part to a separate track or instrument output. You should find yourself getting a very big, realistic sound.

Audio Example 6-36 simulates a four-part trumpet section with a four-part trombone section. Each part was played separately and recorded onto its own track. The four trumpet parts were panned across the spectrum with the lead parts in the center, and the four trombone parts were panned to fill in the holes (Illustration 6-10 through 6-13).

This same kind of technique can be applied to strings, woodwinds, percussion or any other acoustic instrument. One could spend a considerable amount of time and energy trying to achieve a very realistic brass or string sound. It might be easier—and maybe less expensive— to hire a good brass or string section.

Illustration 6-12
Brass Section 3

This placement is the traditional big band brass configuration.

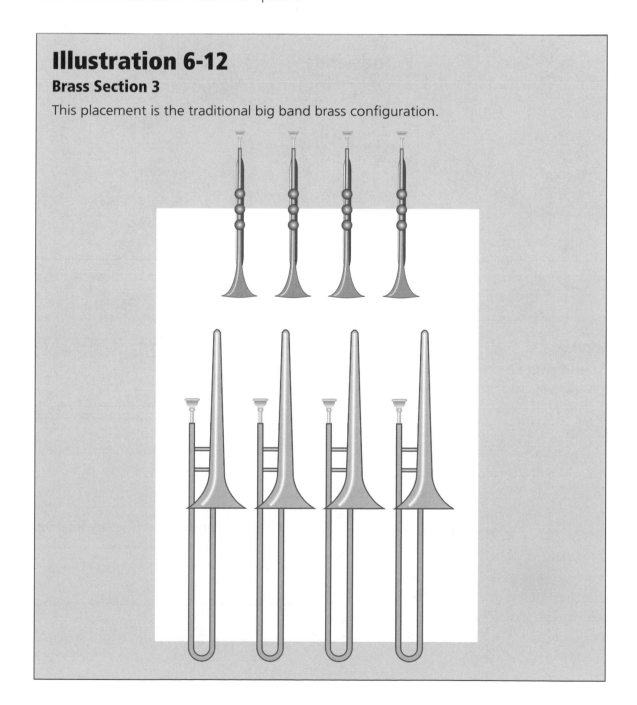

Illustration 6-13
Film Scoring Orchestra
This placement of instruments is the typical for a film scoring session.

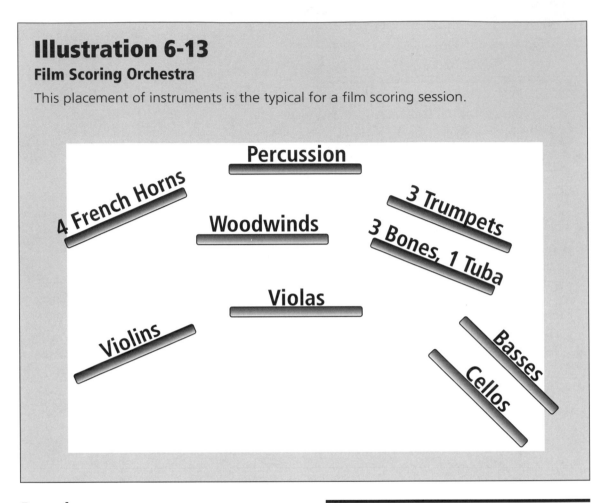

Reverb

Reverberation is a very effective addition to brass sounds, largely because live brass is traditionally heard in a live concert hall. Plate, hall and chamber reverb all sound great. Base your choice of reverb type on the musical needs of the song.

A short plate reverb in the range of .3 to 1 second adds tight textural interest to a brass sound that's similar to the sound of miking the monitor speakers. The high-end response of a good plate reverb enhances the already brilliant sound of trumpets. In Audio Example 6-37, after the first few measures I'll add plate reverb with a .4 second decay time to the trumpet section sound.

Audio Example 6-37
Trumpet Section With .4 Second Plate Reverb
CD-2: Track 28

Audio Example 6-38 demonstrates the same brass part, this time with a hall reverb sound and a three-second decay time.

Audio Example 6-38
Trumpet Section With 3 Second Hall Reverb
CD-2: Track 29

If you have enough effects, try shaping the close sound with a tight plate reverb, then layer

Illustration 6-14
Predelay

This diagram shows the original sound wave, followed by silence—called the predelay time—then the beginning and decay of the reverberation sound.

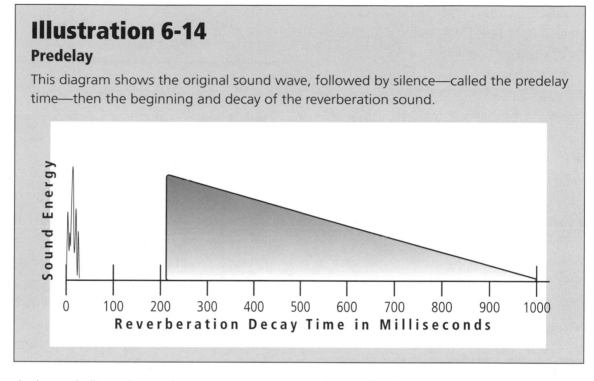

Reverberation Decay Time in Milliseconds

the longer hall reverb over that.

Predelay, the time of a delay before you hear reverberation, is a very useful parameter. The dry sound is heard, then—a number of milliseconds later—the reverberated sound is heard; this is actually a natural effect. When listening to a brass group from the front row of a concert hall, you hear a pretty direct and dry sound first, followed by the slapback off the back of the hall in addition to all the other reflections that make up the natural reverberation.

Predelay in the range of 35 to 75ms gives the dry brass sound a little space before the reverberation kicks in. Longer predelays in the range of 200ms simulate a larger room. Like slapback delay on vocals, the predelay also works well when it has a time relationship to the song (Illustration 6-14).

The brass sound in Audio Example 6-39 uses plate reverb with a two-second decay time and a 50ms predelay. The reverberation is added

after the first few measures.

Audio Example 6-39
Plate Reverb With 50ms Predelay
and 2 Second Reverb Time
CD-2: Track 30

Audio Example 6-40 demonstrates the same brass sound with a warm plate reverb, a 1.5 second decay time and a 250ms predelay that's in time with the eighth note.

Audio Example 6-40
Warm Plate With 250ms Predelay
and 1.5 Second Decay Time
CD-2: Track 31

Exciter

An exciter can help the brass sound cut through the mix without adding the piercing edge that boosting highs with normal EQ can cause. Most exciters have a control that adjusts the exact range of high frequencies that are being excited. This range is dependent on the musical context so it's best to adjust this control while listening to the complete mix. If you're recording the brass parts to the multitrack, it's usually best to print a good, clean brass sound, then add the exciter if it's needed during mixdown.

In Audio Example 6-41, the exciter is added to the brass after the first few bars. Notice how the brass clarity increases after the exciter is added.

Audio Example 6-41 Exciting Brass
CD-2: Track 32

Chorus/Flanger/Phase Shifter

A very subtle chorus can widen a thin and small brass sound, but the chorus-type effects are usually too unnatural-sounding for extreme use. Chorus is a normal sound for a live brass section, and intonation and rhythmic interpretations vary. For a natural sound, be subtle in your use of chorus on brass. Flanger and phase shifter generally don't sound very natural on brass, but these effects can be an interesting addition to a specific musical part in just the right musical setting.

Listen to the simple brass sound in Audio Example 6-42. A slight stereo chorus is added after the first few measures. The result is a more interesting, full sound.

Audio Example 6-42 Brass Chorus
CD-2: Track 33

Delay

Delay can be used successfully to double or triple the brass sound. Use the same approach that we've been using on guitars, vocals and other instruments in this course. Delay times below 35ms combined with and panned apart from the original track make a simple brass sound more impressive, without the harmonic action of a chorus-type effect.

Audio Example 6-43 starts with a very simple brass sound panned to the center. After the first few measures, the brass pans to the left; then I turn up a 23ms delay of the brass on the right. When you set up this kind of sound, be sure to check the sound in mono before you commit to the exact delay time.

Audio Example 6-43 Stereo Brass
CD-2: Track 34

Special Effects

Almost anything can be used for, or turned into, a special effect. Ordinarily, special effects include spacey, wild sounds with lots of extreme processing; sound effects like footsteps, doors and cars; and other sounds that aren't part of the standard instrumental or vocal family.

Creating special effects can be both fun and taxing at the same time. Often, I've known the exact sound I've wanted for a special piece of music, but when I needed to produce it, I couldn't do it. Some different effect sounds—

even brass and synth sounds—require the use of technical features you rarely touch. Be completely familiar with the capabilities of your keyboards and sound modules. There are numerous combinations of wild and crazy sounds possible with most modern keyboards. The better you know your gear, the happier you'll be when it's time to push your equipment's capabilities.

If you have a sampler, you can make some of the most off-the-wall sounds come to life for a particular setting. In my film and video sweetening work, a sampler is a must for creating unique effects. The ability to sample a vocal inflection or scream from the original dialogue, cut it up, turn it around, stretch it out and play it from the keyboard as a textural support for a powerful visual image, is something that can't be efficiently done without a sampler. With a sampler, this kind of technique is pretty easy—if you know how to use your sampler—and it's fast. Speed is *always* a major factor in film and video work.

Use everything you've been taught so far in this course to evaluate and record special effects. Follow this procedure to determine your best plan to record and build special effects:

Evaluate the sound for its transient content. If the attack sounds like metal striking metal or any other two hard surfaces hitting together, be conservative in adjusting recording levels. Don't forget that a strong transient might be 9dB hotter than the average VU level.

Evaluate the sound for its frequency content. If the sound is very thin and the attack is strong, be especially careful not to oversaturate the tape with strong levels. If the sound is full in the low end and the attack is smooth and gentle, be sure the VU levels read between 0VU and +2VU at the strongest part of the track.

Adjust recording levels according to your evaluations. It's time to start trusting and relying on your judgment. Practice recording different sounds at several different levels, just to see what the results are; this will help you make better recordings that have less noise and less distortion.

Use your experience. The simplest sound can be made into a special effect with the addition of enough reverb and other extreme effects processing. At this point in this course, you know how to patch most instruments and effects and you're familiar with what the individual parameters do. Apply this knowledge to extreme special effects; it's good training. When you create and hear the extreme effects, it helps solidify knowledge of subtle effects.

Be creative! Throw caution to the wind. Music progresses because every once in a while someone dreams up a different approach. Whether it's a creative change of instrumentation, effects, orchestration or even a new approach to harmonic, melodic or lyrical content, change happens. Be a part of it; go outside of the boundaries. It's often said in the music business that people either love or hate a potentially successful work; there's no middle ground. So, if you make up a sound or a piece of music that someone tells you they just *hate*, you might have a hit on your hands. Of course, it's more fun when people tell you they love your work.

Conclusion

In our study of string sounds, pads, bell sounds, brass and effects, we're dealing with the frosting on the musical cake. The rhythm section instruments—guitars, bass and drums—provide the cake. They're very important. Even the best frosting can't make up for an awful cake.

Assuming that the rhythm section parts have been recorded and performed well, the frosting is what the listener's attention is continually called to. All of these extra sounds are crucial for indicating musical section changes as well as emotional and textural changes.

Aside from their musical importance, these sounds are often dominant in the mix. Any flaw in your recording of these parts is difficult to cover up. It's worth your time to practice making your recording techniques enhance and support the music rather than detract from its impact.

I'm calling on you to use your judgment more and more in this course—that's just part of the game. If you've followed this complete course, you're developing a sizable repertoire of recording techniques; be creative with their use. Try anything, anywhere, but do it with premeditated intentions. Dream it up, then accomplish it.

7 Panning and Stereo Imaging

Before the 1950s, all commercially recorded and transmitted audio was monophonic. You got one channel, that was it. Our current practical standard is stereo and will probably remain stereo for some time, not necessarily because it's the best system of recreating a natural sound, but because it's what nearly every consumer has and every manufacturer sells. The home entertainment industry has helped the Left-Center-Right approach gain some public recognition, and the theater industry has brought multiple channel audio to the masses, but stereo is still living strong.

When we use the term *stereo*, most of us envision a sound system that plays back through two loudspeakers. Stereophonic sound, though, actually refers to a system that provides the listener with an illusion of directional realism, no matter how many channels or speakers are used. It's the engineer's goal to produce a sound that contains complete directional realism, and that's usually accomplished using just two speakers.

What does *directional realism* really mean? For a recording to sound natural and interesting it must be more than two-dimensional. When sounds are panned left and right in a mix, we can separate the instruments across the left to right spectrum; and when levels are adjusted, we can vary the relative intensity of each ingredient of a recording. But there's much more to shaping the sound of your music than simple volume and left to right adjustments.

Natural acoustic sound is more than two-dimensional. A sound might appear to come from the left or right or one sound might seem louder than another, but also some sounds appear to be closer and others appear to be distant. The human hearing system has an amazing ability to determine directionality and distance. Even though we only have two ears, we can tell if a sound is in front of us, behind us, close to us, far away, to the left, to the right, above us, below us, up high or down low. We can hear very loud sounds, and if our ears were much more sensitive, we could hear the sound of molecules colliding in air.

It's our job to try to approximate the intricacies of the ears' perceptions by sending sound out of left and right speakers. It's possible to give a very dimensional rendition of your music, even when it's played through a stereo system. That's what this chapter is all about.

The possibilities of instrument placement in a mix are far more complex than a simple left to right array of multiple tracks, but through the use of good miking and mixing technique, sounds can be placed in the mix so that they seem to come from left, right, near, far, above, below or even behind.

Depth—the feeling that a sound is close to or distant from the listener—is created through the use of reverberation and delay. This reverberation and delay might occur naturally or be electronically created. We've already covered some of the techniques to make a sound more full throughout the stereo spectrum using delays, chorus and reverberation, as well as room ambience and mic technique.

Stereo imaging is the realization of specific points of origin across the listening panorama of each ingredient of a recorded work. Where we hear the sound coming from and what its acoustical space sounds like are key ingredients in the creation of a pleasing stereo image. If the acoustic guitar sounds like it's coming from

4 feet to the right of center at a distance of 20 feet from the listener at 45° above the horizon in a large concert hall, that's its stereo image. Keep in mind that low frequencies below about 150Hz are omnidirectional, so an effort to give a primarily smooth low-frequency instrument a specific stereo image is usually futile (Illustration 7-1).

Illustration 7-1
Stereo Imaging

Stereo imaging has a three-dimensional perspective. Besides left and right positioning, we perceive sounds as being close or distant, plus we can locate sounds as coming from above or below.

When considering options for a mix, always consider all dimensions and create a mix that's balanced and interesting in each area.

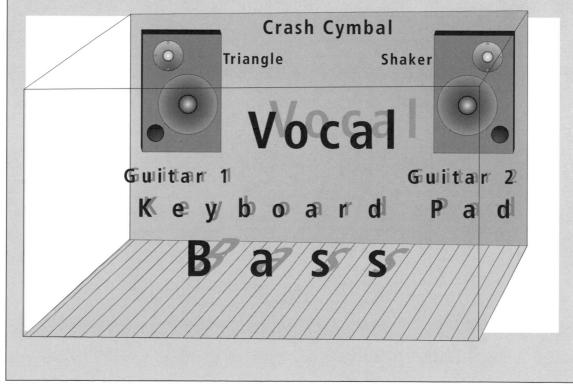

Speaker Position and Choice

When trying to control the stereo imaging and panning in a song, the choice of monitor speakers, their placement, the quality of the amplifier and the listening environment become crucial. It's important when recording tracks to have an accurate monitoring system, but as we reach the point of choosing levels and positions for the ingredients of a completed mix, we must be able to trust that what our monitors tell us is true and accurate.

As I mentioned before, good near-field monitors are more dependable than far-field monitors in most monitoring situations—and that includes final mixdown, where crucial placement choices are made. As a word of advice, get the best near-field monitors you can find and afford. Choose a product that's made by a well-established and respected manufacturer and has an excellent reputation for being reliable and accurate. Each monitor sounds different when

Illustration 7-2
Near-field Monitors

Near-field monitors are designed to be listened to with your head at one foot of a one meter equilateral triangle. The speakers should either be level with your ears or slightly above your ears (around 10°) and aimed at your ears. The fact that the speakers are close to your ears minimizes acoustic coloration of the sound; therefore, you hear a more trustworthy representation of the mix you're creating.

Far-field monitors, which are designed to be listened to from distances greater than 3 or 4', can also be very accurate, but they give excellent stereo representation only if the room that they're in has acoustical accuracy and integrity.

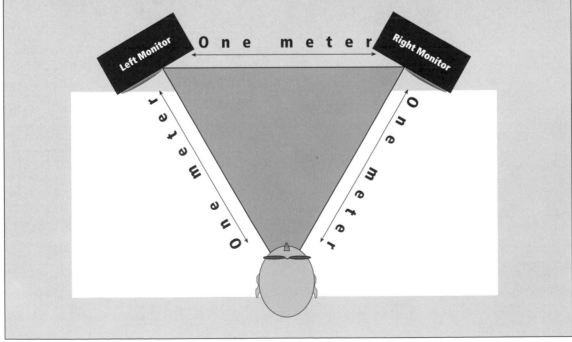

Illustration 7-3
X-Y Configuration

On each of the following diagrams, 0° represents the position of the sound source.

This is the most common stereo miking configuration. The fact that the microphone capsules are as close to the same horizontal and vertical axis as possible gives this configuration good stereo separation and imaging while also providing reliable summing to mono.

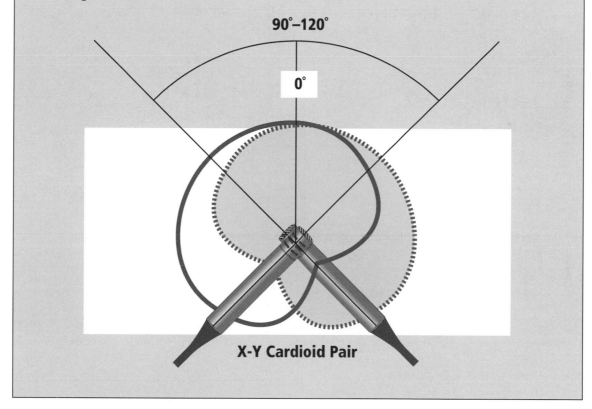

90°–120°

0°

X-Y Cardioid Pair

it comes to stereo imaging and specific panning placements. Your ability to predict how effective or impressive your mix will be when it's played on many types of systems is very dependent on the monitors you use while mixing (Illustration 7-2).

Mic Techniques

Much of the stereo imagery that's included in your recording starts with fundamental mic technique during the initial tracking. In order to

achieve depth, acoustical interest and space in the initial recordings, good mic technique is a must.

On the surface it would seem that, in order to hear the specific stereo location of several instruments recorded at once, we'd need many mics to control their panning placement and to adjust the amount of reverberation separately on each track. It's possible to achieve good results this way, but there is a method that's much more reliable and predictable for recording a

Illustration 7-4
Spaced Omni Pair

This configuration uses two omnidirectional mics. The ambience of the recording environment will color the sound of the recording. This setup is capable of capturing beautiful performances with great life—especially if the recording environment has an inherently good sound.

"D" on the diagram, represents the distance from the center of the sound source to its outer edge. Notice that the distance from the center of the sound source to each microphone is one third to one half of D.

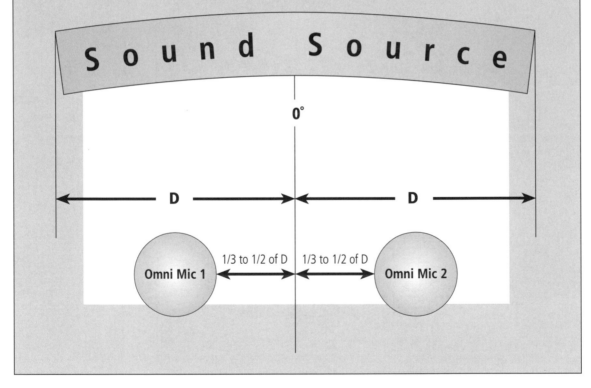

very accurate stereo image, especially in a room that sounds good.

Using two mics, in one of several different stereo miking configurations, can produce wonderfully interesting stereo sounds. It's amazing how clear the difference between left and right and near and far is with most of the standard stereo miking configurations.

Always check the combination of the two mics in mono to guard against phase cancelation.

Coincident miking technique, like the X-Y or MS (mid-side) have the most reliable stereo image when it comes to summing left and right to mono, but there are plenty of situations where these techniques aren't appropriate or practical.

Let's examine a few of the standard stereo miking configurations. Each one of these techniques is field tested and has proven to be functional and effective. Listen very carefully and analytically to these examples. Listen for left/right positioning and for the perception of distance. Are the instruments close or far away? Can you hear a change in the tonal character as the different sounds change position? Do you perceive certain instruments as being above or below other instruments? Can you hear the room sound? In other words, pick these recordings apart bit by bit.

We've heard the X-Y in a number of situations so far in this course. In Audio Example 7-1, listen very closely to the sound of each ingredient of the stereo recording. Listen to the change in the sounds as they move around the room (Illustration 7-3).

Audio Example 7-1 X-Y Configuration
CD-2: Track 35

Illustration 7-5
Spaced Omni Pair With Baffle

This technique retains much of the openness of the regular spaced omni pair, but the addition of a baffle between the microphones increases the stereo separation. When miking a blended acoustical group, this configuration can provide a striking stereo image.

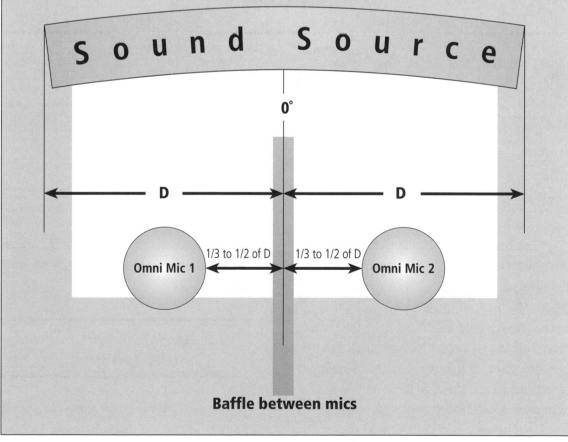

Illustration 7-6
Crossed Bidirectional Configuration

The crossed bidirectional configuration (also called the Blumlein Configuration) has the advantage of being a coincident technique in that the overall sound isn't significantly degraded when the stereo pair is combined to mono. The sound produced by this technique is similar in separation to the X-Y configuration but has a little more acoustical life.

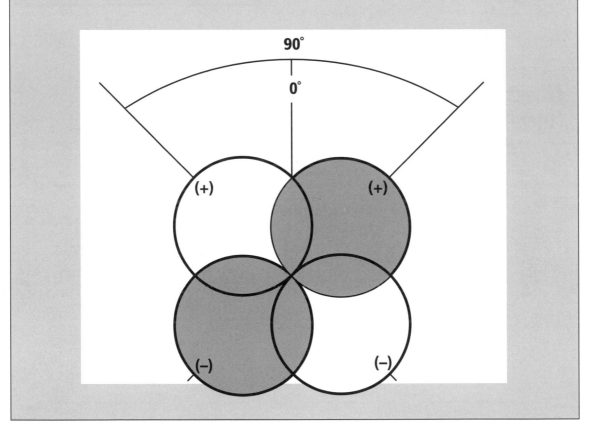

Two omnidirectional mics spaced between three and ten feet apart can produce a very good stereo image with good natural acoustic involvement. When recording a small group, like a vocal quartet, keep the mics about three feet apart; for larger groups increase the distance between the microphones. Use this technique only if the room has a good sound. In Audio Example 7-2, listen closely for the panning placement and perceived distance for each instrument. There's a definite difference in the apparent closeness of these percussion instruments (Illustration 7-4).

Audio Example 7-2 Spaced Omni Pair
CD-2: Track 36

A variation of the spaced omni pair of mics involves positioning a baffle between the two

Illustration 7-7
MS (Mid-side) Configuration

Position the mid mic and the side mic in the closest proximity to each other possible. Both mics should be along the identical vertical axis and as close as physically possible to the same horizontal axis without touching. The MS (mid-side) technique is the most flexible of the stereo miking configurations. Its drawback is that it isn't simple to hook up. You must use a combining matrix that'll facilitate sending the sum of the mid and side mics to one channel and the difference of the mid and side mics to the opposite channel. In other words, you must be able to:

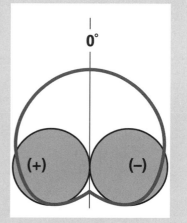

1. Split or Y the output of the mid mic and send it to both channels.
2. Split or Y the output of the side (bidirectional) mic and send it to both channels.
3. Invert the phase of one leg of the side mic split. A *leg* is simply one side of the Y from the side mic.
4. Leave the other leg of the side mic split in its normal phase.
5. Adjust the balance between the mid mic and the side mics to shape the stereo image to your taste and needs.

High quality, double capsule stereo mics typically use this configuration. They demonstrate the advantages of coincident technique—minimal phase confusion between the two microphones. Also, and possibly more important, since the side mic signal is split to left and right—and left and right are made to be 180° out of phase with each other—when the stereo signal is sent through a mono playback system the side mic information totally cancels. This leaves the mid mic signal as simple and pure as if it were the only mic used on the original recording.

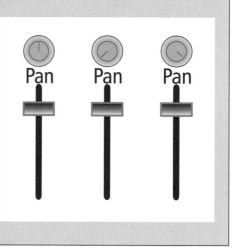

mics, which increases the stereo separation and widens the image. Notice, in Audio Example 7-3, how clearly defined the changes are as the percussion instruments move closer to and farther away from the mics (Illustration 7-5).

Audio Example 7-3
Spaced Omni Pair With a Baffle
CD-2: Track 37

The crossed bidirectional configuration uses two bidirectional mics positioned along the same vertical axis and aimed 90° apart along the horizontal axis. This is similar to the X-Y configuration in that it transfers well to mono, but the room plays a bigger part in the tonal character of the recording (Illustration 7-6).

Audio Example 7-4
The Crossed Bidirectional Configuration
CD-2: Track 38

The MS technique is the most involved of the techniques we'll cover, but it's the best in terms of combining stereo to mono; it also gives a very true and reliable stereo image. Most stereo mics contain two condenser capsules that are positioned in an MS configuration.

To understand how the MS configuration works, first realize that *M* stands for "mid" and *S* stands for "side." The mid mic is aimed at the middle of the stereo image and can possess a cardioid or omni polar pattern. The side mic is bidirectional and is aimed to the sides.

The mid mic is sent equally to left and right. The side mic is also sent equally to left and right but the phase is inverted 180° on either the left or the right side. In stereo, the result of this configuration sounds very similar to the X-Y configuration and results in a very good stereo image. In mono, because the side mic is reversed in phase between left and right, the side information is canceled; that leaves the mid mic as if it were the only mic used. In other words, there's absolutely no phase problem when the stereo image is summed to mono. Listen to Audio Example 7-5 to hear this stereo mic configuration in action (Illustration 7-7).

Audio Example 7-5 Mid-side Configuration
CD-2: Track 39

These microphone configurations are very important when trying to achieve good, natural stereo imaging. Keep in mind that the acoustical environment plays a very important part in the sound of any distant stereo mic setup. If you're not getting the sound that you really need to support your music, try moving your source to a different location. Sometimes that's not always practical, but putting in the extra effort might be worth it. Moving to a different space *will* make a difference in the sound, for better or for worse.

It's also especially important when using stereo mic techniques that the instrument be in peak condition. Subtle nuances within the instrument's sound become more pronounced in these stereo configurations.

There are several standard stereo miking techniques that have been put to good practical use over the years. Some are very specific about the distances at which the mics should be separated as well as the polar patterns. Use these examples to develop configurations that you like and that capture the music in a way that feels good to you. We use many techniques in recording music, but always keep in mind that what we must continually focus on is the emotion of the music and whether we've captured it. Refer to Illustrations 7-8 and 7-9 for other types of stereo miking configurations.

The Head

Another wonderful technique for stereo recording is called the *binaural* technique. This technique uses an actual synthetic head to house two very small condenser mic capsules. The capsules are placed inside the synthetic head, where the eardrums of a real head would be. This synthetic head even has the ear flaps, or pinna.

Recordings made with the synthetic head—called a *binaural mic*—have incredible stereo imaging. When you listen to the recordings through headphones, sounds from all directions can be perceived. Sounds can be localized—their point of origin can be pinpointed—to be in front,

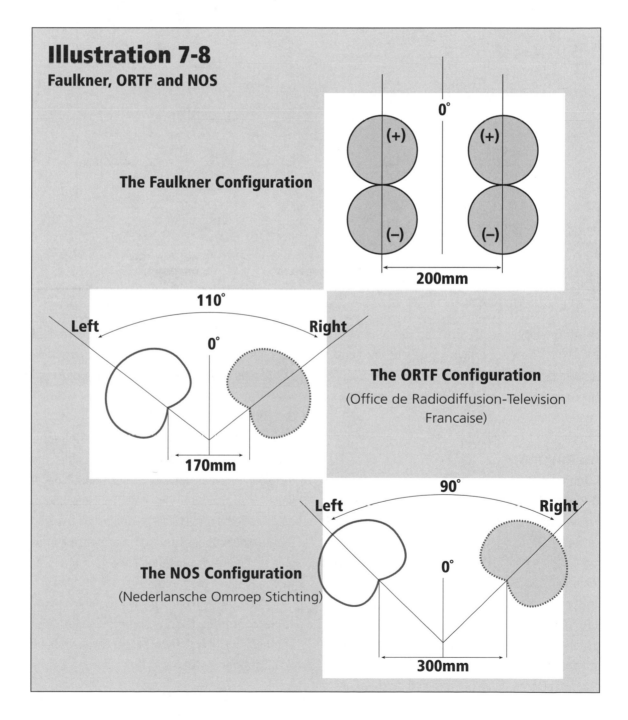

Illustration 7-8
Faulkner, ORTF and NOS

0°

(+)   (+)

The Faulkner Configuration

(−)   (−)

200mm

110°

Left   Right

0°

The ORTF Configuration
(Office de Radiodiffusion-Television Francaise)

170mm

90°

Left   Right

0°

The NOS Configuration
(Nederlansche Omroep Stichting)

300mm

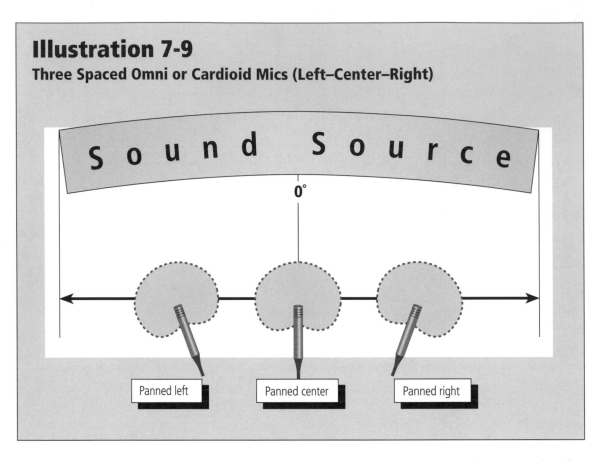

Illustration 7-9
Three Spaced Omni or Cardioid Mics (Left–Center–Right)

Sound Source

0°

Panned left

Panned center

Panned right

behind, above, left, right or anywhere in between. The only drawback to the binaural technique is that the stereo imaging is drastically reduced when the recording is heard on regular monitors.

Assignment

Attend a symphony concert—any one will do. Pay particular attention to the stereo imagery of the orchestra. Try to sit in the center of the concert hall, about 10 to 20 rows back. Listen for all the same things we listened for on the stereo miking examples. I'd guess that you'll be pretty impressed by the sounds you hear when you really listen. Use the orchestra as your benchmark for shaping the sounds and images in your mix. Personally, I do practically no symphony recording; most of my recording situations

are very contemporary and commercial. Still, I learn more from listening to a great live performance than I do from listening to most recordings.

3:1 Principle

When setting up multi-mic recording situations, use this rule of thumb whenever possible: The distance between any two mics should be at least three times the distance from the mic to its intended source. This guideline aids you in placing microphones for minimal phase confusion when the mics are summed to mono—or to one track of the multitrack.

That simply means: If you have microphone A one foot from its source, there shouldn't be another mic closer than three feet to microphone A (Illustration 7-10).

Panning

Let's start with a very simple arrangement of a rhythm section with a single melody line. When all instruments are panned to the center, it's possible for each part to be heard, but the overall sound isn't very natural or spatially interesting. Audio Example 7-6 demonstrates our mono reference point (Illustration 7-11).

Audio Example 7-6 Mono Mix
CD-2: Track 40

With simple panning, we can obviously build a more interesting audio picture. Here's the same piece of music but, as the music plays, I'll pan the guitar and keyboards apart in the left to right spectrum. This is the beginning of—but definitely not the culmination of—a stereo image. Notice how much easier it is to hear everything when these two instruments claim a different space in the soundscape (Illustration 7-12).

Audio Example 7-7 Guitar Right, Keyboard Left
CD-2: Track 41

Illustration 7-10
The 3:1 Principle

The distance between any two mics should be at least three times the distance from the mic to its intended source. If you position a mic 1' from its sound source, there shouldn't be another mic closer than 3' to that microphone.

Use this rule of thumb when setting up multi-mic recording situations. This procedure produces minimal phase confusion when the mics are summed to mono or to one track of the multitrack.

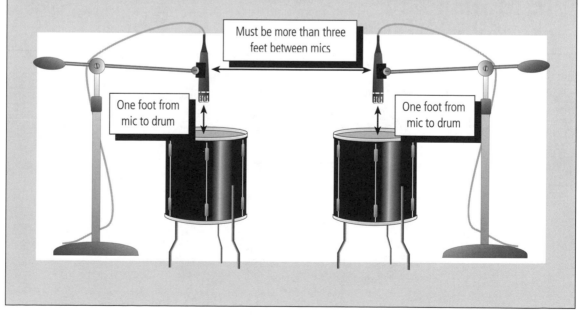

Illustration 7-11
Mono Sound

This is the graphic equivalent of mono sound; it's possible to see everything, though not very easy to look at.

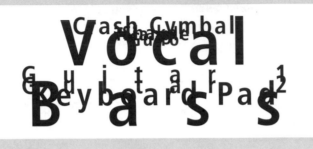

We'll continue to use visual references with the audio examples; they're some of the most important considerations when mixing your music. On the previous audio example, as soon as the guitar and keys moved out of the way, we could hear the bass, drums and melody better; plus we could pinpoint the origin and tonal character of the guitar and keys in greater detail. Panning is important, but even more important is the stereo image you provide for the listener.

In a previous Audio Example, we split the bass across the stereo spectrum. By sending the dry bass track to one side of the mix and panning a short delay of the bass to the other side of the mix, we created a bass sound that seemed to

Illustration 7-12
Guitar Right, Keyboard Left

We consider these audio placements in graphic reference because it provides a means of comparison. When I envision a mix I do exactly that—I visualize the audio components in a three-dimensional thought plane. Now that the keys and guitar are moved from the middle, we not only hear the keys and guitar better, but also the bass, drums and melody.

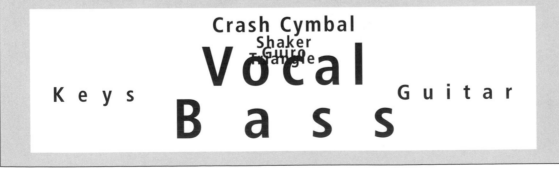

Illustration 7-13
Splitting the Bass

Now we're getting somewhere. The big pieces of the puzzle are all visible. Be sure to check this kind of setup in mono; it can sound truly wonderful in stereo and totally awful in mono.

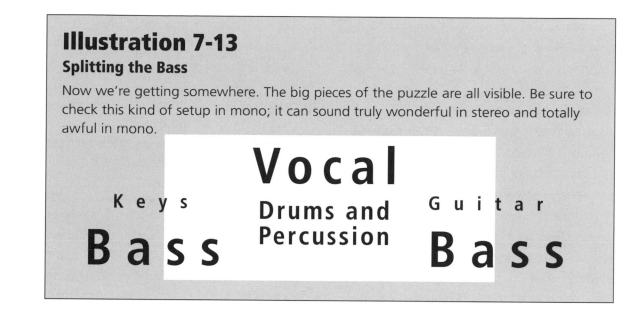

come equally from left and right but didn't seem to come from the center of the mix. In Audio Example 7-8, I've set up a stereo bass sound, with the original panned to one side and a short delay of the bass panned to the other. Using this arrangement, I'll split the bass hard right and hard left. I'll also bring the guitar and keys in to

about 3:00 and 9:00 so they don't conflict with the bass (Illustration 7-13).

Audio Example 7-8 Splitting the Bass
CD-2: Track 42

Illustration 7-14
Adding the Triangle

When we look at this picture, the visual imbalance is instantly recognizable. The audio version of this picture might not seem unbalanced instantly, but eventually a glitch like this will stick out.

Triangle

Vocal
Keys
Drums and
Percussion
Guitar
Bass
Bass

Notice in Illustration 7-13 that each ingredient is claiming a space in the stereo soundscape. So far, we're only dealing with left to right placement of instruments, which might or might not have a natural imagery on their own. We're also only dealing with the two-dimensional left-right/up-down plane. Left to right positioning is adjusted with the pan control. Up and down positioning can be a function of EQ, with the bass frequencies low in the image and the treble frequencies high in the image. Up and down positioning can also be indicated by combining a signal with a short delay of that signal in the same pan position. Notice in the last few illustrations that the bass is placed on the bottom, representing the low frequencies, and the rest of the instruments occupy different top-to-bottom positions. When you're creating your own stereo imagery, always keep these pictures in mind. Strive for a visual balance and it will usually facilitate an aural balance. Listen to Audio Example 7-9. What's wrong with this picture?

Audio Example 7-9 Distracting Pan Position
CD-2: Track 43

You probably caught the triangle on the left that made the mix seem lopsided. This only happened because there wasn't another similarly textured instrument on the right side of the mix to balance things out. This problem seems obvious once you focus on it, but if you aren't thinking visually while you mix, this could end up in the final product. Again, think of your mix in visual terms.

If there was just one triangle and no other similar percussion instrument to offset it, the triangle would need to be placed in the center

of the mix to provide a balanced sound.

Listen to Audio Example 7-10. I'll pan the triangle to the center and adjust the level. Notice how much easier this mix is to listen to (Illustration 7-14).

Audio Example 7-10 Panning the Triangle
CD-2: Track 43

In Audio Example 7-11, I'll add a cowbell on the other side of the mix from the triangle in order to offset the imbalance. Even though I've added an instrument, the mix has a balanced, even sound, and this mix is easier to listen to. The distraction caused by the imbalance no longer exists.

Audio Example 7-11 Adding the Cowbell
CD-2: Track 44

Stereo imagery is much more involved than this simple panning exercise. Panning is important, but reality demands much more than simple left/right comparison. If we are to create a realistic musical image, we must include left, right, up, down, in front, behind, inside, outside and anywhere in between.

Try this exercise. Sit in any normal environment and just listen. Notice the different sounds. Even in a fairly quiet and serene setting, you'll be able to pick out several different sounds. Next, notice where each sound comes from.

The extreme localization accuracy of the human hearing system is amazing. We can very closely pinpoint the origin of each sound we hear. In real life, we're engulfed in a three-dimensional globe of audio stimulation, and in recording that's what we should always try to provide for the listener. Some of the tools required to fully accomplish this feat are either very expensive or haven't been designed yet, but there are several techniques we can use to more closely approach the ideal of three-dimensional audio. Some of the four- and six-channel systems that are becoming common in the film business are very good at providing a surrounding image, but for everyday life most recordists have to primarily consider the normal two speaker stereo system. This chapter focuses on practical and accessible techniques.

There's a lot that can be accomplished on a two speaker system. As I've mentioned before, the dimension of depth can be created with the addition of delays and reverberation. This is a very complex subject and requires you to consider many environmental and psychoacoustic variables. At this point, we'll be keeping things fairly simple and straightforward.

Reverberation

Listen to the reverberation on the snare drum in Audio Example 7-12; I've selected a long decay time. Listen intently to the effect that it creates. Listen to the changes that occur as the reverb fades away. Try to imagine a real room that would sound like this. How big would it be? What kind of surfaces would be around?

Audio Example 7-12 Snare Reverberation
CD-2: Track 45

Audio Example 7-12 was an example of stereo reverberation. Stereo reverb is designed to have slightly different combinations of reflec-

tions and tonal character from left to right. A stereo reverb is helpful in opening up the stereo spectrum and leaving more space for the music. Audio Example 7-13 demonstrates the same reverb sound as the previous example, but this time it's in mono. At the end of the Example, I'll open back up to stereo. Mono reverberation can be very useful when placing an instrument or voice within one area of a large stereo image, but generally stereo reverberation is preferable.

Audio Example 7-13 Mono Reverberation
CD-2: Track 46

When considering placement of an instrument, we must also determine where the listener should be in relation to the instrument. If the instrument is to be placed in a large concert hall, that's only one of the considerations. Do you want the listener to feel that he or she is close to the instrument and inside the concert hall, or do you want the listener to feel as if he or she is standing at the opposite end of the hall from the instrument? Do you want the instrument to be far away and in the corner of the concert hall? Do you want the listener to feel that he or she and the instrument are close together but closer to one side or the other? The list of considerations goes on and on. If you want to create a mix that has clear imagery, you'll have to consider these kinds of options for each instrument or voice in the soundscape.

Now, let's move ourselves and the snare drum around the room. If we want the instrument to appear to be close to the listener *and* in a very large hall, we must consider that the listener would naturally hear a strong, direct sound followed by a slightly delayed reverberation as it comes back to the listener from the hall. Changing the predelay on the reverb and the relative volumes of the reverberation and the direct instrument sound, let's vary the apparent closeness of the listener to the instrument. The longer the predelay, the larger the perceived size of the hall. Listen as I change the stereo image of the drum. I'll start with the drum far away in a large hall.

Then I'll move the drum closer to you, by increasing the level of the direct sound and lengthening the predelay. I'll pan the drum slightly, and while I pan the drum, I'll also vary the balance of the reverberation. As the drum moves left, I'll increase the level of the right side reverb return. Try to picture the placement of this drum in your mind (Illustration 7-15).

Illustration 7-15
Moving the Snare Image Around the Hall

With the mic close to the drum and at one end of the hall, the recorded sound contains mostly direct sound and close reflections. The distant reflections still influence the sound of the drum but aren't always instantly recognizable. In this situation, the reflections from the back wall of the hall are delayed substantially. In a hall that's 150' long, it takes about 265ms for sound to get from the instrument to the back wall, then back to the mic since sound travels at the rate of roughly 1130 feet/second.

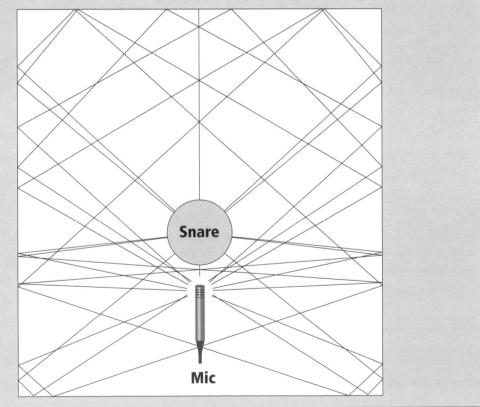

Illustration 7-16
Stereo Distant Mic Setup

This stereo distant mic setup represents a scenario where the reflections might be as strong as the direct sound. The reflections shown are only a small representation of the reflections that occur in reality. Low frequencies carry more energy than high frequencies and therefore can set up repeating patterns of reflections called standing waves. As these patterns combine, they either sum or cancel at specific frequencies, causing acoustic coloration of the sound.

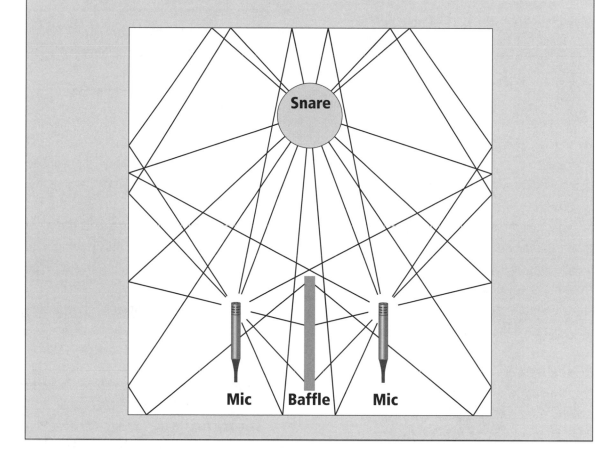

Snare

Mic **Baffle** **Mic**

Audio Example 7-14
Moving the Drum Around the Room
CD-2: Track 47

In Audio Example 7-15, I'll select a smaller reverberation sound and move the snare drum around in that image. Some of the changes are not as noticeable with this smaller room sound as they were with the larger hall sound, but these changes are still a dramatic enhancement of the dry original mono snare sound.

Audio Example 7-15
Moving the Drum Around a Smaller Room
CD-2: Track 47

There are several good applications for these kinds of changes. Film and video sound demands control over sound imagery, and you must be capable of moving the audio image in tandem with the visuals. There are also appropriate settings for these types of movements in music, although most of the time the musical soundscape is stable and balanced.

With your own equipment, select a sound and practice moving it around the stereo image. Try moving the image around different sized environments—from very large to fairly small. Listen very closely to the changes.

With the control available to the modern day engineer, there are plenty of opportunities to create sounds that would never occur naturally; these sounds can be powerful and appropriate. The ability to recognize and create a natural stereo image facilitates much more control in creating usable unnatural stereo images.

Space in a Space

It's common when shaping sounds to combine reverbs and delays to add interest and realism. Combining a small room reverb with a concert hall reverb is common. In the previous chapter, we saw the effect of combining a tight room reverb with a large hall reverb. That technique works very well for designing sounds; the stereo reverberation adds depth to the stereo image.

The combination of effects helps build a pronounced stereo image. When I add a very tight room sound to the marimba in Audio Example 7-16, I increase the acoustic interest of the sound.

Audio Example 7-16
Marimba With Tight Room Reverb
CD-2: Track 48

When I add a large hall sound with a fairly long predelay (around 200ms) the sound takes on a completely different feel.

Audio Example 7-17
Marimba With Large Hall Reverb
CD-2: Track 48

When I add the tight room sound to the marimba, pan the marimba and the room sound toward the right, then pan the large hall sound to the left, I create the stereo image that puts the listener in a small room with the marimba, but there's a door open on the left side of the room that leads into a concert hall. This technique of panning the instrument apart from the large room or hall sound, dry or with a small room reverb sound, is very effective and provides an interesting stereo image in a song or a mix. Listen for the imagery in Audio Example 7-18.

Audio Example 7-18
Marimba Next to the Concert Hall Door
CD-2: Track 48

These images add depth and sound quality to your recordings that can't be achieved in other ways. There's a lot of room for experimentation and innovation with these options.

Listen to the examples of different placements and stereo imaging in Audio Example 7-19. Try to envision the audio space for each of the examples. They will help fine-tune your listening, plus they provide some useful stimuli for creating your own unique sounds. Write down your impression of each example's stereo image, then recreate that image with your own equipment.

Audio Example 7-19 Stereo Images
CD-2: Track 49

When we combine basic panning with reverb in the context of a song or instrumental arrangement, the options for mix placement increase dramatically. If the guitar is panned right, should it be up front and dry in the mix or should it sound like it's coming from behind the rest of the instruments? Should an instrument's reverb be wide and stereo or should it be mono and localized to the point of origin for the instrument? Should the entire mix sound like it's being heard in an auditorium? The list of considerations goes on and on.

Listen to the difference in Audio Example 7-20 as I change the position and reverb on the guitar track. I'm changing the pan position of the guitar and/or the reverb, decay time and predelay. Notice how the stereo image of the guitar changes from close to distant and how the size of the image changes from very small to very large.

Audio Example 7-20 The Roaming Guitar
CD-2: Track 50

Combining Wet and Dry

If you're designing textures with multiple instruments performing the same musical part, it isn't usually necessary to add reverb to all pieces of the texture. In fact, the overall image can change substantially depending on what part of the texture you send to the reverb. If you have similar timbres in the different sounds you're layering, try adding reverb only to certain sounds.

As a practical example, it's common on the chorus of many songs to hear the lead vocal singing along with the background vocals. When this scenario occurs with vocals or other textures, you need to determine which part of the texture you want to be in front of the other parts. With the vocal chorus section, try adding reverb to the background vocals but leaving the lead vocal totally dry. The fact that the background vocals have a similar timbre to the lead vocal will give the impression that there is really reverberation on all of the vocals including the lead part because the reflections will be activated by the other parts. But the overall image will be that the lead vocal seems more present—further forward or closer to the listener—in the mix. This technique is commonly used in the recording industry.

Sometimes we end up combining two or more sounds for a texture, and the sounds are totally different in their frequency content. Reverberation can be applied to either or both sounds; the result of each combination produces a completely different musical feel. Audio Example 7-21 demonstrates a combination of a low-end pad sound with a high-end string sound.

Audio Example 7-21 Low Pad, High Strings
CD-2: Track 51

In Audio Example 7-22, hall reverb is added to the low pad sound, but the high-end strings remain dry. Notice the clarity of the high end and the fullness of the low end.

Audio Example 7-22 Reverb on the Low Pad
CD-2: Track 51

In Audio Example 7-23, with the same sounds used in Audio Example 7-22, plate reverb is added to the high-end strings, but the low-end pad remains dry. Notice the sizzle of the high end and the closeness of the low end.

Audio Example 7-23 Reverb on the High Strings
CD-2: Track 51

Delay

In the chapters on guitar, keyboard and vocal sounds, we used digital delay to widen the image of a single instrument. With the original instrument sound panned to one side of the stereo spectrum and a short delay—below about 35ms—panned to the opposite side of the spectrum, the originally mono image spread across the panorama, leaving more room to hear the rest of the instruments. This technique widens the stereo image, but almost more importantly, it makes room in the mix to hear other instruments and their image in the stereo soundfield. As a quick review, listen to the guitar in Audio Example 7-24. It starts mono in the center, then

I pan it left and turn up a 17ms delay on the right.

Audio Example 7-24
Creating a Stereo Guitar Sound
CD-2: Track 52

Each time you use short delays to widen the stereo image, be sure to keep these three points in mind:

Always check the mix in mono to be sure the combination of the original and the delay don't combine in a way that cancels the predominate frequencies of the track.

If you've hard-panned the delay and the original apart in the mix, be sure that when the mix is summed to mono the instrument is still audible in the mix.

When choosing delay times, keep in mind that short delays—below about 11ms—usually cause the most problems when summing to mono.

Audio Example 7-25
Short Delays From Mono to Stereo
CD-2: Track 53

Sometimes, even if there's no phase problem when summing to mono, the split instrument seems to disappear when the mix goes to mono. The hard-panned split tracks are very visible in stereo, because there's nothing in the listeners' way. As soon as everything comes together in the center in mono, however, the split tracks are simply buried in the mix. The only way to avoid this situation is to avoid hard-panning tracks in the mix. The closer you keep all of the ingredients of your song to the center position, the better the mix will transfer to mono.

It's up to you to decide whether your music should have a huge stereo image or sound good in both mono and stereo. It is possible to get a mix that sounds huge in stereo and still great in mono, but it takes several comparisons, compromises and fine adjustments throughout the mix process. Each instrument must be deliberately placed in the mix, the spread across the stereo spectrum should be very even from hard left to hard right and all stereo images must be aurally calculated and compared to provide width and fullness in stereo while maintaining visibility and clarity in mono (Illustration 7-17).

Delay times above 11ms and below 35ms tend to transfer well to mono, but they still must be cross-checked and fine-tuned in both mono and stereo. Audio Example 7-26 demonstrates a 25ms delay that sounds pretty good in stereo. When I switch to mono, I'll fine-tune the delay time to get the best sound.

Audio Example 7-26
Fine-tuning the 25ms Delay for Mono
CD-2: Track 54

Delay times between 35ms and 50ms often sound very big and impressive in stereo,

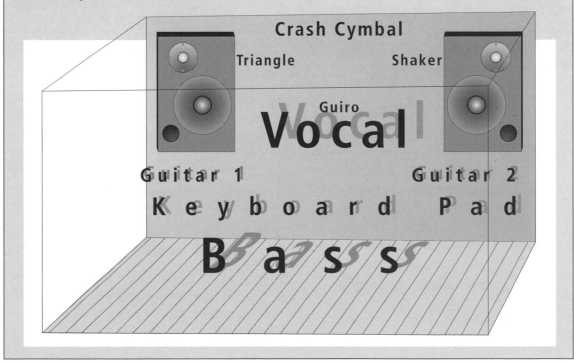

Illustration 7-17
Stereo to Mono Hard Split (Stereo Image)

In this stereo image, the guitars are clear and visible because they're hard-panned out of the way of the rest of the instruments.

Crash Cymbal

Triangle   Shaker

Guiro

Vocal

Guitar 1   Guitar 2

Keyboard Pad

Bass

Illustration 7-18
Stereo to Mono Hard Split (Mono Image)

Once the mix is summed to mono, the guitars are hidden among the rest of the orchestration. The only way to minimize this situation is to avoid hard-panning in the stereo mix. The closer in to the center position you keep each ingredient of the mix, the better the mix will sound in mono. You must compromise and constantly cross check your mix if you want a product that sounds good in both stereo and mono.

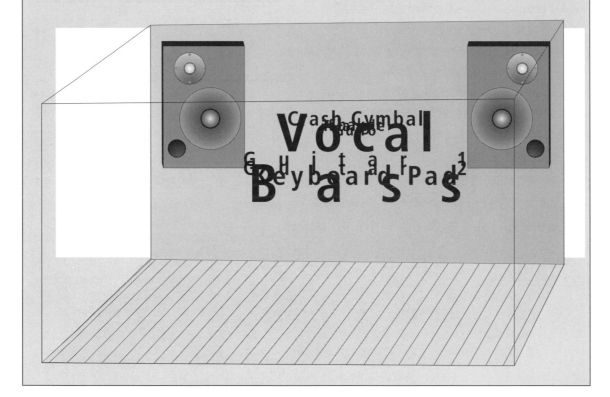

but when they are summed to mono they tend to sound roomy with a very short slapback effect. Audio Example 7-27 demonstrates a 50ms delay, cross-checked from stereo to mono.

Audio Example 7-27
Fine-tuning the 50ms Delay for Mono
CD-2: Track 54

In understanding the stereo image, it's helpful to realize that when these short delays are panned apart, our ears will prefer the original over the delay. A phenomenon known as the Haas Effect indicates that the delay is suppressed by as much as 8 to 12dB. In other words, our hearing system is doing its best to ensure that localization is cued from the initial, direct sound wave. If we want to split an instrument in the mix and we want that instrument to sound like it's coming equally from both left and right, we have to turn the delayed signal up higher in actual level than the original. The amount depends on the amount of transient and the overall sound quality of the instrument.

Panning

If the wide stereo image has been created with a good 16-bit or better digital delay, the sound quality of the delayed signal should be nearly identical to the original sound. To increase the stereo effect, try equalizing the left and right side differently. Listen to the split of a simple keyboard sound in Audio Example 7-28. The original is panned right and the delay is panned left. On the left, 8kHz is boosted and 4kHz is cut; on the right, 8kHz is cut while 4kHz is boosted. In this way, the difference between left and right is enhanced; the frequencies that I've selected should be well represented in nearly all possible monitor systems.

Illustration 7-19
Psychoacoustic Chart

How does the image change with the addition of a short delay panned to the same position as the original sound?

Perceived Change	17ms	15ms	11ms	7ms	3ms
Comes from above	Audio Example 7-29	Audio Example 7-30	Audio Example 7-31	Audio Example 7-32	Audio Example 7-33
Comes from below					
Sounds thick					
Sounds thin					
Sounds good					
Sounds bad					
Other					

Short delays are good for widening images, but they're also useful for creating more subtle changes. If short delays, below about 17ms, are combined with the original dry signal in the same pan position, the image can seem to rise or lower on the vertical plane.

Depending on the tonal character of the instrument you're recording and the accuracy of your monitors, these short delays produce different effects. On the chart in Illustration 7-19, keep track of the perceived differences you hear in Audio Examples 7-29 through 7-33. Listen to the acoustic guitar part in Audio Example 7-29. It starts clean and dry, then a 17ms delay is slowly added. The original guitar and the delay are both panned to the center position.

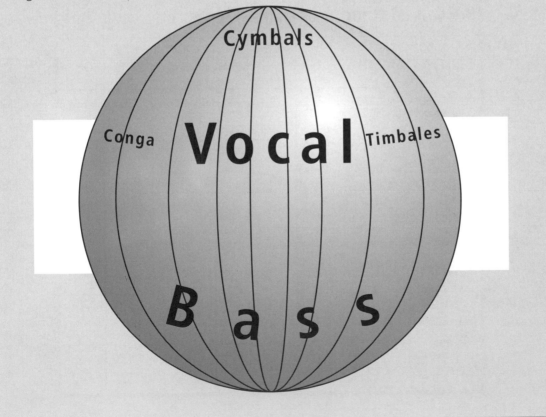

Illustration 7-20
Global Map

Envision your mixes from a three-dimensional, global perspective. Stereo imaging and panning work together to place each ingredient of your music in a specific position. Through the use of the tools available to you—delays, reverbs, etc.—you can give the image width and depth.

Audio Example 7-29 17ms Delay
CD-2: Track 56

Audio Example 7-30 demonstrates the same example, this time with a 15ms delay. Notice the audible vertical position of the guitar as the delay is added. Does it rise or lower?

Audio Example 7-30 15ms Delay
CD-2: Track 56

Audio Example 7-31 demonstrates the same example, this time with an 11ms delay.

Audio Example 7-31 11ms Delay
CD-2: Track 56

Audio Example 7-32 demonstrates the same example, this time with a 7ms delay.

Audio Example 7-32 7ms Delay
CD-2: Track 56

Audio Example 7-33 demonstrates the same example, this time with a 3ms delay.

Audio Example 7-33 3ms Delay
CD-2: Track 56

The previous five Audio Examples are designed to provoke your thoughts on positioning and stereo imaging. When we listen with ears tuned to analyze these subtle sound differences, we're just beginning to hear the music.

Use these techniques to serve the purpose of the music. If some of these simple techniques can add to the musical power and impact and provide a clear visual image, they're serving their purpose well.

Combining each of the topics we've discussed in this chapter starts to become a bit of an organizational mental task. We've learned how to move instruments closer, farther away, into more than one acoustical space at a time and up and down along the vertical axis.

In your head, develop a global picture of each mix. Keep track of the three-dimensional positioning of each ingredient. Create a balanced visual image; it'll help you produce a mix that's easy to understand, powerful and fun to listen to (Illustration 7-20).

Chorus/Flanger/Phase Shifter

The use of stereo chorus, flanger and phase shifter effects can definitely widen an image. As we've discussed previously, these effects—although pleasing in stereo—can spell trouble in mono. They can be more trouble than a simple delay because their constantly changing and sweeping delay times cause sweeping changes in the frequencies that sum and cancel. These effects produce excellent results when adjusted to optimize their impact in both stereo and mono.

Monitors and Your Stereo Image

Keep in mind that the stereo image will change depending on the monitor system. If many of your stereo placement cues are indicated by very high frequencies, everything will sound fine as long as your music is being heard on a system that reproduces the very high frequencies. As soon as your music is heard on a below par system with limited highs, the image that you've worked so hard to create will probably be gone. This is a frustrating fact that we all must face.

If you check your mixes on large, medium and small speakers, you should be able to build a mix that has good imaging and transfers well to most monitor systems. It's all a matter of compromising a little here and there for the good of each listening situation.

High quality near-field reference monitors are typically your best tool for accurate mixing. The monitor du jour changes, but it's never a secret. I have my current favorites, and I wouldn't think of mixing on speakers I used regularly ten years ago. That's normal for this industry. Read the trade magazines and talk to your local pro audio dealers; they'll always know what the gear of the day is.

Conclusion

This chapter includes some very important ideas and tools for you to consider during the construction of your music. Where and how we place the ingredients of a mix can make or break the emotional appeal of the music. Practice these concepts on your own music. Time and time again I've seen and heard each one of the points we've covered in this chapter play an important role in sound shaping.

8 The Total Recording Session

My goal in this chapter is to demonstrate and highlight some procedural do's and don'ts. We'll work from basic room considerations all the way through to the final recording of the final musical part to the multitrack. We'll cover each step thoroughly, but some of the basic patches and techniques will reference previous chapters of the *AudioPro Home Recording Course*. We've covered quite a bit of information in each chapter, and it's finally time to start putting everything together in a logical and productive way.

I'd also like to mention that I've used my own home setup as the project studio to work through this recording session. I've done this almost exclusively throughout this course so that the sounds that I demonstrate are similar to what you can expect to achieve in your setup.

Planning

The technique that will net you the most creative use from your equipment is preplanning. In the professional recording world, it's the producer's fundamental job to plan ahead. The musical vision for the final product is his or her primary concern. What kind of sound should the final product have? How many tracks are available on the multitrack? How many channels are available on the mixer? Should the tracks be played live? Who should play them? Could the song be recorded more powerfully with the aid of some computer-assisted or sequenced parts? Should

there be background vocals? How should the background vocals sound? What should the instrumentation be? Should there be a solo section? Who should play the solo? All these things need to planned ahead of time. Organization is the key to getting the kind of recorded sound you want (Illustration 8-1).

Tracks

Once you've sketched out the arrangement and decided on the musical content of the song, it's best to make up a track sheet, indicating the final tracks for the song. Refer to Illustration 8-2 for a simple 8-track track sheet. For more track sheets in 4-, 8-, 16- and 24-track configurations refer to Volume 1, Chapter 6 of the *AudioPro Home Recording Course*.

Envision the Final Product

Once you've mapped your song out on a track sheet, it becomes obvious that some things can't be accomplished without this crucial step.

For the song we will be working on in this chapter, I'd like to end up with a big, full keyboard sound; an electric guitar part that has a large, impressive sound; an acoustic guitar part; lead vocals and a large stereo backing vocal sound; plus, I want a good, solid drum set sound with a few different percussion parts.

Those expectations are only realistic if I use a sequencer referenced to time code. In this way, the synth and drum machine parts never

Illustration 8-1

Planning Chart

Use this chart to help plan the number of tracks you'll need to get the desired final sound. Your song might have totally unique requirements, but try to anticipate as many of the features of your particular piece of music as possible. This type of preplanning will help calculate what it'll take to get the sound you want.

Instrument/Voice/ Consideration	Sounds required		Number of tracks
Type of sound for final product	❏ Pop rock ❏ Orchestral ❏ Brass band ❏ Grunge	❏ Country ❏ R & B ❏ Jazz ❏ Other	
Lead vocal	❏ Solo ❏ Solo with overlapping lines	❏ Duet	
Guitar sound	❏ Acoustic ❏ Dist. rhythm ❏ Stereo ❏ Nylon string	❏ Clean electric ❏ Dist. lead ❏ Mono ❏ Other	
Piano	❏ Acoustic ❏ Rhodes-type ❏ Mono	❏ Electric grand ❏ Stereo ❏ Other	
Synth	❏ Strings ❏ Bells ❏ Stereo ❏ Special effects	❏ Brass ❏ Analog synth ❏ Mono ❏ Other	
Drums	❏ Kick ❏ Toms ❏ Crash ❏ Special effects	❏ Snare ❏ Ride ❏ Hi-hat ❏ Other	
Percussion	❏ Triangle ❏ Conga ❏ Bongos ❏ Special effects	❏ Claves ❏ Tambourine ❏ Shaker ❏ Other	
Backing vocals	❏ Single Part ❏ Sm. group mono ❏ Sm. group stereo ❏ Massive live	❏ Sm. group stereo ❏ Lg. group stereo ❏ Layered and huge ❏ Other	
Solos	❏ Guitar ❏ Sax ❏ Flute	❏ Keyboard ❏ Trumpet ❏ Other	
Hand claps	❏ Large stereo	❏ Small mono	
Sound effects	❏ Stereo	❏ Mono	
Time code	❏ SMPTE	❏ Sync pulse	
Sequenced parts running from time code	❏ Keys ❏ Guitars ❏ Percussion ❏ Sound effects	❏ Synth ❏ Drums ❏ Solos ❏ Other	

need to actually be recorded onto the multitrack. Refer to Illustration 8-3 to see the track sheet as planned for the final completed recording to multitrack.

The setup in Illustration 8-3 is fairly common for an 8-track session using a sequencer and time code. Notice that track seven is empty. Anytime you're recording to an analog multi-

Illustration 8-2
Generic Track Sheet

Multitrack Track Sheet								
Title	1	2	3	4	5	6	7	8
Title	1	2	3	4	5	6	7	8
Title	1	2	3	4	5	6	7	8
Title	1	2	3	4	5	6	7	8

track, try to leave the track next to the time code blank. Two possible problems commonly occur when tracks are printed next to time code.

The time code leaks into the adjacent channel on the mixer, producing an unacceptable continual chatter behind the music as the time code goes on and on and on.

If an instrument with heavy transient information is printed next to code, the transients can leak onto the time code track and either confuse the time code reader or actually damage the time code track, rendering it useless during parts of the song. When this happens, the sequencer might stop and start at

Illustration 8-3
Track Sheet Layout

Multitrack Track Sheet								
Title	1 Backing vocals	2 Backing vocals	3 Guitar fills	4 Electric guitar	5 Lead vocal final	6 Acoustic guitar	7	8 SMPTE 1:00:00:00
Title	1	2	3	4	5	6	7	8
Title	1	2	3	4	5	6	7	8
Title	1	2	3	4	5	6	7	8

places that you don't want any stopping and starting. Sometimes erasing the problem track next to time code fixes the problem; sometimes the transients have actually become part of the time code track. The only way to fix this problem is to actually regenerate the time code.

If you're lucky, you can patch the existing time code track into the input of your code generator and the generator will be able to exactly reproduce the code, letting you record the regenerated code to a different track. This procedure keeps the sequence in sync with the analog tracks, and all is well. You just have a clone of the original time code track, at a different location, on a different track.

If the code has been damaged very severely, you'll need to print an entirely new track of code. Once you've done that, you'll need to find the new start point for the sequence. This can be tedious and frustrating, but most new sequencing software packages provide the control necessary to perform this kind of repair activity. See your manual or call product support if you have a seemingly insurmountable problem like this and you've tried all of the options that you can think of.

This brings up a bit of a sidebar. If you're using computer software for sequencing or for any other purpose, purchase it legally and aboveboard. Not only is it the right thing to do, but you'll receive all the proper documentation with the software, you'll be notified of bugs that might exist in a current software version, you might even get free upgrades of the software occasionally and, last but not least, you'll be able to call the software support team to find out the best way to get yourself out of a bind. Believe me, one of those panic calls can be worth several times the cost of the software.

Pirating software is a tempting activity for a new computer owner, but it's illegal, unfair to the author of the software, unfair to the manufacturer of the software and, in the long term, not a productive way to use software.

Instrument

Tuning

Remember to always keep those instruments in tune and at the peak of their condition. An instrument that's out of tune can destroy the power and texture of an otherwise good recording. Tuners are relatively inexpensive these days so there's no excuse for bad intonation. Before the session, tune all keyboards and guitars to the same tuner. If you're using an acoustic piano, be sure that it's tuned; check the tuning reference to your tuner. A piano can be in tune with itself but still be a cent or two out of tune with the standard pitch reference of A 440. If your tuner reads slightly off dead center—in tune—when the piano plays, you'll need to tune all the rest of the instruments to that same slightly-out-of-tune reference.

Strings

Be sure your guitars have new or fairly new strings. Some bass players like the sound of old bass strings, but on electric guitars and acoustic guitars, you'll get better-sounding recordings if the strings are new. Old guitar strings also tend to lose consistent intonation up and down the neck. This can be a real problem on some songs in some keys.

Getting the Recorder Ready

Cleaning and Demagnetizing

Once the tracks are planned out and you're sure that your instruments are in tune and in good repair, it's time to start getting the technical details in order. The first order of business is cleaning and demagnetizing the tape recorder; this is one of the most crucial steps involved in producing high quality recordings. A machine that's dirty and has heads that are magnetized produces recordings that are noisy, distorted and inaccurate. That's never good!

Digital and analog recorders differ in their maintenance needs. Many digital machines use a rotating head, video recorder-type mechanism. These transports are easy to clean on a periodic basis. Using a VHS or 8mm video cleaning tape helps keep things operating well. Don't overuse cleaning tapes, though; they are abrasive, and too-frequent use damages the rotating head.

It's best to occasionally have your rotating head machine cleaned and serviced by a factory-authorized service agent. They'll take the machine apart, do a thorough cleaning of all serviceable areas and verify functionality throughout the machine. Check the manufacturer's specifications for maintenance and adhere to them; it will pay off in the long run.

If you're using a computer-based recorder, the only maintenance you'll need to worry about is maintaining plenty of available space on your hard drives, removable media drives and backup systems.

Demagnetizing the Analog Tape Machine

Though digital recorders are the norm for many setups, analog machines offer warmth and smoothness that surpasses the current state of digital recording. Analog recorders also require the most regular maintenance. In order to function optimally, certain adjustments and routines must be regularly performed and verified.

As a rule, you should clean analog tape recorder heads about every four to eight hours and demagnetize them every eight to sixteen hours, depending on the activity of your sessions. You can't hurt anything by doing this too often so if you have a question about whether or not it's time to perform these routine duties, go ahead and do them.

- Turn the tape recorder off.
- Take any tape off the recorder.
- Plug the demagnetizer in at least three feet away from the tape recorder and at least three feet away from any tapes. If the demagnetizer has an on/off switch, be sure that you're holding the demagnetizer at least three feet from the recorder when you switch the demagnetizer on.
- Once the demagnetizer is on, start moving slowly toward the recorder (the accepted speed is about one inch per second).
- Move slowly through the entire tape path. Start at the supply reel—on the left—then move slowly along the tape path. Most demagnetizers have rubber or plastic tips, so feel free to touch metal parts with the demagnetizer; be most careful with the heads. If you touch the heads with the demagnetizer, make contact away from the center of the head, where the gap is. When you develop the right touch with the demagne-

tizer, you can usually get very close to the head without actually touching it. Never touch the heads with a metal-tipped demagnetizer that's not covered with rubber or plastic.

- When you encounter tape guides, idlers or heads, move slowly up and down the guide, idler or head a couple of times.
- Continue along the tape path until you've reached the take-up reel (on the right).
- Once you've covered everything, draw the demagnetizer slowly away to a distance of at least three feet.
- Switch the demagnetizer off.
- Turn the tape recorder on.

Be certain that the demagnetizer isn't turned off while it's close to the heads. The demagnetizer is a magnet that dominates the magnet field around the heads and constantly changes polarity back and forth from north to south in response to the 60-cycle alternating current that comes from the wall outlet. As the demagnetizer is pulled slowly from the head, the head has been subjected to equal strengths of north and south magnetism; hence, the resulting net magnetism is zero. If the demagnetizer is turned off when it's very close to—or touching—the head, the heads see a strong north or south impulse. The result is a magnetized head that'll require three or four cycles of demagnetizing to be free from magnetism (Illustration 8-4).

Illustration 8-4
Demagnetizer/Degausser

Demagnetizing the analog recorder is one of the simplest and most important preparatory procedures in analog recording.

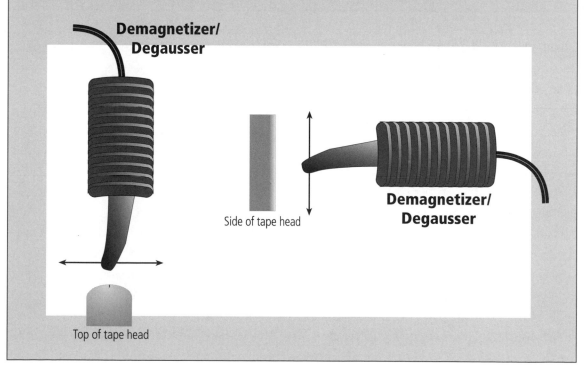

Demagnetizer/ Degausser

Side of tape head

Demagnetizer/ Degausser

Top of tape head

Illustration 8-5
Cleaning the Recorder Head

Use a cotton swab soaked in denatured or 99% pure isopropyl alcohol to clean the recorder heads. Use up and down movements that follow the direction of the head gap.

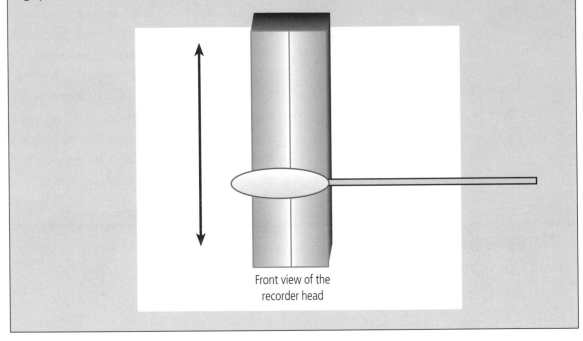

Front view of the
recorder head

Cleaning the Analog Recorder

Once the tape path has been demagnetized, clean all tape path surfaces with the solutions suggested in your equipment owner's manuals. Heads can be cleaned with isopropyl alcohol, but be sure it's at least 90% pure. Most drugstores carry 99% pure isopropyl alcohol, which works very well for heads and other metal parts. Denatured alcohol is also commonly used. Rubbing alcohol is only 70% pure and contains too many impurities to act as a good cleaner.

Dip a cotton swab, like a Q-Tip, in the cleaning solution; then swab the parts in the tape path. Be sure to move up and down the recorder heads in the same direction as the gap; this increases the cleaning action and decreases the chance

of damaging the head gap (Illustration 8-5).

Tones on the Analog Recorder

If the technical stability of your tape recorder is suspect, have it checked out by a capable technician. The owner's manual will usually have a procedure for setting the EQ and alignment of the machine. This is very important and you should become comfortable with performing these kind of adjustments. However, I recommend that the first time or two you try this kind of setup procedure, you have your work checked out by a technician, just to make sure you're on the right track.

When you're sure that the tape recorder is going to do the best job it can, you can be sure that you're on the right track to getting the best recordings possible.

Many mixers have a built-in tool called a tone oscillator or tone generator. This has real value as you get deeper into the recording process. The oscillator produces test tones (simple sine waves) that we can use as reference tones for EQ and level adjustments.

Audio Example 8-1
Oscillator Generated Sine Waves
CD-2: Track 57

If your mixer doesn't have an oscillator, pick one up at your local electronic supply store. They can be purchased at a fairly low cost and can be simply plugged into your mixer.

The simplest and most fundamental use of the tone generator involves setting the oscillator to produce a 1000Hz—or 1kHz—tone. Audio Example 8-2 demonstrates a 1000Hz tone.

Audio Example 8-2 1000Hz Tone
CD-2: Track 58

A 1000Hz tone is considered an average reference. If a normal musical source is peaking around 0VU, the average of all the energies at all frequencies is typically 0VU.

A 1kHz tone should be simultaneously sent to all of the output buses of the mixer. Adjust all of the output bus levels to read 0VU from the same oscillator send; then adjust all the tape recorder inputs to read 0VU while the mixer output buses read 0VU. Only when this scenario has been completed, can we trust that the meters on the mixer accurately represent the levels the recorder needs to receive.

When the adjustments are set and the recorder has been cleaned and demagnetized, record about 30–45 seconds of the 1kHz tone on all tape tracks. If your recorder is set up correctly, you should be able to record 1kHz at 0VU on all tracks and then play the tape back with the meters reading 0VU.

The reason we record this tone is twofold:

- We can see if the tape recorder output levels are set properly on playback.
- When it's time for mixdown, we can adjust the levels of the tape recorder outputs to read 0VU from this tone, optimizing the capabilities of the tape recorder. Without this procedure it's very difficult to optimally play your tape back on different machines. For each machine your tape is played on, you can adjust the output levels to read 0VU for each channel; this is your assurance of most accurately representing the impact of your music.

Along with a 1kHz tone, record about 30 seconds of a 10kHz tone and a 100Hz tone. Record these tones at 0VU. Their purpose is to verify the accuracy and consistency of the high and low frequencies. If your recorder is set up properly, any frequency recorded at 0VU will play back at 0VU.

Tones on the Digital Recorder

Tones on the digital recorder are used primarily for reference levels. Typically, 30 seconds of a 1kHz tone is adequate for overall level adjustments. Digital recorders have an accurate and steady enough frequency response that it isn't necessary to record 10kHz or 100Hz tones for high- and low-frequency adjustments.

Media Selection

Magnetic Tape/Video Tape

The tape you use makes a big difference. If you're using any magnetic tape-based recording system, always use the current industry standard tape; don't try to save money on tape! If you're going to spend hours and hours of your time recording a piece of music that's coming straight from your heart and soul, don't risk messing it up by buying tape that's second best.

All major professional tape manufacturers have excellent formulations and continue to upgrade their products. Ask a knowledgeable salesperson at a store that specializes in professional audio needs which tape is currently best for your situation. Try the two or three most highly recommended tape formulations, read about them, and form your own opinion about what works best with your setup.

Recordable CDs/Hard Drives

My experience has been consistent with all types of storage media for audio. Cutting costs by sacrificing quality is the most expensive route to follow. If you buy the cheapest disks you can find, you run a higher risk of disk errors and manufacturing defects. Many of the discount media are simply rejects from reputable manufacturers. All media has a failure rate; any disk holds a chance for defect. When it comes to data loss, keep your exposure low; always back up your data and always use premium quality media.

Tape Storage Is a Critical Consideration

If you always follow these recommendations, your tape should be safe:

- Keep your tapes away from speakers. The speaker's magnet could destroy all of your hard work by erasing your tape.
- Don't store your tapes in extreme heat or cold. If the temperature is uncomfortable for you, it's probably not good for your tape.
- Control the humidity of the area where you keep your tapes. A lack of humidity is fine; but if you store your tape in a humid area, it can destroy your recorded tracks.
- Keep tapes away from doors that lead outside. The constant temperature and humidity changes are very damaging.
- Don't place or leave your tapes in the trunk of your car. This might seem obvious, but I've seen some pretty bad-looking tapes as a result of this kind of treatment.
- Don't leave tapes in exposed sunlight (for instance, in your car on a sunny day); it doesn't even have to be hot to cause damage. The sun can ruin your tapes in the car even on a chilly, sunny day.
- Once you understand that tape doesn't respond in a positive way to heat, cold and humidity, use common sense and good judgment to keep your tapes out of these conditions.

Time Code

As you're planning your session, you need to decide whether the music and facilities available to you demand all live performances or whether you'll want to include MIDI-sequenced instruments. Strive to include every technological

Illustration 8-6
Live Recording Track Sheet
This represents a possible track sheet of a recording without the aid of a sequencer.

Multitrack Track Sheet								
Title	1 Backing vocals	2 Backing vocals	3 Electric guitar	4 Acoustic guitar	5 Lead vocal final	6 Bass guitar	7 Mono keyboard	8 Mono drums/perc.
Title	1	2	3	4	5	6	7	8
Title	1	2	3	4	5	6	7	8
Title	1	2	3	4	5	6	7	8

advantage at your disposal in a musically supportive way. Musicians often turn their noses up at certain tools that are provided by some technological breakthrough because they question its musical authenticity. Though their skepticism might have merit, there's also a lot to be said for the added texture and refinement facilitated by these newer tools.

One particularly useful tool is the MIDI sequencer, locked to time code. With the current flexibility of a computer with good software, MIDI parts can be added to almost any song, either sequenced ahead of time or played against a live track. In effect, you are adding more live tracks to your tape recorder.

If we take the traditional approach of a total live recording with no sequencer assistance on the song we're working through, we're immediately limited to eight tracks. We can bounce parts down from a group of tracks to one or two tracks, but every time we bounce down, we lose quality; plus we typically end up

with all mono tracks, since in the 4- and 8-track worlds, stereo mixdown is a luxury that's rarely justifiable. Refer to Illustration 8-6 for a representation of what we could accomplish if all parts were recorded live—without the aid of a sequencer locked to time code.

If we use time code and have a mixer with some extra channels, we can dramatically increase the dimension of our recordings. The MIDI sequence never needs to be printed to tape; it can just follow along in reference to time code. In mixdown, the ability to use sounds direct from the synth and drum machine—instead of having to print to tape first—dramatically increases sound quality. Combining some of the stereo sounds from your sound modules with tracks recorded to the multitrack produces a much more impressive and dimensional sound than would be possible without this technique.

I've seen many situations where this approach has helped create recordings that were far more impressive than they would have been

Illustration 8-7
Live Recording Track Sheet

This track sheet shows the same song as Illustration 8-6, except the SMPTE time code track is used to control all of the stereo keyboards, sound modules, and drum machines.

Multitrack Track Sheet

Title	1 Backing Vocals	2 Backing Vocals	3 Guitar Fills	4 Electric Guitar	5 Lead Voc. Final	6 Acoustic Guitar	7	8 SMPTE 1:00:00:00
Title	1	2	3	4	5	6	7	8
Title	1	2	3	4	5	6	7	8
Title	1	2	3	4	5	6	7	8

Now we have the multitrack audio tracks plus the benefit of the mono or stereo sounds from the sequence, possibly including:

Stereo bass	2 tracks - stereo	**Med. low tom**	1 track - mono
Stereo guitar	2 tracks - stereo	**Low tom**	1 track - mono
Kick drum	1 track - mono	**Support snare**	1 track - mono
Snare drum	1 track - mono	**String pad**	2 tracks - stereo
Hi-hats	1 track - mono	**Organ pad**	2 tracks - stereo
Triangle	1 track - mono	**Brass**	2 tracks - stereo
Shaker	1 track - mono	**Guitar effects**	2 tracks - stereo
Crash	1 track - mono	**Vocal ooo...**	2 tracks - stereo
High tom	1 track - mono	Total =	25 tracks
Med. high tom	1 track - mono		

without it. On our recording for this chapter, we'll use SMPTE time code and a computer-based sequencer locked to that code. Refer to Illustration 8-7 for an example of the sounds and tracks possible when using SMPTE and a sequencer in conjunction with an 8-track multitrack—as opposed to the sounds we could include in Illustration 8-6.

The beauty of this kind of recording is that we don't have to commit to level settings, pan adjustments, instrument tuning or any other MIDI controllable parameter until the final mixdown. Only in mixdown do we have the proper perspective to make these adjustments. Using the sequencer for your recordings can dramatically increase your ability to create a mix that'll sound good on any system.

Audio Example 8-3 represents a typical track that could be controlled by the sequencer throughout the recording process. If you start with this foundation and then add live guitars, vocals and solos, you'll have a pretty decent-sounding recording.

Audio Example 8-3 MIDI Sequence to Build From
CD-2: Track 59

Striping SMPTE

Print the SMPTE track at the beginning of the session. It's best to record the code throughout the entire length of the tape rather than trying to stop and print code at the beginning of every song on the reel. This process of recording time code is called striping. For more about time code, refer to Volume 1, Chapter 6 of the *AudioPro Home Recording Course.*

To stripe SMPTE time code, all you need is a SMPTE generator. Many MIDI interfaces come complete with a SMPTE reader/generator, but they can also be purchased separately. SMPTE is almost always recorded on the tape track with the highest number so for our purposes, we're going to stripe track eight.

I've used many different SMPTE readers and generators and I've seen suggested recording levels ranging from -10VU to 0VU. Follow the procedure outlined by the manual for your

particular piece of equipment and experiment to see what really works with your recorder.

The problem with recording time code too cold is that it's more likely to drop out or be disrupted if the tape wears on the edge, although time code that's been recorded colder won't tend to bleed into the next track as much. Sometimes when code is recorded too hot, it becomes audible in the final mix. That's not good because SMPTE code sounds like Audio Example 8-4. The advantage to recording the code a little hotter is that it tends to be more durable over time and more reliable. I've found that recording time code at -3VU is a pretty good compromise for my setup. A few test runs will show you what's best for yours.

Audio Example 8-4 SMPTE Time Code
CD-2: Track 60

Getting the Sequencer to Follow SMPTE

Once the tape is striped, it's time to get the sequencer to follow the code. Plug the output of the time code tape track into your SMPTE reader; in the case of our example, the reader is part of my MIDI interface. If the patch is correct, we'll be able to see the time code displayed on the reader as the tape plays back. The reader will stop when the tape stops (Illustration 8-8).

Tightening the Arrangement

It's important to preplan the arrangement of the music. Choose the musical ranges and amount of activity in a way that lets each part work

Illustration 8-8
Sync Screen and SMPTE Reader

When the tape is played back, be sure the SMPTE reader is set to accept and re-sponds to the time code that's been striped. The reader should stop when the tape is played back.

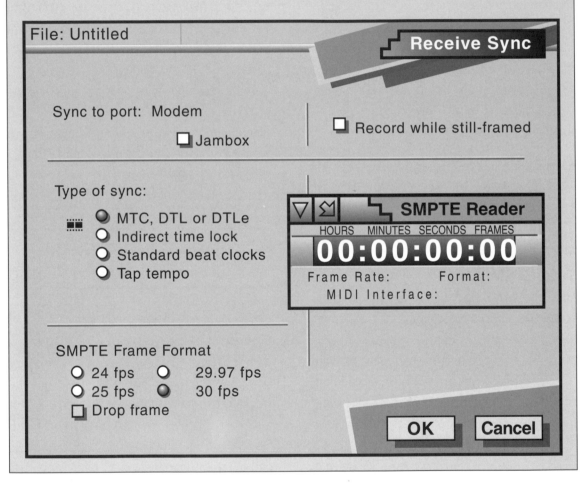

together for a song—instead of fighting for attention during the song. Craft parts so they enhance, but don't detract from, the melody. The listener can really only hear a few things at one time anyway so having lots of parts going on at once is a waste (Illustration 8-9).

Once the sequence is done, you're ready to record the multitrack parts. Use the multitrack for whatever live performances you need. These might include real guitars, lead vocals, backing vocals, percussion, strings, brass, solos or any other acoustic instrument or voice.

Contents of Arrangement

For our recording, we'll use sequenced keyboard and drum machine parts, and on the multitrack, we'll record lead vocals, backing vocals, electric rhythm guitar, acoustic guitar and lead guitar.

Reference Lead Vocal

I've striped track eight of the multitrack with SMPTE time code, and I've set up the sequencer to run from the time code. Audio Example 8-5 demonstrates the full sequence for this song.

Audio Example 8-5 The Sequence
CD-2: Track 61

It's very common to record a reference vocal track. This doesn't have to be the final lead vocal track but it does need to be in tune. It should also have the correct phrasing for any part that will be sung with the backing vocals. The lead vocalist often wants to wait to perform the final lead vocal until all of the filler parts have been added. Sometimes the addition of guitars, backing vocals and lead fills is more

Illustration 8-9
Musical Activity Planning

Craft the supportive musical parts so they enhance but don't detract from the melody. This chart shows one method you can use to preplan the activity of each ingredient in your song. Notice that when the vocal is active, the instruments are less active; also notice that the intro needs to have activity to give the listener something to specifically focus on. This kind of planning and thinking can mark the difference between amateur recordings and music that sounds like a hit.

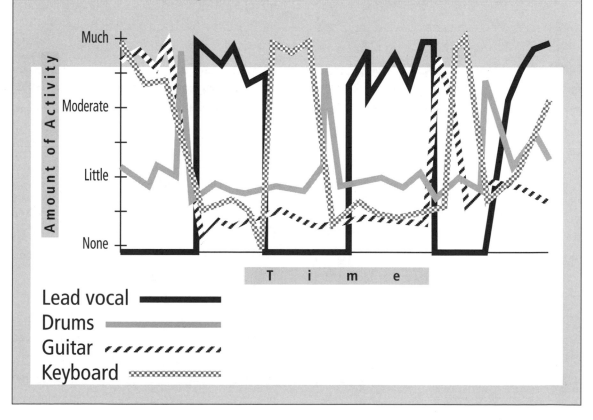

Lead vocal ▬▬▬
Drums ▬▬▬
Guitar ///////////
Keyboard ▨▨▨▨▨

inspiring for the lead vocalist than the basic tracks, and the performance might contain more heart and soul than the original reference track. On the other hand, sometimes the first track the singer lays down has the most life and emotion. Be flexible in your handling of this. I find, on many sessions, that the first lead vocal take is the one I use in the final mix. I might need to dump the track into the computer and adjust some intonation or timing problems, but that first take is often the one the singer has been waiting for months to sing; it's exciting.

Since the reference vocal could end up being the final track, spend a little time setting it up so that what you record is usable.

Patch the vocal mic through a compressor and set the ratio between 3:1 and 7:1—I'll use a 4:1 ratio on this example. Set a medium-fast attack time and a medium-slow release time. Finally, adjust the threshold so that when the singer sings the loudest part of the song, you read about 6dB on gain reduction. Once the compressor is set and you're reasonably sure that the record level is set properly, record the reference vocal. Always record the first take! You have nothing to lose by pushing the record button; you're not erasing anything and you're not causing any more wear on the tape.

I know there are a couple of places where the singer really belts it out in the song that we're recording, so I'll ride the fader a little during the track. By that I mean I'll turn the record level down very slightly when I know the singer's going to get louder, and then I'll turn the record level back up, after the loud part. There is an art to riding a fader during a take. Try to anticipate the flow of the melodic line and the momentum of the singer. Make very smooth changes, and make them very slowly. It's not always neces-

sary to ride the fader when recording a track, but this technique—which involves you, the operator acting as a human compressor—can help your vocal recordings sound more consistently clean and understandable. Audio Example 8-6 is a little bit of our reference vocal that I've printed to track six.

Audio Example 8-6 Reference Vocal
CD-2: Track 62

Backing Vocals

On this song, I'd like to end up with a big backing vocal sound with a minimum of singers. In order to accomplish a large vocal sound, we'll need to record several tracks of the backing vocal parts. We'll never have the tracks available to get this kind of sound once the guitar parts and the final lead vocal part are recorded, but since we've preplanned our recording, we know that now is the time to record these tracks.

To accomplish this technique, print a reference rhythm track from the sequence; record the entire rhythm track from the sequence to one or two tracks of the multitrack. The balance should be adjusted so the backing vocalists hear what they need to in order to sing with the proper phrasing and intonation. The reason we print the sequence to one track of the multitrack is because, in a minute, we'll be changing the tape speed and singing the backing vocal parts along with the pitch changes that are caused by changing the tape speed. This produces a very big backing vocal sound. However, if the sequence was simply following time code, the pitch wouldn't change as the tape speed changed, and the results wouldn't be pleasing to the ear. In this case, I'll print the sequence reference track to track seven. Normally, for the reasons I mentioned earlier, it's best to avoid printing anything next to the time code; but in this case, since this is only a reference track and won't be used in the mix, I'll print very cold to tape. The strongest part of this track will peak at about 7VU because I don't want to disrupt the time code on track eight by recording the signal too hot onto track seven.

Also, if you are using a digital multitrack, it's acceptable to print audio on the track next to time code; you should have no problems at all. Only in the analog realm is this a concern.

It's our goal to end up with two backing vocal tracks that we can pan apart in the mix for a large stereo sound. Before we get to those final two tracks, we'll actually record six tracks of backing vocals. This process can be followed in any situation. If you only have one backing vocalist, you can create a pretty impressive sound. If you have two, three, four or even five backing singers, you can end up with a huge sound using this technique.

The first thing that we're going to do is record the backing track onto three separate tracks (in this case tracks three, four and five). This lets you stack up harmonies by recording separate parts on each track. Remember, listen to the reference sequence track during this procedure and not to the MIDI sequence following time code.

You'll get the most out of this technique if you use the vari-speed on the multitrack. If you don't have a vari-speed, follow these procedures without the speed changes. You'll still end up with a good backing vocal sound.

Record track three with the vari-speed set to normal speed.

Audio Example 8-7
Backing Vocal One: Normal Speed
CD-2: Track 63

Next, on track four, set the vari-speed so the multitrack is playing slightly faster than normal. You don't need to speed the machine up much for this technique to work. Raise the speed just barely enough to hear a pitch change in the tracks. Now record the backing vocals onto track four at the new speed. Notice in Audio Example 8-8 that the pitch is only very slightly higher than that on track three.

Audio Example 8-8
Backing Vocal: Vari-speed Up
CD-2: Track 63

Once those parts are satisfactory, we'll record another pass through the backing vocals onto track five. This time slow the playback of the multitrack down slightly below normal speed. Again, you don't need to set up a dramatic speed change—just enough so that the pitch is barely lower than normal.

Audio Example 8-9
Backing Vocal: Vari-speed Down
CD-2: Track 63

When the machine is set back to the original speed and the three tracks are blended together, the texture will be much more interesting than if the tracks had been recorded at the same speed. If I record the same singers on each pass but at a different speed, the harmonic content of the singers changes slightly once the speed is returned to normal. There's more of a chance that a few singers will sound like a lot of singers when there's a slightly different harmonic content on each recorded track.

Bounce to Track One

Now that the three backing vocal parts have been recorded, let's bounce those down to track one. If you have a 4- or 8-track recorder, this process of bouncing—or ping-ponging—tracks becomes a useful and necessary technique. Set the inputs of your mixer channels to receive signal from the multitrack on channels three, four and five. Using the bus assign, send channels three, four and five to output bus number one. Finally, patch the output of bus one to the input of tape track one and put the recorder into record on track one; if this is already connected in your system, simply put tape track one into record.

Set up the blend and balance of the tracks you're bouncing. It's best to monitor mixer channel one only so you can hear the mix of the tracks you're bouncing exactly as they're going to tape (Illustrations 8-10 through 8-12).

Once the three backing vocal parts have been bounced to track one, erase over the original backing vocals with a completely new set of backing vocals. The parts and the singers can

Illustration 8-10
Bouncing Tracks (Ping-ponging)

Here's the basic procedure for bouncing tracks, also called ping-ponging. In this case, we're bouncing tracks 3, 4 and 5 to track 1:

- Use the bus assigns to bounce tracks. Don't use a simple three-way Y adapter.
- Set the channel inputs of 3, 4 and 5 to tape so the tape recorder track playback levels are controlled by the faders.
- Adjust the mix of these tracks so they sound blended and smooth; ride the mix if necessary.
- With the bus assign buttons, assign 3, 4 and 5 to output bus 1, which should be patched to the input of tape track 1.
- Set tape track 1 to record.
- Adjust the level of this submix of tracks 3, 4 and 5 to read about 0VU at the strongest part of the track.
- Record the bounced vocal mix to track 1.

If you make a mistake on a section, simply rewind a bit, punch that section in, then move on. It's a simple procedure to get the mix of the bounced tracks set for one section, move on to the next section, set up for it and record again.

Here's another very important point: Clean up the sounds between the actual musical parts while you're performing the bounce. This is the perfect opportunity to get rid of the giggles, breaths and editorial comments from the background singers.

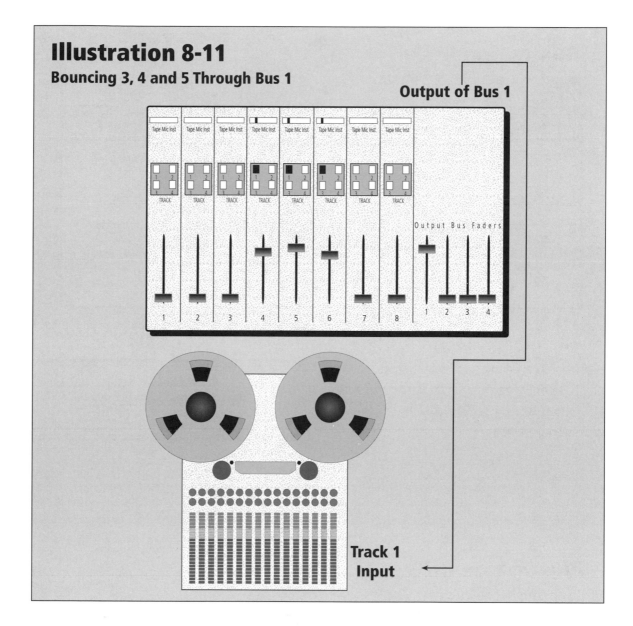

Illustration 8-11
Bouncing 3, 4 and 5 Through Bus 1

Output of Bus 1

Output Bus Faders

Track 1
Input

be the same, but the fact that the performances are different adds to the fullness of the sound. This time we'll also slightly vary the speed of two of the tracks while recording. Again, this speed change should be so minimal that you can hardly hear the pitch change. Once the recorder is taken out of vari-speed mode, the vocal tracks that were recorded slightly slow and slightly fast have a different harmonic structure than the track recorded and played back at normal speed

(Illustrations 8-13 and 8-14).

Some formats and particular models of multitrack recorders don't have enough channel separation to be able to bounce to adjacent tracks without causing a squeal or feedback. If you have this problem, you'll need to juggle your track planning a bit—just another item to add to your preplanning session.

Audio Example 8-10 demonstrates the sound of the completed backing vocals. We've

Illustration 8-12
Bouncing Tracks Track Sheet

Multitrack Track Sheet								
Title	**1** Tracks 3, 4 and 5 combined to track 1	**2**	**3** Backing vocal 1 - Recorded slightly slow using vari-speed	**4** Backing vocal 1 - Recorded slightly fast using vari-speed	**5** Backing vocal 1 - Recorded at normal speed	**6** Reference lead vocal	**7** Reference rhythm section	**8** SMPTE 01:00:00:00
Title	1	2	3	4	5	6	7	8

recorded six separate tracks at different speeds and have bounced them down to two separate tracks that we can pan apart in the mix for a wide stereo sound.

Audio Example 8-10
The Completed Backing Vocals
CD-2: Track 63

Illustration 8-13
Bouncing More Vocals

Multitrack Track Sheet								
Title	**1** Tracks 3, 4 and 5 combined to track 1	**2** Tracks 3, 4 and 5 combined to track 2	**3** Backing vocal 1 - Re-recorded slightly slow using vari-speed	**4** Backing vocal 1 - Re-recorded slightly fast using vari-speed	**5** Backing vocal 1 - Re-recorded at normal speed	**6** Reference lead vocal	**7** Reference rhythm section	**8** SMPTE 01:00:00:00
Title	1	2	3	4	5	6	7	8

Illustration 8-14
Completed Bounce

Multitrack Track Sheet								
Title	**1** Tracks 3, 4 and 5 combined to track 1	**2** Tracks 3, 4 and 5 combined to track 2	**3**	**4**	**5**	**6** Reference lead vocal	**7** Reference rhythm section	**8** SMPTE 01:00:00:00
Title	**1**	**2**	**3**	**4**	**5**	**6**	**7**	**8**

Electric Guitar to Track Four

Now let's start working on recording the guitars, electric guitar first. Be sure the guitar is perfectly in tune and that the tape speed is set to normal. At this point, we'll listen to the sequenced parts from the sequencer as it follows time code rather than from the recorded reference rhythm section track. Once we're hearing the sequenced part as it's locked to time code, we can adjust levels of the individual parts, if need be, to aid in the performance of the upcoming live tracks.

On this guitar part, I want a clean sound, with a feeling of motion and continual interest. I've chosen a Strat sound. As we've seen in previous chapters, there's the option of recording with a microphone on an amplifier or direct into the mixer. In this case, I'd like a close and clean sound, and I've found a sound on the multi-effects processor that I like a lot. I'll patch the guitar into the effect, then plug the effect directly into the mixer. This lets me tweak the EQ a bit and then send the guitar to track four with the bus assign.

The effect I've come up with is actually a combination of compression at a 4:1 ratio—showing around 6dB of gain reduction at the strongest part of the track—a little slapback delay, stereo chorus and some hall reverb with a .75 second decay time.

Since I'm recording to an 8-track and since I only have a couple of good reverbs in my system, I'll print this guitar with reverb, being careful not to add too much. I can always add a touch of one of the main reverbs I've connected to an auxiliary bus into the mix if the guitar needs to blend a little better. However, if I add too much reverb to the track now, the only way I can get a dryer sound in the mix is to rerecord the guitar part. Depending on the part and how long it takes to record the first time, rerecording can be a pain (Illustration 8-15).

Audio Example 8-11 demonstrates the sound of the guitar as I've printed it to tape.

Illustration 8-15
Adding the Electric Guitar

Multitrack Track Sheet								
Title	**1** Tracks 3, 4 and 5 combined to track 1	**2** Tracks 3, 4 and 5 combined to track 2	**3**	**4** Electric guitar	**5**	**6** Reference lead vocal	**7** Reference rhythm section	**8** SMPTE 01:00:00:00
Title	**1**	**2**	**3**	**4**	**5**	**6**	**7**	**8**

Audio Example 8-11 The Electric Guitar
CD-2: Track 64

Punch-Ins

Any time we start recording human beings playing live musical parts, we're probably going to need to deal with an occasional mistake. Thankfully, multitrack tape recorders let us punch into record on the fly. This means that while we listen to an existing track—our electric guitar on track four, for instance—we can press record and that track can instantly go into record. We've talked about this before , but I'd like to reiterate the importance and convenience of the punch-in; use it to your advantage.

I teach a lot of recording classes, and one of the most common hesitations I see in students is with punching in. It seems that, most of the time, beginning students would rather record an entire track over rather than risk the stress of punching in at the wrong time on a track that's nearly completed. But once you get the hang of punching in, it's pretty easy and almost stress-free, especially at home. On top of that, it can be one of your biggest time savers. Being able to piece a part together, section by section, instead of having to technically master a part to the point where you can actually play the whole thing from beginning to end, is often the only way to get a track done.

I mention this as a word of encouragement and as a gentle nudge to jump in with both feet. Practice this technique with confidence at home and then put your neck on the line in the middle of a session with other musicians.

Acoustic Guitar to Track Five

I'd like a simple and clean acoustic guitar track on this song. I'd really like the clarity of the transient from the pick hitting the strings, and since I know that condenser mics record transients far better than other mic types, I'll use a simple condenser mic on this steel-string acoustic guitar.

The mic is about six inches in front of the guitar and almost directly above the point where the neck joins the body, pointed at the guitar. This position should get a good balance of lows and highs.

As we move the mic around the acoustic guitar, we hear more lows directly over the sound hole, more mids at the tail end of the guitar and more highs over the neck of the guitar.

I've cut at 80Hz to get rid of the extreme lows that won't be needed in the context of this song. I've also put a slight boost of about 2dB at 8kHz to increase the clarity of the sound. Other than that, the EQ is pretty natural as it comes into the board.

Since this part is in the context of several MIDI tracks, the electric guitar track and the lead and backing vocals, I'm going to compress the acoustic guitar slightly. I'm not using extreme compression, but I know from experience that a little compression as I'm recording will result in a part that's easier to hear in the context of the mix. It will also have less apparent noise than if I hadn't used a compressor.

I've set a 3:1 ratio with about 4dB of gain

reduction at the strongest part of the track. I've also set the attack time to medium-slow so that the attack of the notes will be exaggerated in relation to the body of the sound. This technique gives the guitar sound better definition (Illustration 8-16).

Audio Example 8-12 demonstrates the sound of the acoustic guitar as it is on the multitrack. Notice that there's no reverb or delay effects added at this time. On this and other naturally acoustic instruments, it's always best to print to the multitrack without effects if possible.

Audio Example 8-12 The Acoustic Guitar
CD-2: Track 65

Final Vocal to Track Three

We only have two tracks left to add to our preplanned song: the lead vocal and the lead guitar. In my original plan, I wanted to save the

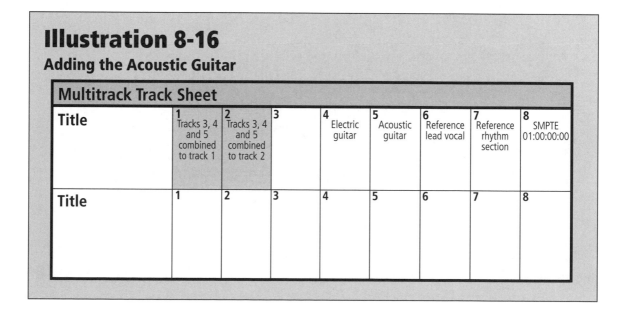

Illustration 8-16
Adding the Acoustic Guitar

Multitrack Track Sheet							
Title	**1** Tracks 3, 4 and 5 combined to track 1	**2** Tracks 3, 4 and 5 combined to track 2	**3**	**4** Electric guitar	**5** Acoustic guitar	**6** Reference lead vocal	**7** Reference rhythm section	**8** SMPTE 01:00:00:00
Title	1	2	3	4	5	6	7	8

Illustration 8-17
Adding the Lead Vocal

Multitrack Track Sheet								
Title	**1** Tracks 3, 4 and 5 combined to track 1	**2** Tracks 3, 4 and 5 combined to track 2	**3** Final lead vocal	**4** Electric guitar	**5** Acoustic guitar	**6** Reference lead vocal	**7** Reference rhythm section	**8** SMPTE 01:00:00:00
Title	1	2	3	4	5	6	7	8

lead vocals until as close to the end of the process as possible. We've made it almost to the end, but now is the time to add the lead vocals instead of the lead guitar for two reasons:

• First, if we record the lead guitar now, when we record the lead vocal it'll be necessary to eliminate the reference vocal while we record the final lead vocal. It's best to have the ref-

Illustration 8-18
Punching In

This mistake needs to be replaced by punching into record after "Paradise," then out of record before "your."

Bad Take

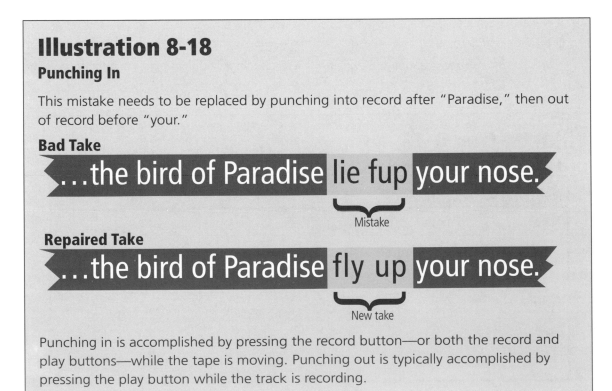

…the bird of Paradise lie fup your nose.

Mistake

Repaired Take

…the bird of Paradise fly up your nose.

New take

Punching in is accomplished by pressing the record button—or both the record and play buttons—while the tape is moving. Punching out is typically accomplished by pressing the play button while the track is recording.

erence vocal available while recording the final vocal. As soon as you erase the reference vocal, the singer will either forget the order of the lyrics or go into deep depression because one of the licks on the reference track was the best he or she had ever sung, and they'd really like you to bounce that lick onto the final lead vocal track. If you can keep that reference vocal until the final lead vocal is done, you'll often be very glad you did.

• Second, many times the lead guitar fills between the lyrics on one or more of the verses or choruses. This can only be done effectively against the final lead vocal track. A good player will do everything possible to both enhance and stay out of the way of the lead vocal. The singer might sing the lead track with a completely different interpretation on the final take than on the reference take, and if the lead guitar is played against

Illustration 8-19
Patching the Compressor (Review)

Connect the send of the mixer to the input of the compressor/limiter, then connect the output of the compressor/limiter to the return on the mixer.

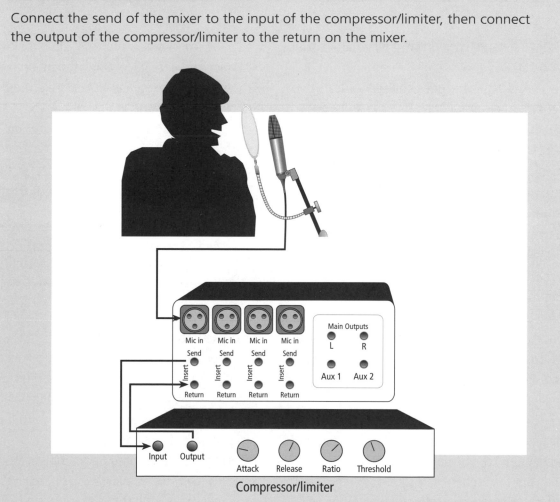

Illustration 8-20
Adding the Lead Guitar

Multitrack Track Sheet								
Title	**1** Tracks 3, 4 and 5 combined to track 1	**2** Tracks 3, 4 and 5 combined to track 2	**3** Final lead vocal	**4** Electric guitar	**5** Acoustic guitar	**6** Guitar fills	**7** Reference rhythm section	**8** SMPTE 01:00:00:00
Title	**1**	**2**	**3**	**4**	**5**	**6**	**7**	**8**

the reference vocal track, it might ultimately be useless.

Anyway, here goes the lead vocal; I'm recording this as naturally as I can. I'm using a good condenser mic plugged into a compressor. The compressor is set with a 4:1 ratio, a medium-fast attack time and a medium-long release time. I've set the threshold so that there is about 6dB of gain reduction at the strongest part of the track. I haven't printed any effect or EQ with this track. Now I'll be able to shape the vocal sound as I need to in the mix without having to compensate for problems that I've created while recording the track. If you print the vocals with extreme effects or reverb, it's kind of like shooting in the dark. Unless you're mixing, you have nothing to base major sound shaping on. This is especially true of vocal recording.

I've recorded from a distance of about ten inches, and I've used a pop filter between the singer and the microphone. Also, keep in mind that the atmosphere you create for the singer affects the emotional interpretation of the lyric.

The lead vocal is probably the most crucial track for punching in. Often the entire track is great with the exception of a couple of words. Try punching in those words before you start recording large sections over; you can do it (Illustration 8-17 through 8-19)!

Audio Example 8-13 demonstrates the sound of our lead vocal track.

Audio Example 8-13 The Lead Vocal
CD-2: Track 66

Lead Guitar to Track Six
And now that the lead vocal is done, it's time to record our final track: the lead guitar. There's a section designed for a guitar solo, but there are also several spots where the guitar can fill in holes. Record the guitar fills and solo over the reference vocal track onto track six.

It's really the arranger's job to design the accompaniment so that there's always a point of interest, but sometimes there'll be a couple of holes that need a focal point, or maybe the arranger actually wanted licks from a solo instrument to fill these holes. Try to create a fill part that's not too busy; if there's too much going on with the fill track, it becomes ineffective. Use licks only when and where they're really needed. Since we have the lead guitar on a separate track, we can always leave some of the licks out in the mix. If you have a question about a par-

ticular spot in the song, go ahead and record a lick or two as an option. As a rule, filler tracks work better when they've been structured and planned to fill specific holes in the arrangement. If the player just lets the licks fly throughout the tune, during the mix you're burdened with the task of sifting through all the licks to find what's really needed. Some of the licks that need to be included may not work well when the track has to be turned up or down in time to stay out of

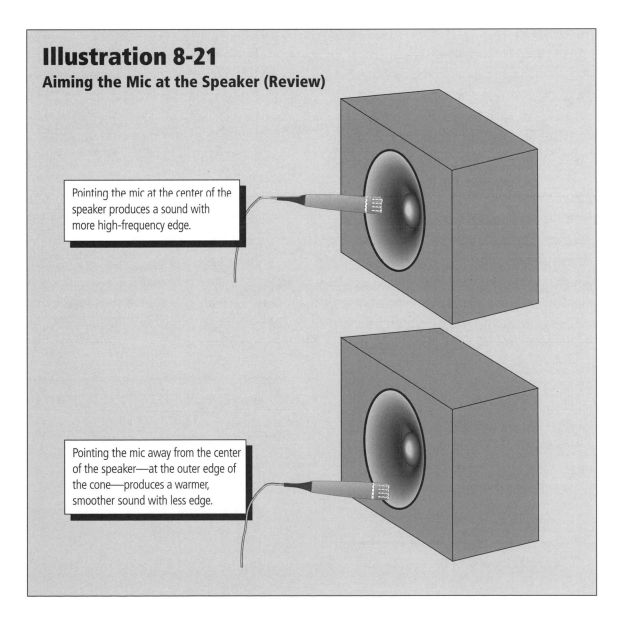

Illustration 8-21
Aiming the Mic at the Speaker (Review)

Pointing the mic at the center of the speaker produces a sound with more high-frequency edge.

Pointing the mic away from the center of the speaker—at the outer edge of the cone—produces a warmer, smoother sound with less edge.

the way of the lead vocal or other focal point.

I've plugged this guitar through a compressor, tube-type distortion, a chorus and a delay. This is a pretty typical lead guitar effects combination; I'll go ahead and print everything to tape. The one ingredient that I'll be a little cautious about is the delay. If I include too much delay at this point, the track might end up sounding muddy and distant when we get to mixdown. The only way to fix that problem is to rerecord the lead guitar track. Not a fun thought when you're deep in the middle of a long, tedious mixdown.

It's standard to print the guitar with whatever compression and distortion the guitarist is using for the basic sound. Guitar compression and distortion can't be accurately reproduced during the mixdown.

I'm plugged into a guitar amp and have placed a moving-coil mic about a foot in front of the speaker. Always experiment with mic placement in your own situation to include the amount of room sound that works best for your guitar sound. In this case, I have quite a bit of effect on the guitar already and I'm just miking the guitar amp to get the benefit of the sound of a tube amplifier so I'll keep the mic relatively close to the speaker.

I've also pointed the mic about halfway between the center and the outer edge of the speaker. Remember, the highs and attack come from the center of the speaker and the warmer, fuller sound comes from the outer edge of the speaker (Illustrations 8-20 and 8-21).

Audio Example 8-14 The Lead Guitar
CD-2: Track 67

Conclusion

During this recording session, we've seen how preplanning is the key to getting the most out of the equipment and available musical resources. If we'd saved the backing vocals for last, we simply couldn't have gotten the large group vocal sound because there wouldn't have been enough tracks. By planning from the beginning, we were able to tell what was coming up and then plan accordingly.

Each ingredient of a musical work is important, and although as engineers we need and want to see that we get the best and cleanest sounds on tape, we must keep the emotional impact of the music primary in our thoughts. Plan ahead and know the capabilities of the equipment available to you; only then will you be free enough from the technical details to be able to monitor and contribute to the emotional impact of the music.

Now that we have the tracks completed, its time to mix down and prepare the master mix for duplication. That's our topic for the next and final chapter of the *AudioPro Home Recording Course*.

Audio Example 8-15 All Tracks Together
CD-2: Track 68

9 Mixdown to Master to Product

I n this chapter, we'll go through the mixdown process, from choosing the mixdown machine all the way to the preparation of the final mixed master for duplication.

Mixdown is the end of the journey for your song and this is the final chapter of this book. During mixdown, we must draw on nearly all of the information we've studied in this course. I'll often refer to other chapters, and I've included a review of some of the most pertinent information that we've covered in the *AudioPro Home Recording Course*. This review is included as a refresher if you've been following this course chapter by chapter. For those of you who've jumped into this course at the end, the review will fill in some information to help you get more from this chapter—though to truly benefit from this course you'll want to get the depth that each chapter offers.

It's common for musicians to spend hours and hours recording tracks only to run out of time, energy and money when mixing starts. This is the opposite of what should happen because there are so many options and complex considerations in mixdown that determine the final impact of your song.

Often a song that's been labored over during the recording process is destroyed by a poor mix. It's also common for a lackluster recording job to be polished into a very punchy and exciting musical work during the mixdown process. When you have recorded great tracks and are using good, intelligent mixing techniques, the magic can happen.

If you're budgeting for a project, leave as much time as possible for mixing. In a small setup, leave two hours minimum to mix each song. It's not out of the question to spend four or five hours per tune when you begin focusing on the small details that become important in the mix, even in a 4- or 8-track studio—especially when combined with a MIDI system following time code. In the 24 plus track world, I can spend between 6 and 16 hours per song just in the mixdown process, depending on the complexity of the song and the budget.

Keep in mind that the choices you make during mixdown are nearly all subjective. There isn't a specific list of procedures that'll result in the perfect mix every time. Decisions on levels, EQ, effects, panning or any other variable in the song are subject to your musical preference, taste and experience. Each time you adjust one variable, you'll probably be affecting one of the other variables. Practice, experience and well-informed musical and technical decisions result in confident, appropriate and often very exciting and innovative mixes.

Mixdown Machine

Selecting a 2-track recorder to store your final mix on is very important. Many home setups use cassette as the final master 2-track. This, though cost effective in most cases, is a fading medium that lacks the competitive edge of a good analog reel-to-reel recorder or one of the many digital formats currently available. If you've been printing your mixes to cassette, I suggest an upgrade as soon as it's financially feasible. If your mixed stereo master isn't in a format that allows maximum dynamic range and clarity with minimum noise and distortion, you're doing your music extreme injustice.

Digital recorders are becoming reasonably priced in many formats. Check the prices and availability of DAT (digital audio tape), DCC (digital compact cassette), recordable CDs and mini-discs, optical drive recorders and any of the computer-based hard drive recorders. Over a period of a few months, the price of any of these mediums can dramatically decrease while the availability dramatically increases.

Prices for new analog reel-to-reels are typically higher than the least expensive new digital recorders, but check the used equipment market because the digital revolution is driving the price of used analog recorders down. Analog has taken a bit of a beating, but it still remains the recording medium of choice for many projects. With the newest tape formulations and some good Dolby or dbx noise reduction, an analog recorder can approach or equal a digital recorder in dynamic range and signal-to-noise ratio. Many world-class engineers who can afford the very best of everything still prefer the sound of analog over the sound of digital. It has even become fairly common to print tracks or mixes to a good analog recorder, to get the analog sound, and then immediately dump the mix, or tracks, to a digital recorder for long term storage and/or manipulation.

As another good alternative to cassette, don't forget to try printing your mixes to the hi-fi tracks of your video recorder. The audio specs on hi-fi tracks are much better than most analog recorders at any price, even without noise reduction.

Some of the analog-to-digital converters, designed to store full digital information on a standard VHS or Beta video tape machine, are fading into the sunset with the onset of newer formats, but they still do a good job. Sony and Nakamichi have the most common systems of this type.

Listen to these rough mixes of our song for this chapter. This is the exact same mix, printed to four different mediums.

- The first mix was recorded to DAT.
- The second was printed to an analog 2-track with no noise reduction.
- The third mix was printed to a cassette using Dolby B noise reduction.
- The fourth mix was recorded to a cassette without noise reduction.
- The fifth mix was recorded to the hi-fi tracks of a video recorder.

Each of these mix versions had to go through the same process to get to the CD you're hearing. All editing was performed in the digital domain and then the final edited version was digitally recorded back onto the final master DAT which was sent to the duplication facility.

Listen for the differences in these mixes. Refer to Illustration 9-1 for a list of points to consider while evaluating these mixes.

Audio Example 9-1 The DAT mix
CD-2: Track 69

Audio Example 9-2
The 1/4" Half-track Reel-to-Reel
CD-2: Track 70

Audio Example 9-3 The Cassette With Dolby B
CD-2: Track 71

Audio Example 9-4 The Cassette Without Dolby
CD-2: Track 72

Audio Example 9-5
The Hi-Fi Tracks From a Video Recorder
CD-2: Track 73

Basic Procedure for Alignment (Mixdown and Multitrack)

Review Chapter 8 for the cleaning and demagnetizing procedure. This is one of the most important procedures to help you get the best mix possible from your setup!

Machine alignment and EQ settings are tedious and often confusing at first, but if you expect to progress in a positive way in engineering, you'll need to eventually master these more technical procedures. If you're feeling totally inept in this regard, pay the price to hire a very good technician to set your recorder up properly. Ask if you can be present during the procedure. You'll pick it up pretty quickly once you see someone go through the steps. You'll at least pick up some of the basic maintenance routines that are easy to perform and will keep your recorder in reasonably good shape.

Even experienced engineers occasionally hire a top notch technician to make sure that the recorder is performing to its optimum specifications. It isn't always practical to own some of the high-end equipment that's capable of ensuring that everything is just right.

Most recorder manuals spell out the manufacturers alignment and EQ procedure. Rather than trying to combine all manufacturers' procedures into one generic list, I recommend that you read your owners manual thoroughly and practice the procedures recommended therein.

By the way, these procedures apply to analog recorders, like reel-to-reel and cassette. Digital recorders are much more stable mediums and aren't limited in their basic operation by the same constraints as analog magnetic tape recorders. Maintenance is minimal on a digital machine, and any adjustments or repairs are best left to factory qualified service technicians.

Playback Alignment

The purpose of playback alignment is to set your recorder playback levels in relation to an accepted standard in the recording industry and ensure that basic head positioning is correct. This procedure should be followed for your analog multitrack and analog 2-track mixdown machines.

One fundamental tool in this process is a professionally manufactured reproduction calibration tape. These tapes are available in all analog formats. They contain several different frequencies—sine waves—recorded at very specific magnetic strengths, measured in a unit called a Weber, in particular, a billionth of a Weber, called a *nanoWeber*. The actual magnetic impulse applied to the magnetic tape by the record head is called *flux*. The magnetic strength, measured in nanoWebers, is called the *reference fluxivity*.

Illustration 9-1
Recorder Evaluation

Listen to the demonstration of five different recording formats in Audio Examples 9-1 through 9-5. Evaluate each category with your highest level of discernment.

Rate each category: 1 = Poor, 2 = OK, 3 = Good, 4 = Very Good, 5 = Best

Evaluation	DAT AE 9-1	Reel-to-Reel AE 9-2	Cassette Dolby B AE 9-3	Cassette No Dolby AE 9-4	Hi-Fi VHS AE 9-5
Highs					
Mids					
Lows					
Transients					
Distortion					
Wow and flutter					
Noise					
Clarity					
Dynamics					
Subjective feel					
Emotion					
_____					
_____					

All frequencies on the reproducer calibration tape are recorded at the same reference fluxivity. The goal of the playback alignment procedure is to get the same reading on your tape recorder output meters for each frequency on the calibration tape.

Record EQ

The purpose of the record alignment procedure is to adjust input, record levels and record equalization. Once the record alignment is finished, you should be able to record any frequency at 0VU into the recorder and get 0VU out of the recorder on playback.

The alignment and EQ procedure can also include adjusting head position and bias levels (see your tape recorder manuals for procedures).

If your tape recorder has been adjusted properly in relation to a standard reproducer calibration tape, you're on the road to producing recordings that are compatible with any other conscientious engineer's equipment in the world.

Reference Tones

Adjusting the tape recorder outputs to the mixer inputs is an important step. If your mixer doesn't have input level controls for each channel, you should at least set up your multitrack recorder so that its VU meters read 0 from the output of the reproducer calibration tape reference tones. This can be done with the internal calibration level adjustments or the main output levels on the machine.

If you're serious about high quality recordings, you should have your equipment calibrated by a technical specialist, or you should make it your goal to learn how to calibrate your gear yourself.

One vital step in setting up for a mix is adjusting the output of the stereo mix bus to match the input of your 2-track recorder.

If your board has a tone oscillator, send a 1kHz tone to the stereo bus output VU meters and adjust the oscillator level for a 0VU reading. The tones produced by the oscillator are simple sine waves.

If your mixer doesn't have a built-in oscillator, purchase one at the local electronics supply store. Prices and features vary, but for this purpose, a simple and inexpensive oscillator will do fine. Simply patch the oscillator into any mixer

channel and assign the channel to the stereo bus. Be sure the pan control is centered and, assuming the stereo bus output fader is up to normal operating range, adjust the input fader for a 0VU reading on the stereo bus output VUs.

If the output of the stereo bus is patched to the input of your mixdown recorder, and if the recorder is in record/pause or input mode, a reading should register on the mixdown recorder input meters.

If you're using an analog mixdown machine, adjust the input level of the recorder to read 0VU from the same 1kHz tone that's coming from the mixer output.

If you're using a digital mixdown recorder, like a DAT recorder, the 0VU that's coming from the board VU meter should read between -18 and -12 on the digital recorder meter. The key with any digital recorder is to get as close as possible to 0 on the digital meter at some point in the song. If you reference 0VU to -18 on the DAT meter, you'll always have plenty of headroom, but you might not be using the full resolution of the digital recording system.

If you only reach half the maximum level on a digital recorder, it's almost as if you are only using half the system bits—instead of 16-bit digital recording, you might be realizing only 8 bits. That's not good; fill up the digital meters to ensure ultimate digital audio clarity. I often reference 0VU to -12 on the DAT meter.

Once this is done, you can be sure that what you see on your mixer's stereo meters will be what the inputs of the mixdown machine sees.

Reference Tone

Since you have the oscillator on and working, now is the time to print reference tones. This involves recording three tones onto your stereo master: 1kHz, 10kHz and 100Hz.

1kHz is recorded as a standard reference tone. 1kHz at 0VU is used as a benchmark level for the average level of a mix that has been printed with its levels around 0VU. We can use this 1kHz tone as a reference in making dubs of our master mixes. Setting the record level on the dubbing machine is usually as simple as playing the 1kHz tone from the master into the dubbing machine then adjusting the dub machine record level to read 0VU. This process is much quicker than trying to play through the entire song to accurately set the levels. The primary requirement for this procedure is that you've recorded the mixed master without allowing the mix level to go past +1 or +2VU.

1kHz is also used by the duplication/product manufacturing facility for this general level setting. They'll also use the 10kHz and the 100Hz reference tones to adjust their equipment for accurate high-frequency and low-frequency content. In this process, they can match their playback EQ more closely to the playback EQ of your tape recorder. If your mixdown recorder is inaccurate in the highs and/or lows, this will show up when the duplication engineer plays the tones you've recorded back on his or her playback machine. Even if the duplicator needs to artificially boost or cut certain frequencies to match your reference tones, you'll end up with a much more satisfying final product simply by nature of the fact that you sent a reference of what you thought 0VU of highs, mids and lows should be.

I almost always print 0VU of 1kHz at the beginning of each song's group of mixes. This is a convenient way of verifying levels when assembling all of the mixes into an album.

When the edited master is finished—and all the songs are in their proper order and spaced correctly—the reference tones are included, but only at the beginning of the album master. The reference tones should be separated from the first song by 10-15 seconds.

Starting the Mix/Zeroing the Board

- Make sure that you start each mix with your mixer in a neutral state. Switch all EQs to bypass or, if there aren't bypass switches, set all EQ to flat.
- Match 0VU out of the multitrack to 0VU on the mixer.
- Match the stereo outputs of the board to the stereo inputs of the mixdown machines.
- Print 30 to 45 seconds of a 1kHz tone, 10kHz tone and a 100Hz tone at the beginning of your master reel—at 0VU. This is necessary on the final mixed master for use by the duplication facility, and it will help you in making dubs for your own use.

Some of these basic technical and mechanical adjustments might seem unnecessary or too much of a bother, but attention to these details will make your recordings sound better.

The importance of adjusting your recording equipment to perform to its optimum specifications equates exactly with the importance of tuning any other musical instrument. As I've mentioned before in this course, if we can make several small points better in our recordings, the result will be a substantially and noticeably better recording.

Tape Choice

Always use the highest quality and most highly regarded tape possible for your masters, especially in the analog domain. The recording tape market is competitive so when one major manufacturer produces a newer and quieter product, the other major manufacturers release a similar product. There is a huge difference in the noise level and durability of many of the currently available products.

Read trade magazines and talk with salespeople or other engineers to keep up on what's hot in the tape market. In the past few years, 3M 996, Ampex 499, Scotch/3M 226 and Ampex 456 have been the most popular and consistent tapes. Trying to save money by finding a great deal on an off-brand tape is never a good idea. This is, after all, the fundamental storage medium for your music, and you might be spending hours of your life and chunks of your soul to produce it—so buy the best.

Outboard Gear to Have on Hand

Any or all of these choices for outboard equipment are valuable in most mixing situations. Most people build their arsenal of effects and processors a little at a time.

If you're building your setup a piece at a time, one good multi-effects processor will go a long way. As we've seen before in this course, with one processor you might need to print some of your sounds to tape with effects, but try to save the main reverb or effect for the mixdown. The more effects you accumulate, the more you can save for mixdown.

A second multi-effects processor can really boost the power of your setup. A simple delay or dedicated reverb is also a good choice for an addition to your setup. Basically, the more involved and advanced your recordings become, the greater your chances of extravagant equipment needs.

But remember, if you overuse effects and processing, you run the risk of producing a confusing and vague sounding mix. Too much reverb is detrimental to the punch and impact of a mix, too much delay confuses a mix in much the same way. Too much compression can produce a mix that sounds thin and lacks the punch of a mix that has strong dynamic range.

Other effects that are useful to have available in a mix are a digital delay; more reverb; a compressor, stereo compressor or EQ specific compressor/enhancer like the Aphex Dominator; and gates.

Depending on your setup and the amount of noise coming from your tape recorder and instruments, multiple gates might be a valuable addition to a clean, noise-free, punchy sound. Many high-end, world-class boards have a gate built in to every channel. I've done several mixes where I've used up to 16 or so gates on a 24-track mix. Some tracks just aren't suited to gating, but many are.

Parametric and graphic EQs are sometimes the only solution to many sound shaping problems. Having these tools available, although they're not always essential, can save the day.

Exciters can also be useful in many situations, but I've done an awful lot of mixes without using them, even when there's been a handful of them available.

Another valuable tool is the real-time spectrum analyzer. This uses a calibrated microphone to visually show you the frequency content of your music. One version of a spectrum analyzer shows a series of 31 LED meters. Each meter responds to a specific frequency. These LEDs typically respond to the frequencies available on a 31-band graphic EQ. If there's too much or too little of a frequency or frequencies, you can see it on the LEDs. Other analyzers register these frequencies using onscreen computer graphics. Some even show a graphic representation of decay over a time period.

Spectrum analyzers can be very useful. Prices vary from about four hundred dollars to several thousand, but even the simplest and least expensive can still indicate some inherent problems with your mixes—or your sound system.

Tape Speed

Analog tape speed is measured in inches per second, sometimes just called *ips*. Standard music recording speeds are 7 1/2 ips, 15 ips and 30 ips.

Faster tape speeds result in better signal-to-noise ratio, less wow and flutter, and better high-frequency response. If your tape recorder has two tape speeds, use the faster of the speeds for recording music. If you're recording dialogue, the slower of the tape speeds can work well enough and will conserve tape.

The exception to this rule of thumb comes when choosing between 15 ips and 30 ips. Faster tape speeds also change the low-frequency response, and many engineers prefer to record at 15 ips using good quality noise reduction because they like the extra punchy low end at 15 ips. Other engineers prefer 30 ips because of the more accurate high frequency at the higher tape speed.

Automation

In the mix that we're doing in this chapter, we won't be using computer-assisted automation. The primary advantage to automation lies in its ability to help you shape and form a mix as you go; the computer ends up making all the moves for you. For now, it's best to keep things as simple as possible, but as your experience and skills progress, you'll find that automation will become a very useful and often necessary tool for producing an acceptable mix.

Automation is a means of integrating a computer system into your mixing process. In this process, you can record fader and mute changes into the computer's memory. After you've performed the move once, the automation system memorizes it, and from that time on, the computer performs that move for you every time the mix plays. This is a big bonus when you're building a mix. Automation gives you the ability to make new level changes while you hear the old level changes. This is like giving you several more hands to use during the mix.

When we studied dynamic processors, the key operator in a compressor/limiter or a gate/expander was the VCA (voltage controlled amplifier). In most automation systems, the VCA is also the circuit doing the work. As the fader moves up or down, a changing voltage is sent to the VCA. These voltage changes are represented by a binary code that's stored in the computer memory. These voltage changes are played back into the automaton VCA, and the VCA responds by turning the appropriate channel up or down at the precise moment that you did. In this system, the faders don't move on playback, but the levels are being changed by the computer.

Voltage changes are either converted to binary information and stored directly on the one track of the multitrack master or stored in computer memory and referenced to the SMPTE time code track printed on the multitrack master.

Another system of automation is called *moving fader automation*. In this system, fader motion is still converted to voltage and stored in computer memory, but instead of a VCA changing the level on playback, the faders are actually moved by voltage-controlled motors that reside within the fader housing.

Moving fader automation eliminates the need for the addition of another amplifier (the VCA) in the circuit. From the purist's standpoint, it's always best to eliminate as many amplifiers from the signal path as possible. It's commonly agreed that the most sonically pure mixes in the analog domain come from moving fader automation systems.

With the newer full digital consoles or digitally controlled analog consoles, it's common for every control on the console to be fully automatable in real time throughout the song. This includes faders; mutes; pans; bus assignments; auxiliary sends; EQ; and even compression, limiting, gating and expanding. With this kind of control, your mixes can take on a completely new dimension and intellectual depth. Every move is represented by a unique binary code. The computer simply remembers all the codes and references to SMPTE, and at a specific SMPTE time the computer replays the binary code. It's a very simple premise, though it is sometimes taxing on the computer's ability to remain stable. Save often!

Multiple Sets of Monitors

As we've discussed before, it's best to mix using a good set of near-field monitors. You'll also want to check your mixes on far-field monitors and very small radio-like speakers to verify that your mix sounds good on a variety of sound systems. Remember, it's our goal to produce mixes that sound good on any system they're played on. They don't need to sound exactly the same, but they should sound good. The more accurate your sounds are as you're tracking on

the multitrack, the easier the mix will go. If you spend the time getting clean, solid, exciting sounds onto the multitrack, you'll be a happier person during mixdown.

Comparison to Other Projects

A very effective mixing technique involves comparing your mix to a mix that you love the sound of or one that's held in high regard by the audio community at large. Plug a CD into one of your mixer's aux or tape inputs or into two channels of your main mix bus, and have it there and ready to switch on for comparison. Turn the CD on occasionally to check the basic sound of your mix. Evaluate highs, mids and lows along with effects and basic orchestration. It helps if the reference mix is similar in style and feel to the song you're mixing.

You'll often be surprised by the results when you try this. You might be amazed at how bad your mix sounds in comparison. You might also be amazed at how good your mix sounds. Comparison is inherent to the music business, so it's best to make them while there's still an opportunity to make changes.

The Spherical Approach to Panning and Positioning in the Mix

We should think of a mix as a three-dimensional sound field. Refer to Chapter 6 of this book for a detailed description of this three-dimensional perspective. This is a very important part of the mix process, and I highly recommend developing this kind of 3D mindset.

EQ: The Cumulative Effect

If we boost the kick drum, bass guitar and rhythm guitar by 4dB at 100Hz, they might each sound fine alone, but the cumulative effect of boosting the same frequency on all of these instruments wouldn't be good. The result is an artificially hot mix—a mix that doesn't sound as strong or loud as it should.

As an example, listen to Audio Examples 9-6 and 9-7: two mixes of the exact same instruments on the same song. In Audio Example 9-6, the drum, bass and rhythm guitar tracks are mixed for even volume, without the addition of equalization on any of the tracks. I've adjusted the master level of the track so the mix reads +1VU at the strongest part of the track.

Audio Example 9-6 No EQ on the Rhythm Section
CD-2: Track 74

Audio Example 9-7 demonstrates the same parts with each instrument boosted by 6dB at 100Hz. This might seem to sound OK on some songs or some systems, but there's definitely an adverse effect on the overall mix level and sound quality. This mix also reads +1VU at the strongest part of the track. Notice how much softer the high-frequency instruments sound, even though the mix level reads the same as the previous mix. This is because the lows are controlling the mix levels.

Audio Example 9-7
Boosting 100Hz on the Rhythm Section
CD-2: Track 75

Boosting the same frequency on different instruments has a cumulative effect on the overall mix level. We should be able to compensate for this fact in an intelligent way. The ideal procedure, when combining EQ, is to compensate for a boost in one instrument by cutting the same frequency in another instrument. For example, if the bass guitar needs a boost in the low frequencies at 100Hz, try cutting 100Hz on the kick drum. If the kick drum needs more lows, boost 60Hz and then cut 60Hz on the bass guitar. If the guitar is added to these instruments, chances are there's no need to include the lows at all. Try cutting below 150Hz on the rhythm guitar track. When we compensate for boosts in EQ by cutting at the corresponding frequency on a different instrument, we end up with mixes that sound louder at the same master mix level; we also create mixes that sound better on more systems. If we boost 100Hz on all the tracks and the mix is played back on a system that is very responsive at 100Hz, it's obvious that there will be a problem with the sound of the mix on that system.

Listen to Audio Example 9-8. I've set the EQ so that the instruments complement each other. Notice that this mix sounds smoother and louder than the other mixes of the same rhythm section parts, even though the master mix level still reads +1VU at the strongest part of the track.

Audio Example 9-8 Complementing EQ
CD-2: Track 76

Now listen to Audio Example 9-9. I've edited the three different versions of the same rhythm section together; you'll hear a little of each version. Notice the difference in the volume between versions even though each version was recorded so that +1VU is the strongest reading on the track.

Audio Example 9-9 Comparison
CD-2: Track 77

Mixing Theories and Building Concepts

It's best to approach each mix as a separate musical work. For the most natural and believable mix, imagine the music as if it were being played by a live group. For panning, imagine where each instrument would be onstage. It's most typical in a live band to have the drums and bass in the center with the keys to one side, rhythm guitar to the other side and the lead vocals in the middle. Any instrumental solos are typically placed in the center of the mix, as if the soloist had stepped forward for the solo. There are, of course, infinite variations of precise placement in a live performance situation and multiple instrument combinations, but imagining your recorded music as a live group will result in consistent success and believability.

Mix Approach

- Focus on the drums and bass first. If these ingredients are punchy, balanced and supportive, most of the work is done. This combination defines the structure and boundaries of the mix.
- Next, add the lead vocal. Start working on fitting the lead vocal together with the bass and drums. Once this combination is solid, you might be surprised at how full and complete the sound is. Many times we keep adding tracks to get a full sound when what we probably need most is to get rid of some tracks and set up a good mix.
- Then, start adding ingredients in order of importance. Once the bass, drums and lead vocal are working together, you'll find it easy to tell what the level of the primary guitar and keyboard should be; just don't ruin the punch and drive supplied by your initial mix.
- Add all the miscellaneous percussion and sound effects after everything else is up. Use only what you need. Try not to run over the lead vocals with an instrument or solo. If the lead vocal is on, you probably don't need another lead instrument fighting for the limelight. Focus as you mix. Determine what is the most important thing at each point in the song and highlight it in the mix.

The Arrangement

If the arrangement has been structured with the final product in mind, and if you've been disciplined enough to record only the parts that really need to be in the song, mixing is a much easier and more streamlined process. That's why arranging and production experience is so valuable to the success of a project.

There are a lot of situations when it's valid to record a few tracks that you might or might not use in the mix. Often those tracks will be turned up for just a portion of the song, at just the right time. In that context, it can be very valuable to record extra parts.

There's also definite value in planning your song out in detail before you start recording and then sticking to that plan throughout the recording process—although, of course, you must also allow for creative freedom in the heat of the recording moment.

Keep this in mind. There should always be

one focal point that stands out to the listener at each point of the mix. As the mixing engineer, you must always give the listener a point of interest. This approach produces mixes that are fun and easy to listen to because they maintain interest, captivate and pull the listener through the song. Keeping a focal point normally involves many level, panning and effect changes throughout the song.

Timing is critical when adjusting levels. Developing the touch necessary to change levels and to turn tracks on and off just at the right time takes practice. Selecting when and where to make a crucial change often requires the ability to push a button, turn a knob or move a fader at a precise moment or within a very specific time period.

If you've written a complete song and you'd like to get people to listen to the whole thing, give them a mix that builds from the beginning to the end and always has one focal point. Include some exciting and possibly surprising sounds, and structure your arrangement with the goal of keeping your listener's focus on the tune.

Remember this: If you're turning channels on and off and you've simplified to the point where there's only one or two instruments in the mix, it should sound like those were the only instruments you recorded. They should sound full and interesting, and the rest of the tracks should be off so they aren't adding tape or mixer noise. Ideally, only the tracks or channels that are being heard in the mix are turned on. Even if there isn't music on a track, having it on adds to the overall noise or lack of clarity, and it can ruin the impact of your music.

Characteristics of a Good Mix

Strong and Solid, But Controlled, Lows

It's extremely important to build a mix that's distributed evenly in the lows. If the kick is boosted at 100Hz, the bass should not be boosted at 100Hz—in fact, most likely the bass should be cut at 100Hz. Always consider the ramifications of boosting or cutting the same frequency on two or more instruments. If you're limited on your mixer to simple two-band, fixed frequency cut/boost EQ, you must use good mic choice and technique along with educated EQ choices during recording of tracks.

Mids Distributed Evenly Among Various Instruments

Too much midrange results in a "honky" sound, while too few mids results in a hollow, empty sound.

Strong, Smooth Highs That Are Easy to Listen To

A mix that has one particular high frequency boosted on several instruments can take on an abrasive and irritating character. Highs must be distributed evenly.

Balance

A mix that sounds like it's stronger on one side than the other can be distracting. A good way to check the balance of a mix is on headphones. I'll usually listen to a mix on the phones just before I print the master. Headphones are very telling when it comes to stray instruments that might distract if not placed properly.

Depth

A mix can sound OK if it's two dimensional (just left-right), but when a mix sounds three dimensional—or if the sounds seem distributed from near to far as well as left to right—it becomes much more real sounding. Reverb and delays add depth. It's typically best to have one instrument define the near character and one instrument define the far character. A simple dry percussion instrument is usually a good choice for the closest instrument. A synth string pad or guitar part might be a good choice for the most distant sounding instrument. These choices are all dependent on the desired musical impact.

Width

A stereo mix is more interesting if there is one or two instruments defining the far left and far right boundaries. These boundaries might be far left and far right, but care must be taken to ensure that the mix sounds good in both mono and stereo. Mixes with boundaries closer in toward the center position—3:00 and 9:00 or 10:00 and 2:00—transfer very well to mono, but they aren't as fun to listen to in stereo.

Momentum

If a song maintains the same intensity and texture from start to finish, it probably won't hold the listener's interest. As a mixing engineer, you should always strive to give the song the appropriate flow. That might include starting from just one instrument and the lead vocal and building to a full orchestration with exaggerated effects, or it might include subtle changes throughout the song that are barely noticeable but add enough to maintain the listener's interest.

Consistency

A mix is only good if it sounds good on any system it's played on. Too often a mix will sound really good in the studio or on your own recording setup, but when you play the mix in your car, your living room, the club sound system, the radio or on your friend's mondo home entertainment complex, it sounds embarrassingly bad. Use near-field reference monitors to monitor most of your mix and, as a cross-check, include some larger far-field monitors and some very small radio-like monitors in your setup. Being able to check your mix on two or three sets of speakers can make the difference between good, usable mixes and bad, waste-of-time mixes.

Sounds Good in Stereo and Mono

Continually cross-reference the sound of your mix in stereo and mono. As I've mentioned several times, an instrument, sound or mix can sound great in stereo but terrible in mono. Some of the slight delay or chorus changes that make a mix sound good in mono make practically no difference to the sound of the mix in stereo.

Approaches to Mixing That I've Found Ineffective

- Quickly get all of the tracks to sound good together and then add the lead vocal.
- Turn everything up and adjust until it sounds good.
- Get the rhythm section sounding good first, then the filler keys and guitars, then the backing vocals, then the lead vocals.

Signs of an Amateur Musical Recording

Avoid these characteristics in your mixes:

- **No contrast**—The same musical texture throughout the entire song
- **A frequent lack of focal point**—Holes between lyrics where nothing is brought forward in the mix to hold the listener's attention. A new mixing engineer will often set up the basic rhythm section mix and then leave it completely alone throughout the tune. During the vocal passages there's a focal point, but when there's no vocal, listeners will tend to lose interest and probably fade away from your song.
- **Mixes that are noisy and lacking in clarity and punch**—Although a new engineer will often attribute this to bad tape or a questionable tape machine, it's usually a result of bad mixing technique.
- **Mixes that sound distant and are devoid of any feeling of intimacy**—This is usually the result of too much reverb or overuse of other effects. As a rule of thumb, there should always be at least one instrument in each mix that is dry; this serves as a point of reference for the listener. With at least one dry sound, the mix takes on much more of an intimate character than if everything has reverb. Remember, reverb is a tool that adds distance and space to a sound, so if every ingredient in a mix has reverb, the entire mix will sound distant.
- **Inconsistency in levels**—No one likes to listen to a song that all of a sudden reaches out and bites. It's fairly common for a lead vocalist to sing with subtle compassion and feeling one second and in the next breath go full blast, full volume. If the mixing engineer isn't blending the loud and soft passages in some way, the listener becomes distracted, or worse, annoyed by the blaring loud passages and nearly inaudible soft passages.
- **Dull and uninteresting sounds**—Learn what's considered good for your style of music and then start practicing. Practice getting the appropriate sounds for whatever style of music you're working with.

Basic Setup Procedure

Once You Select and Prepare the Multitrack and Mixdown Machines

- Plug the outputs of the multitrack into the line inputs of your mixer. If you're using an analog multitrack, be sure you're in playback mode (sometimes called repro or tape). If you're in sync, simul-sync, sel-sync or overdub mode, the sound quality could be dramatically diminished. Some tape machines don't offer any of these options (Illustrations 9-2 through 9-4).
- Be sure you've selected *line* at the input of each of the multitrack channels on the mixer.
- Assign all channels of the mixer to a stereo bus. Some mixers have a dedicated stereo bus that's fed by the main faders. Some mixers require the use of two of the multitrack bus assignments to send your mix to the 2-track mixdown recorder.
- Plug the outputs of your stereo mix bus into the inputs of your 2-track mixdown recorder (Illustration 9-2).
- If you're mixing to an analog multitrack recorder, be sure the correct head is selected for best playback reproduction (Illustrations 9-3 through 9-5).

- If your multitrack master was recorded using noise reduction, make sure that you're either playing back on the same machine you recorded on with the noise reduction on or playing back on a machine equipped with exactly the same kind of noise reduction. Dolby A, Dolby B, Dolby C, Dolby SR and dbx noise reduction are not cross-compatible. If your tape has been encoded using one method, it must be decoded using the same method.

- Build a list of moves for the duration of your song, referenced to the tape counter or time code, if available (Illustration 9-6).

- A lyric sheet is very useful. Mark your moves, with the tape counter number, by the lyric

Illustration 9-2
Basic Mix Setup

Assign all channels to a stereo bus—like buses 1 and 2. Most mixers let you pan between odd and even numbered buses; typically, odd is left and even is right.

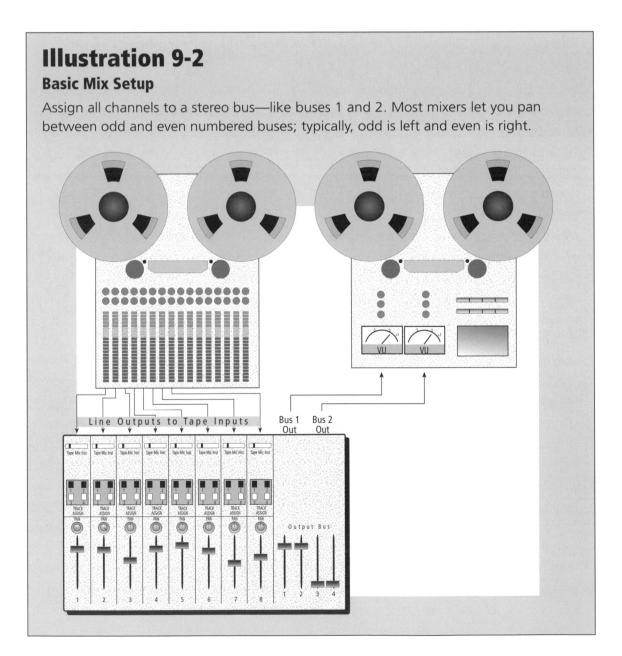

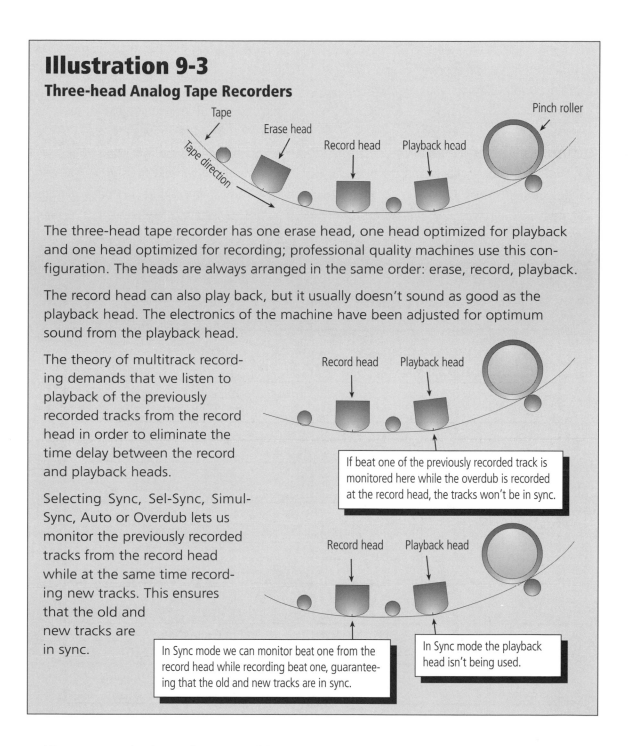

Illustration 9-3
Three-head Analog Tape Recorders

Tape

Erase head

Record head

Playback head

Pinch roller

Tape direction

The three-head tape recorder has one erase head, one head optimized for playback and one head optimized for recording; professional quality machines use this configuration. The heads are always arranged in the same order: erase, record, playback.

The record head can also play back, but it usually doesn't sound as good as the playback head. The electronics of the machine have been adjusted for optimum sound from the playback head.

The theory of multitrack recording demands that we listen to playback of the previously recorded tracks from the record head in order to eliminate the time delay between the record and playback heads.

Record head   Playback head

If beat one of the previously recorded track is monitored here while the overdub is recorded at the record head, the tracks won't be in sync.

Selecting Sync, Sel-Sync, Simul-Sync, Auto or Overdub lets us monitor the previously recorded tracks from the record head while at the same time recording new tracks. This ensures that the old and new tracks are in sync.

Record head   Playback head

In Sync mode we can monitor beat one from the record head while recording beat one, guaranteeing that the old and new tracks are in sync.

In Sync mode the playback head isn't being used.

(Illustration 9-7). It's usually easier to follow the lyrics than just numbers, but often a simple list of counter numbers, in the order that they occur, with specific notes is the ideal approach.

• If a fader or any other control is constantly moving from one position to another, mark the two or three positions on the board with a grease pencil. These marks are easily removed and provide instant visual cues.

Everyone develops a preference for how they work best. Try several approaches and use the one that works best for you. Organization is the key.

Arranging During Mixdown

You might be making some radical musical changes in your mixes. Once you've critically evaluated the options, you could end up turn-ing off everything but the acoustic guitar and the lead vocal for the just the intro or the first quarter of the song; you might leave some tracks completely out of the song or just include them on the choruses. The options are vast.

Spend some time analyzing your rough mixes. It's very important to listen to your song with analytical ears before you begin the final mix. This could take a few hours, but it is defi-

Illustration 9-4
Mix Moves: The List Approach

Counter Number	Channel Number	Control Position	Notes
0021	5	-5	Intro Keyboards
0036	5	-9	
0036	3	ON and -1	
0048	3	+1	Fader moves on "tears"
0102	3	OFF	
0109	7	+2.5	Guitar Solo
0210	7	OFF	End of Guitar Solo
0211	3	ON	
0222	5	+1	Keyboard Fill
0224	5	-5	
0312	1 and 2	ON and -2	Backing Vocals Enter

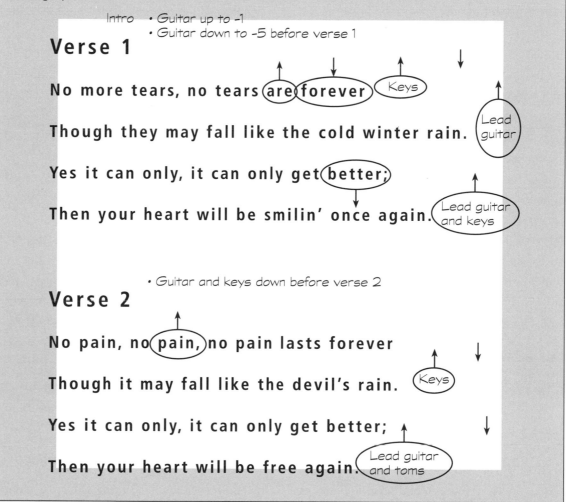

Illustration 9-5

Mix Moves: The Lyric Sheet Approach

Use up and down arrows to indicate instrumental or vocal level changes; circle the change points.

nitely time well spent. Try to consider all options; make a list of different ideas and attempt to separate your heart from the song. If you listen as though you were hearing the song for the first time, you might come up with ideas that add a fresh, new interest to your music. One of the things that takes quite a while during mixdown is experimenting with different approaches to the music.

Multiple Mixes

Don't be afraid to try something really "out there" with your song. Go ahead and work through your ideas; print each idea to tape. I like to print as many versions of each song as I can come up with. Sometimes you'll listen to all of your final mix versions and fall in love with the one that seemed like your least favorite in the studio. You might even end up editing parts of different versions together.

I start laying mixes to the mixdown machine as soon as each version is even close to complete. Often your first impressions of balance, pan and level are the most natural and will best suit the song; and printing that primal, gut-level mix frequently pays off. While you're in the middle of mixing is the time to try different things that come to mind or to simply cover your bases. It's much quicker and easier to print mixes when everything's set up than to reset later. If you have a question about whether or not the bass is too loud or soft when the mix is played on your buddy's mondo home stereo, print the song once with the bass louder and once with the bass softer. You could end up with several mixes of each song—it's common to end up with 10 or 20 or more. Chances are good that you'll be happy with one of the versions, and you'll possibly save yourself from personal embarrassment and wasted time.

Mix Versions

These are some of the basic types of mixes I consistently print:

- **The "gut-level" version**—This is my first reaction to the music and how it should go together. Sometimes these instinctive mixes are the most punchy and real-sounding. Always print your first guess. You might use it less than 10 percent of the time, but on those occasions where it's the best mix, you'll be the hero for having had the foresight to print it.
- **The guitar version**—Heavy on the guitars, often with no keys except when they're absolutely necessary.

- **The keyboard version**—Heavy on the keys, often with no guitars except where they're absolutely necessary.
- **The very streamlined version**—Take away everything except the lead vocals, then add just the instruments that have to be there to provide harmonic structure.
- **The "build" version**—This one starts simply with parts being added as the music requires, until the end, when all tracks and instruments might be included.
- **The bigger build version**—This typically represents a more subtle but definite build. Try thinning out the intro, then possibly leaving the backing vocals and the keys out on the first verse and chorus. Next, bring the strings in, then some extra percussion, etc.
- **The vocals up version**—I like to print each version with the vocals a little louder than normal. I don't always print this one, but if there's any question in my mind I'll just do it.
- **The bass up or bass down versions**—Bass can be one of the toughest instruments to judge at first. Monitor speakers are very important in the accuracy of your low-frequency judgments. Only time, practice with your own equipment, and cross references with other systems will give you confidence that what you hear in the studio is compatible with what you'll hear in the real world. If you have any question at all about the bass, print versions with the bass louder and/or softer.
- **Solos louder or softer versions**—If there's any question, just do it. Sometimes you'll end up with the perfect solo level except for that one high note that kills. If you have a version with the solo turned down, you can always edit that part of the solo in

from the "soft solo" version. Like I said before, part of the beauty of having all these mixes is the flexibility to mix and match parts later.

- **The no backing vocals version**—Just in case! Sometimes the simple version without backing vocals has more punch and believability. This version is also handy for editing purposes. Maybe you'll want the backing vocal out during the first half of the song. If you don't print a no backing vocals version, you'll need to set everything back up, try to get together everything you like about the current mix, then print the version without the backing vocals. You'd be better off investing the time to just print this option in the first mixing session.

- **The instrumental version without backing vocals**—This is mostly for editing flexibility.

- **The instrumental version with backing vocals**—With the popularity of instrumental "trax" and karaoke, there might be a need for the instrumental version of your song. I've found a definite need to print these, especially in the pop, country and Christian markets. It's painless to turn the lead vocal off and spend the three or four minutes printing this version, but it's usually painful and expensive to go back later to duplicate your complete master mix without vocals. Saving time is always good! Besides, when these versions are needed and you've shown the foresight to have them instantly available, you look good and you solidify the ever important client-artist relationship. If you happen to be the client *and* the artist, it's still important to have this kind of foresight.

Building the Mix

Let's start building the drums on our song. See Illustration 9-8 for the tape recorder track sheet and a list of the MIDI tracks used on this song.

Kick Drum/Bass Guitar

The kick and snare are panned to center and each have their own channel on the mixer. Giving these instruments separate mixer channels from the rest of the drums and percussion makes a big difference in the punch and impact of the mix. Often the snare needs plenty of big sounding reverb; it's better to have the flexibility to reverberate the snare alone, without applying reverb to all of the drum sounds at once. Center position is almost always the best place for these instruments. If the kick and snare are off to one side or panned apart, your mix won't seem to have a solid point of origin, and the low-frequency content of the kick could cause its side of the mix to read hotter on the stereo meters.

On this song, I want a solid and punchy kick without an overly exaggerated slap. I'll boost the lows at 80Hz, cut the mids at 250Hz and leave the highs flat. These are only suggestions based on the sound of the instruments. Though the techniques are common on these types of instruments, the actual frequencies you alter, if any, are subject to the instruments you're working with and your personal musical taste.

I want the snare to be full and clean. I like the sound of this snare pretty well, but I'll boost 5kHz by 2 or 3dB just to help the clarity of the sound once the song starts coming together. I'll add a little bit of a plate reverb, with about a one second reverberation time, to the snare. I'm assuming that you've gone through the individual instrument sound chapters in this course and have several basic sound-shaping techniques at your disposal.

I've got the cymbals, toms and percussion all coming from two outputs of the drum machine, and on the mixer I've panned these two channels hard right and hard left. Individual instrument panning must de done within the drum machine. I'll bring up the drums starting with the kick and snare, rough in their levels and EQ, then work in the rest of the drums. The panning of the cymbals, toms and percussion is adjusted to achieve a balanced feel from left to right.

Illustration 9-6
Possible MIDI Tracks

Through the use of MIDI along with your multitrack, you can control and record a lot of tracks. This is an example of a very realistic possibility for our song in this chapter; we have 6 recorded tracks on the multitrack and 25 tracks of MIDI instruments.

Multitrack Track Sheet

Title	1 Tracks 3, 4 and 5 combined to track 1	2 Tracks 3, 4 and 5 combined to track 2	3 Final lead vocal	4 Electric guitar	5 Acoustic guitar	6 Guitar fills	7 Reference rhythm section	8 SMPTE 01:00:00:00
Title	1	2	3	4	5	6	7	8

Stereo bass	2 tracks - stereo	**Med. low tom**	1 track - mono
Stereo guitar	2 tracks - stereo	**Low tom**	1 track - mono
Kick drum	1 track - mono	**Support snare**	1 track - mono
Snare drum	1 track - mono	**String pad**	2 tracks - stereo
Hi-hat	1 track - mono	**Organ pad**	2 tracks - stereo
Triangle	1 track - mono	**Brass**	2 tracks - stereo
Shaker	1 track - mono	**Guitar effects**	2 tracks - stereo
Crash	1 track - mono	**Vocal Ooo...**	2 tracks - stereo
High tom	1 track - mono	Total =	25 tracks
Med. high tom	1 track - mono		

Audio Example 9-10 Building the Drums
CD-2: Track 78

Pan the Cymbals for a Natural Sound

It isn't natural to hear one cymbal completely from one side and another completely from the other, so avoid this kind of panning.

It is natural to imagine the drum set occupying a particular zone in the mix. The drum set is usually in the center of a band, but it still has a little spread across the center zone. I've found that panning the cymbals between about 10:00 and 2:00 in the mix provides enough of a spread to hear separation, but not so much that the drums sound too wide.

Live Toms

If you're mixing a live drum set, and you've got the toms on a separate track or tracks, it's not usually a good idea to just leave the tracks turned up to their normal settings all the time. The ringing of the tom heads and the leakage of the rest of the drums into the tom mics can severely decrease the close, punchy sound of the kick and snare mics.

Try applying the gating techniques that we discussed earlier in this course to the toms.

If you have any automation available, it can come in handy, on the tom tracks in particular. I prefer to listen through the entire song, noting where the tom fills are and then find each fill and write the fader moves into the automation. This saves having to set up the gates, which are usually touchy on the tom tracks and lets me blend the tom tracks in and out at a rate that's less distracting than the gate might be.

Many mixers have MIDI automated mutes. This simply lets you write the channel on and off into your sequence—a very useful and convenient feature.

Drum Machine Toms

If you've printed the drum machine toms to tape—and especially if the tom tracks are an important and strong part of the mix—gate them. Drum machine tracks are extremely easy to gate, and the tape noise between the tom hits is worth getting rid of.

Drum Set Overheads (Live)

Blend in the overhead mics just enough to fill in the sound of the kit and the cymbals. Cut lows below about 150Hz. The punch and lows of the set come from the close mics.

Overheads are primarily for transient definition on the cymbals and other percussion included in the drum kit.

If there are two overheads, boost a different high frequency on each mic. I like to boost 10 or 12kHz on one and about 13 to 15kHz on the other.

Bass

Once the drums are roughed in, we can move on and add the bass guitar. Fine-tuning the drum sounds will have to wait until the mix is further along and we can hear how the sounds are combining.

You'll need to assess the bass sound in your song. If it needs more lows, don't boost the same frequency that you boosted on the kick drum. Try boosting 150Hz on the bass if you boosted 80Hz on the kick, or vice versa. If you boosted 80Hz on the kick, you're best off to cut 80Hz on the bass, and if you boosted 150Hz on the bass you're best off to cut 150Hz on the kick. This approach results in a more controlled low end.

If you need to boost highs in the bass for clarity, find a frequency that works, but don't use a frequency that's predominant in any of the percussion instruments. Also, the bass is almost always panned center. The lows in its sound contain a lot of energy and can control the master mix level. If the bass is panned to one side, the entire mix level will be artificially hot on one side. This would be senseless, since bass frequencies are omnidirectional; even if you had the bass panned to one side, the listener might not be able to tell, anyway.

In Audio Example 9-11, I'll add the bass to the drums and adjust its EQ to fit with the drum sounds.

Audio Example 9-11 Adding the Bass
CD-2: Track 79

As I mentioned before, one of the biggest concerns you should have in a mix is how the lows fit together. If they accumulate, your mix will be muddy and boomy; in other words, it won't sound good. If you've been able to fit the pieces together well, your mix will sound full but very controlled and clean. Low frequencies are the most difficult to monitor accurately because many near-field reference monitors don't reproduce the frequencies that can cause most of the problems. In order for far-field monitors to work properly, they should be in a room that has a smooth, even frequency response.

When combining the bass and drums, remember that the kick drum and bass guitar rarely have reverb, though the snare and toms often do. Also the hi-hat, shaker, overheads or tambourine hardly ever need reverb, while drum machine cymbals and some percussion instruments, like congas and some very sparse percussion parts, can benefit from the appropriate reverb sound.

Lead Vocal

A lot of mixing might be required on the lead vocal track. The primary focal point of the mix is almost always the lead vocal. Because of this, it has to maintain a constant space in the mix. The style of the music generally determines exactly how loud the lead vocal should be in relation to the rest of the band; once that's been determined, the relationship must remain constant.

In a heavy R&B or rock song, the lead vocal is often buried into the mix a little. The result of this kind of balance is rhythmic drive and punchy drums; the bass and primary harmony instrument are accentuated.

In Audio Example 9-12, I've mixed the vocal back a bit. When the volume is turned up on this kind of mix, the rhythm section is very strong and punchy.

Audio Example 9-12 The Vocal Back Mix
CD-2: Track 80

In Audio Example 9-13, I boost the vocals in the mix. When the vocals are forward in the mix, it becomes very important to avoid vocal passages that are very loud in relation to the rest of the track. Notice how the vocal becomes difficult to listen to as it gets too loud on this passage.

Audio Example 9-13 The Vocals Louder
CD-2: Track 81

In a country or commercial pop song, the lead vocal is usually loud in the mix, allowing the lyric and emotion of the vocal performance to be easily heard and felt by the listener.

When the lead vocal is being mixed, there are many times when one word or syllable will need to be turned up or down; sometimes the changes are more general. This is the point where you, as the mixer, need to have a copy of the lyrics. The more organized you can be, the quicker your mix will go.

Chances are you'll have several changes to make during the mix, and the lead vocal will probably contain many of them. Mark the tape recorder counter numbers on the lyric sheet at each verse, chorus, interlude and bridge; this will help speed things up, no matter what. As you develop a list of vocal level changes, write them on the lyric sheet next to, above or below the lyric closest to the move. Lead sheets are very convenient for keeping track of mix moves.

Compression

If the lead vocal track is very inconsistent in level, try running the track through a compressor. I suggest a fairly high compression ratio, between 7:1 and 10:1 with a fast attack time and a medium release time. Adjust the threshold for gain reduction on the loudest notes only; most of the track should show no gain reduction. Our purpose here is to simply even out the volume of the track without extreme compression.

Expander

Often the noise between the lyric lines is blatantly irritating—especially if you've boosted the highs for clarity. An expander is a convenient tool that helps get rid of all noise between vocal lyrics. Set the expander's threshold so that it turns down only when there is no vocal. Set the attack time to fast, the release time to medium and the range to infinity.

Listen to the vocal track in Audio Example 9-14. After the first eight measures, I'll switch in the expander. Notice the decreased tape noise after the expander is switched in. This technique is most useful when using an analog multitrack, but it's also useful in the digital domain to get rid of room ambience and miscellaneous noises.

Audio Example 9-14
Expander on the Lead Vocal Track
CD-2: Track 82

Vocal EQ

If you used proper mic choice and technique to record the vocals, you might not need any EQ in the mix. If you need a little, it's safest to make subtle changes. If you boost or cut dramatically, it might sound OK on your mixing setup, but you'll be increasing the chances of creating a mix that could sound bad on some sound systems.

The basic vocal sound should be full, smooth and easy to listen to. Don't create a sound that is edgy and harsh. There isn't much need for the frequencies below 100Hz, since those are covered by the rhythm section instruments, so it's usually best to roll off the lows below 100 or 150Hz—or to use a highpass filter.

If there's a lack of clarity, try boosting slightly between 4 and 5kHz.

Exciter

Another tool that will add clarity to the vocal without using EQ is an exciter. Be careful not to overuse the exciter or your vocal will sound harsh and edgy. If used in proper proportion, an exciter can add a pleasing clarity. I'll add the exciter after the first four measures in Audio Example 9-15.

Audio Example 9-15
Exciter on the Lead Vocal Track
CD-2: Track 83

Simple Delay

On the vocal in Audio Example 9-16, I'll add a single slapback delay in time with the eighth note triplet to help solidify the shuffle feel. Since I know the tempo of the song is one quarter note equals 95 beats per minute, I'll look on the delay chart in Volume 1, Chapter 2 of the *Audio-Pro Home Recording Course,* to find that the delay time for the eighth note triplets is 210ms. Listen to the mix with the vocals. After a few measures, I'll add the delay. Notice how much more interesting the sound becomes. This delay is panned center with the vocal.

Audio Example 9-16
Simple Slapback on the Lead Vocal
CD-2: Track 84

As your equipment list grows, try setting up two or three aux buses as sends to two or three different delays. This way they'll all be available at once, and you can pick and choose what to send to which delay and in what proportion. This technique requires restraint and musical taste to keep from overusing delay, but it's a convenient way to set up. I'll set each delay to a different subdivision of the tempo; I usually use a quarter note and eighth note delay and sometimes a sixteenth note or triplet delay.

Add Backing Vocals

As we build the backing vocal sound, we must consider the musical style plus the production style. Sometimes it's appropriate to double the backing vocals with a digital delay or chorus. Sometimes it's appropriate to use a reverberation time of about 2.6 seconds. Sometimes it's OK to use a one-second reverb. At other times it's appropriate to use one single backing vocal track dry, just as it was recorded.

Background vocals often include the same kind of effect as the lead vocal but in a differing degree. Usually there's more effect on the backing vocals than the lead vocal. If the lead vocal has less reverb and delay, it'll sound closer and more intimate than the backing vocals, giving it a more prominent space in mix.

These choices are purely musical. For your songs to come across as authentic and believable, you or your producer must do some stylistic homework. Listen to some highly regarded recordings in the same style as your music; listen through the lyrics. Focus on the kick drum sound. Does it have reverb? Is it punchy in the low end? Does it have a present or exaggerated attack? Where is it panned in the mix?

Go through this process with each instrument in the mix that you're evaluating. See Illustration 9-9 for a checklist to be used when evaluating musical styles.

Backing vocals don't usually need to be thick in the low end, so I'll roll off the lows between 100 and 150Hz. Audio Example 9-17 demonstrates the backing vocals on our song,

soloed. After the first couple of measures, I'll cut the lows at 120Hz.

Audio Example 9-17
The Backing Vocals Cut at 150Hz
CD-2: Track 85

Illustration 9-7
Sound Evaluation Chart

Instrument	Reverb	Highs	Lows	Mids	Attack	Pan	Fullness	Comments
Kick								
Snare								
Toms								
Cymbals								
Conga								
Tambourine								
Shaker								
Clave								
Misc. perc. 1								
Misc. perc. 2								
Lead vocal								
Back. vocals								
E. guitar 1								
E. guitar 2								
Acoustic gt.								
Bass guitar								
Piano								
Strings								
Brass								
Keys 1								
Keys 2								
Keys 3								
Effects keys								
Dialogue								
_____								
_____								
_____								

Listen to the vocals in Audio Example 9-18 along with the rhythm section and the lead vocal.

Audio Example 9-18 Add the Backing Vocals
CD-2: Track 86

Backing vocals should support the lead vocal without covering it. If the parts are well written, background vocals should nearly mix themselves. Well-written parts fill the holes between the lead vocal lines without distracting from the emotion and message of the lyrics; they also support the lead vocal on the key phrases of the verse or chorus while offering a musical and textural contrast. There's an art to writing good backing vocal parts that are easy to sing, make musical sense and aren't corny.

Practice and diligence pay off quite well when it comes to these very important parts. If the drums, bass, lead vocal and backing vocals are strong and mixed well, most of your work is done.

Comping Keyboards and Rhythm Guitars

It's standard to pan the basic keyboard and guitar apart in the mix. Often, these parts work well when panned to about 3:00 and 9:00, as they are in Audio Example 9-19.

Audio Example 9-19
Keyboard and Guitar Panned Apart
CD-2: Track 87

Since it's typical that the guitar and keys have been recorded with effects, there's often

not much to do to get these parts to sound rich and full. If you've followed this course from the beginning, you should know several techniques to help shape the sounds of these instruments.

If there's just one basic chord comping part, it's often desirable to create a stereo sound through the use of a delay, chorus or reverb.

Filling in the Holes With the Guitar or Keys

There's often one instrument that provides the bed—or constant pad—for the song, and another instrument that's a little less constant that can be used to fill some of the holes that might crop up.

This might be one case where the mixing engineer becomes the musical arranger. It could be best if an instrument is only included during certain sections of a song, even though the instrument was recorded throughout the entire song. The process of mixing involves musical decisions.

Deciding exactly what needs to be where is one of the most important parts of the final mix. If too many things are going on at once during a song, the listener can't effectively focus on anything. Frequently, during a session, the basic tracks will be very exciting and punchy, and everyone in the studio can feel the excitement and energy. Eventually, as more and more parts are added, everyone can feel that the music's punch and energy have been buried in a sea of well-intended musical fluff. That's not very exciting.

The old standby rule of thumb continues to pertain in music: Keep it simple. The more musical parts you include, the harder it is to hear the music. See Illustration 9-10 for a look at a couple of standard intellectual approaches to building a mix.

On this song, we have a keyboard comping part and an acoustic guitar comping part. I recorded both parts all the way through the song, even though it'd probably be cleaner if there were only one of these parts going on at a time. Now that we're mixing, I'll listen to this mix and decide which part should be playing when. There might be a spot toward the end where both should be playing. Listen for yourself. Audio Example 9-20 demonstrates the rhythm section and vocals with both the guitar and keys comping. Notice how they sometimes work well together but that often they get in each other's way.

Audio Example 9-20 Mix With Guitar and Keys
CD-2: Track 88

Audio Example 9-21 demonstrates the song with just the keys comping. I've removed the guitar so that the keys can be stronger and punchier in the mix without detracting from the rest of the orchestration.

Audio Example 9-21 Keys Comping
CD-2: Track 89

Audio Example 9-22 demonstrates the song with just the guitar comping. I've removed

Illustration 9-8
Two Schools of Thought

There are traditionally two popular approaches to mixing:

1. One school uses a full rhythm section sound and adds several different textures and small musical ideas throughout the music to add color and pizazz. There are often lots of layered keyboard textures, large vocal group sounds and big string and brass sounds.

2. The other school uses a more basic rhythm section sound but concentrates on optimizing each ingredient, not only from a technical and sonic standpoint, but also from a musical developmental standpoint. They'll construct the very best musical part they can for each instrument, then spend time to make sure the instrument sound is as good as it can be.

Each of these theories has its place in the musical world and can be extremely effective in the hands of experienced professionals. Both techniques can be very time consuming. When you add more and more parts to your music, each part must have its own special place, and it must dovetail in with the rest of the music in a way that doesn't detract from the musical feeling and emotion. On the other hand, when you limit the number of instruments in a song, every note of every track must be crafted to help maintain momentum and musical focus throughout the entire song.

the keys so that the guitar can be stronger and punchier in the mix without detracting from the rest of the orchestration.

Audio Example 9-22 Guitar Comping
CD-2: Track 90

For the sake of comparison, listen to all three mix versions edited in a row. Notice the difference in space, feel and emotion as one version transitions to the next.

Audio Example 9-23 Mix Comparison
CD-2: Track 91

Lead Parts

It's common to include a lead instrument part; this is typically a guitar, keyboard or sax. It often runs throughout the song filling holes and, essentially, adding spice and emotion while maintaining flow and interest. If you get the player to play only what's needed on the lead track, your mixing job is easier. Often, when the lead parts are recorded, the total scope of the song, arrangement or orchestration hasn't been defined. In this case, I'll let the lead player fill all the holes he wants, then pick and choose what to include in the mix. If you let the lead part fill all holes between the lyrics, verses or choruses, the element of surprise or contrast is lost. There's an art to finding the appropriate spots to include the lead licks; but remember, at any point of the song there only needs to be one focal point.

Lead parts are usually good to include in the intro, leading into a chorus, between verses and choruses, sometimes between lyric lines and in the repeat choruses at the end of the song.

In the song we're using in this chapter, there's an acoustic rhythm guitar, a simple electric lead part and a solo guitar part. Different songs and styles demand different instrumentation. The electric guitar part here is used to fill throughout the song. A part like this can be turned on and off as needed or you can just let it fly through the entire song. This part provides a focal point between the lyric lines. Listen to the song without the electric part, in Audio Example 9-24, and notice that the holes between the lyrics lack focus.

Audio Example 9-24 No Electric Guitar
CD-2: Track 92

Audio Example 9-25 demonstrates the same part of the song, but now I'll include the electric fills. Notice how this maintains interest and helps the flow of the song.

Audio Example 9-25 With Electric Guitar
CD-2: Track 93

The solo part is used for contrast in the intro, at the solo section and in the end during the repeat and fade section. Listen to the intro without the guitar solo part in Audio Example 9-26.

Audio Example 9-26 Intro Without Solo
CD-2: Track 94

When the solo is included in the intro, it

helps give a focal point and define the style and emotion of the song.

Audio Example 9-27 Intro With Solo
CD-2: Track 94

Solos

As a note on solos, keep in mind that it's often good to put the same effects on the solo as the lead vocal. This adds continuity to the emotional flow and acoustical space of the song. Solos are almost always panned center to help keep the focus.

Mix Levels

A good mix for commercial playback will always be hanging around 0VU with the strongest part of the song registering up to +1 or +2VU; the weakest part doesn't usually go below about -5 minimum. For a song that is going to be heard on radio or TV, you need to keep the mix as close to 0VU as possible so the quiet parts aren't lost or distractingly inaudible.

When you're recording a symphony, piano or other wide dynamic range source, it can be very difficult to keep levels around 0VU; with these types of sources, that wouldn't be natural sounding or easy to listen to. If you're mixing to a digital 2-track and your music will be heard primarily on CD, there's plenty of room for including a wide dynamic range; in this context a wide dynamic range can be fantastic. Some of my favorite symphony recordings include passages that are barely audible, even on CD, followed immediately by very strong full ensemble passages.

However, most of what the normal record-

ist works with is commercial in nature and should maintain a constant and strong mix level. In contemporary music, contrast is usually most effective when demonstrated by changes in orchestration rather than changes in ensemble volume. Taking a full group and cutting immediately to a single acoustic guitar is often very effective and a great dynamic change, even though the mix levels might stay constant.

Fades

The majority of recordings end in a simple fade out. The fade is a good way to end a song while sustaining the energy and emotion of the choruses or end section. Sometimes an ending adds too much finality and resolve; it detracts from the continuity and flow of an entire album. Other times endings are the perfect resolution of the song, album or section of an album.

Seven to fifteen seconds is the typical range of fade lengths. If the fade is too short, the end seems even more abrupt than an actual ending. If it's too long, the continuity of an album can be lost or, if the tune is heard in a car or other noisy environment, most of the fade will be covered up, creating the feel of a huge gap between songs.

Fades should begin right after the beginning of a musical phrase and be smooth and even throughout the length of the fade. Don't get excited toward the end and duck out too quickly; also, don't try to feather the last bit so smoothly that the average listener won't be able to hear the last four or five seconds of the fade.

I like to time the fade so that there's an interesting fill or lick just before the end. This gives the listener the feeling that something is going on after the fade. If the listener imagines that the band keeps playing, the emotion and energy of the mix should continue even though the song is over.

If there are lyrics during the fade, try to finish the phrase just after a key lyric such as the last word of the chorus or a crucial vocal fill lick. Don't cut an idea off with the end of the fade. End between ideas.

For a fade to begin naturally, start the fade after the beginning of a musical section. Often the length of the fade is determined by the length of the musical section happening during the fade.

The fades in Audio Examples 9-28 through 9-31 are for time only so that you'll get the feel of each fade length.

Audio Example 9-28 demonstrates a 7 second fade.

Audio Example 9-28 7 Second Fade
CD-2: Track 95

Audio Example 9-29 demonstrates a 10 second fade.

Audio Example 9-29 10 Second Fade
CD-2: Track 95

Audio Example 9-30 demonstrates a 15 second fade.

Audio Example 9-30 15 Second Fade
CD-2: Track 95

Audio Example 9-31 demonstrates a 5 second fade.

Audio Example 9-31 5 Second Fade
CD-2: Track 95

Preparing the Mixed Master for Duplication

Editing

If you've completed mixing all ten or so songs for your album, it's time to get everything into a form that the duplication facility can work with.

If you'll be compiling all of your songs, you'll need to do some sort of editing. Editing can be performed by actually cutting the analog master with a razor blade and taping the pieces back together again or by using a computer-based digital editor. You might want to edit for these reasons:

- To put your songs in the correct order.
- To adjust spacing between songs.
- To remove a section or sections of a song. If you've recorded the "album" version of a song and end up needing a shorter, more commercial version, you could end up cutting a five-minute song down to a three-and-a-half minute song; this is quite common.
- To reuse a section at another time in the song. Sometimes one chorus section will be good and one will be bad. You could end up copying the good chorus section and using it in place of the bad one. This is also common with single phrases, lines or lyrics.
- To lengthen a song. When you've been disciplined in your recording procedures and have produced a perfect three-and-a-half minute

song, someone is bound to request the "dance" mix that should be six minutes long or longer. In this case, you'll need to grab bits of your song, remix them in several different ways then reassemble the pieces into something much longer than the original piece of music.

Special effects are also possible with editing. You can achieve sounds that you can't during mixdown, like backward sections.

If you're using a digital editor, time and pitch changes can be made fairly effortlessly.

Editing is very important in the professional audio world and requires a lot of practice whether you're actually cutting and splicing tape with a razor blade or using the newest digital editor.

If you've printed several mixes of your songs, you'll need to select the mix of each song that's perfect for your album, and then you'll have to decide on an order for the songs. Song order is an important part of the flow and impact of any album. With the right song order, a listener can be pulled through an entire album with ease. If the order is wrong, the listener might be lulled to sleep or end up so emotionally jostled that they're left with a bad feeling about the whole album.

The actual order is often determined by the style and personality of the artist. Many albums include the third song on side one as the title song. Sometimes the title song is the first song. Sometimes the title of the album doesn't come from a song, but from the intellectual theme of the album. These are artistic choices that reflect the personality of the artist.

Always include the tones that you originally recorded on your 2-track masters—1kHz, 10kHz and 100Hz, all at 0VU. These are very

important for the duplication facility to recognize the settings of your equipment.

Adjust spacing between songs according to the energy and pace demanded by the energy of the music. A standard space between songs is four seconds. When you're dealing with fade outs, begin the four-second space from where the mix totally loses its presence, which might be sooner than the point that the last drop of music has passed. Generally, the more contrast between songs, the longer the gap between the songs.

If your project is going to be printed to CD, you have one order of songs to consider and one musical and emotional flow. If your project is going to cassette, you'll need to plan two separate sides that have their own flow, emotion and life. A very important point for the logistics of cassette duplication is the comparative lengths of side A and side B. Side A should be slightly longer than side B. If side A is longer, the cassette can be listened to completely with minimal gap between side A and side B. If there is dead space it should be at the end of side B.

Mastering

After you've completed the mixing and editing and just before the duplicators get your tape, the mastering engineer will fine-tune any inherent problems with your music. The mastering engineer might re-EQ your song, run it through a compressor or an exciter or simply adjust levels of the songs to help you end up with a more competitive and respectable product. This is a very important step for your music, and spending a little extra money on a respected and noteworthy mastering engineer is worth it.

Different Mixes

Listen to the different mix segments in Audio Examples 9-32 through 9-38. Take note of the things you like and dislike about each. Most of the techniques and options in this chapter are included somewhere in these mixes. Once you've completed reviewing these mix segments, listen to Track 99 on CD-2 for a complete take of the Full Blown Mix from Audio Example 9-32.

Mix 1—The full blown mix—includes everything

Audio Example 9-32 Full Blown Mix
CD-2: Track 96

Mix 2—The keyboard mix

Audio Example 9-33 Keyboard Mix
CD-2: Track 96

Mix 3—The acoustic guitar mix

Audio Example 9-34 The Acoustic Guitar Mix
CD-2: Track 96

Mix 4—The building mix

Audio Example 9-35 The Building Mix
CD-2: Track 97

Mix 5—The simplest mix

Audio Example 9-36 The Simplest Mix
CD-2: Track 97

Mix 6—The electric rhythm mix with solos

Audio Example 9-37 The Electronic Rhythm Mix
CD-2: Track 98

Mix 7—The only-what's-absolutely-necessary mix

Audio Example 9-38
Only What's Necessary
CD-2: Track 98

Each mix has a different feel. What you like depends on your musical taste and judgment.

Conclusion

The techniques contained in this course give you enough knowledge to accomplish almost any type of sound. It's possible to learn recording techniques, as well as musical skills and arranging tricks, but in the end it's up to the individual to provide the combination of all techniques, along with some God-given talent, to produce a solid work that sounds good, has a flow, maintains interest and conveys real human emotion. If you've been following this course diligently from the beginning, you have a good foundation on which to build your recording. By no means should you consider this "enough" knowledge to get you by, though. The great part about music and recording is that there's always something new around the corner. We'll always be learning and creating new sounds and music.

Glossary

active direct box: In addition to matching impedances, this direct box contains electronic circuits designed to enhance the lows and highs that might have been degraded by the impedance matching process. These direct boxes are more expensive than non-active boxes, but they generally help facilitate a cleaner, more interesting instrumental sound.

active electronics: Electronics, within the bass or guitar, designed to increase high- and low-frequency clarity and output. Instruments with active electronics usually have a characteristically punchy low end and a clean high end.

adjacent track: The track with the next highest or next lowest number; for example, track four is adjacent to tracks three and five.

arco: On a stringed instrument, this indicates that the notes are bowed rather than plucked.

automation: Computer-assisted mixing system in which the computer remembers the engineer's moves during mixing and duplicates them on replay.

backing vocals: The supporting vocals in a song; vocals other than the lead vocal. Sometimes one backing vocal is sufficient, and sometimes two or more singers might record the same parts on two or more tracks of the multitrack. Also called background vocals.

bass strings: Approximately the lower two octaves of the standard 88-key piano when referring to treble, mids and bass. Also, the lower half of the strings when only referring to the treble and bass strings.

binaural: A very realistic and directional stereo mic technique in which an actual synthetic head houses two very small condenser mic capsules. The capsules are placed inside the synthetic head where the eardrums of a real head would be. This synthetic head even has the ear flaps—called *pinna*. The directional realism of binaural miking is most impressive when heard through a good set of headphones and is not as impressive when heard through speakers.

Blumlein configuration: A coincident stereo miking technique that uses two bidirectional microphones positioned on the same vertical axis—as close together as physically possible—pointing equally at the sound source but aimed 90° apart.

Bösendorfer Grand: The brand name of a piano considered to be one of the best available. Bösendorfer is noted for a clean, clear sound with a very good-sounding low register. It's also noted for an extended low end on the keyboard, containing more notes than the standard 88-key piano.

bouncing, bouncing down, ping-ponging: The process of rerecording a group of already recorded tape tracks onto one track of the same multitrack or one track of a different multitrack. This technique is common on machines with few tracks. Once the group of tracks has been bounced to a single track, the tracks previously occupied by that group are available for recordings of other instruments, voices or sound effects.

bridge: The point of rest for the strings at the opposite end of the bass or guitar from the neck. Normally a fairly massive metal bracket that the strings fasten to. The bridge saddles are the moveable pieces of the bridge that the strings lie across on their way from the point of attachment to the head. Intonation of the instrument is adjusted by moving the bridge saddles toward or away from the neck.

cent: 1/100 of a half-step.

clean sound: Typically a sound that has no distortion or effects. Also a sound that is an exact reproduction of the original sound source.

clone: A direct digital copy. An identical numerical copy of the binary code from a digital source. A copy that is made from the digital output of a digital source to the digital input of a digital recorder is a *clone*.

coincident stereo mic technique: Stereo mic technique using two microphones that lie as closely as physically possible on the same horizontal and vertical axis. X-Y and MS are the most common coincident stereo miking techniques.

comping: Musically, this is a consistent and rhythmic accompaniment part generally played on a guitar or keyboard.

dead spots: Notes, or frets, on a bass or guitar that don't sound as loud or resonate as much as the rest of the notes. Many basses have dead spots around the fourth or fifth fret on the first (smallest) string; new strings can help hide this problem. Also, a compressor can help even out the level of all the notes, thereby minimizing the dead note problem.

DiMarzio: A brand of instrument pickup. Typically has a hotter output than a *stock* pickup.

directional realism: Perception of points of origin for audio ingredients heard in a recording that the listener finds believable and possible. Recorded sound that puts the listener in a believable acoustical and musical environment. Hearing sound from a recording in the same way it could be produced acoustically, including a natural, comfortable balance of highs to lows, left to right, and the perception of nearness and distance.

drown the mix in reverb: To include a lot of reverb in the final mix. A figurative phrase relating to the fact that a sound that has no reverb is said to be *dry* and a sound that has reverb is said to be *wet*. Drowning a sound or a mix in reverb means making it very wet.

dub: To make a copy. Also, the actual copy itself.

edit: To remove, shift, insert, duplicate and rearrange the order of musical sections once the mix is complete. This is accomplished by cutting the master tape with a razor blade and taping the pieces back together with a special splicing tape or by using a digital editor to numerically shift parts of the song around in the editor/computer memory.

electric piano: A piano using electronic pickups that amplify the sound of a string or metal wire being struck by a felt hammer. An electric grand piano contains real piano strings that are struck and amplified. A Fender Rhodes electric piano contains individual metal wire rods, called tines, that are struck and amplified. Synthesizers and samplers are not electric pianos, though they can almost always produce the sound of an electric piano.

exciter: A processor that boosts the even numbered harmonics of a signal. This adds high-end presence and crispness to a sound without an increase in loudness. This is often used on drum overheads, lead vocals, backing vocals and some guitar and keyboard sounds. An exciter is rarely used on an entire mix in recording but can add a desirable presence to a complete live mix; or for live vocal monitors, it can increase the understandability of a monitor mix without increasing the chance of feedback. Boosting the even harmonics produces a crisp, bright sound in the exciter. On the other hand, if the exciter boosted the odd harmonics it would create a dampened, dull sound—not very exciting.

The Faulkner Configuration: A stereo miking configuration using two bidirectional microphones facing straight ahead, toward the sound source. The mics are traditionally about 200mm apart.

felt pick: A regular guitar pick made from felt, usually the same shape as most picks. The felt is about 1/8" thick. Felt picks have a warmer sound than plastic picks. The sound is similar to the sound of the bass being plucked with the fingers of the right hand. This is a good tool for guitar players covering the bass part because they can use their picking technique and approximate the sound of normal bass technique.

flux: A magnetic impulse.

fundamental: The harmonic that indicates the note name and defines the frequency of the sound wave.

generation: A copy of an analog tape or a digital tape that has gone from digital to analog, then from analog to digital. A digital copy made from the analog outputs of a digital source patched into the analog inputs of a digital recorder, rather than using all digital connections. A master tape is the first generation, whereas the submaster is second generation.

global sound map: A three-dimensional mental picture of audio placement, including left/right, up/down and near/distant positioning.

guitar MIDI controller: A guitar that converts the string's pitch data to MIDI note data. This process lets the guitarist play any keyboard sound available from the guitar. Guitar controllers also transmit velocity and pitch bend data, making the guitar controller a very useful and valuable programming tool.

The Haas Effect: Indicates that the delay of a sound is suppressed by as much as 8 to 12dB. Our hearing system does its best to ensure that localization is cued from the initial, direct sound wave. In order for a simple delay to be panned apart from the direct sound and heard as equal in volume to the original sound, it must be higher in actual level, or amplitude, than the original sound.

hammers: The felt beaters on a piano that actually hit the strings.

hard-left and hard-right: Pan settings that are all the way left or all the way right.

harmonics: Simultaneously sounding whole number multiples of the fundamental frequency. If the fundamental is indicated as a variable by the letter "f," the harmonic series is calculated as f times 1, f times 2, f times 3, f times 4, etc. Harmonics combine with the fundamental to create the unique tonal quality of each instrument.

harmonizer: A processor that can receive a musical pitch at its input and change the pitch by as much as one or two octaves at the output. Most harmonizers change pitch either in half-step increments or in one cent increments. An example of a half-step is from C1 to C#1 on the keyboard. (A cent is 1/100 of a half-step.)

head: The part of the bass or guitar that holds the tuning machines. On basses that have the tuning machines at the bridge end of the instrument, the head is the other end of the instrument from the bridge.

hum tone: A *partial* that is one half of the fundamental frequency; this occurs on many bell sounds.

intonation: On a fretted instrument, it's possible to have the open strings in tune but the fretted notes out of tune. Adjusting the length of the string by sliding the bridge pieces that the strings lie in toward the neck or away from the neck adjusts the intonation. Setting the intonation on a fretted instrument can be tedious and is usually best left to trained professionals.

localization: The ability of the ears and the brain to work together to indicate the point of origin of sounds. Even though a stereophonic sound system normally uses two channels of audio playing back through two loudspeakers, the recording engineer can use good mic and mixing techniques to indicate very specific points of origin for each ingredient of a mix. Positioning includes controlled placement from left to right, up to down and close to distant.

long stick: On a grand piano, the longer of two support posts that prop the lid open over the strings.

machine alignment and EQ: On a tape recorder, alignment refers to the process of verifying and achieving the exact physical positioning of each contact point in the tape path (heads, hubs, tape guides and idlers, etc.). Adjusting the EQ on a tape recorder involves adjusting the machine electronics so that all frequencies play back and record in accordance with a specific reference level. This is an involved, though essentially routine and easily performed, procedure. Most tape recorder manuals document the exact method for alignment plus the necessary tape and equipment requirements.

master: Not a copy. The first generation mix of a song or project, usually in stereo form. Engineers often specify the number of tracks for the master, such as 2-track master, 8-track master or 24-track master.

mid strings: The strings that contain the middle notes of the piano. The strings within about an octave and a half of middle C.

MIDI: The abbreviation for musical instrument digital interface. This interface converts keyboard, outboard gear and other electronic equipment parameters into a binary, numerical form that can be remembered and manipulated by a computer or sequencer.

mixdown machine: The audio recorder that receives the mixed audio signal from the board. Usually stereo, this machine can be analog or digital in format.

monophonic: Single channel audio. Many AM radio and vintage television programs are monophonic.

moving fader automation: Automation where the faders actually contain a small motor that can physically move the fader; this motor is controlled by voltage. Fader movement during mixdown indicates a change in voltage, and the computer records the voltage changes. On replay, the computer transmits the voltage changes to the motorized fader and the fader moves in the exact same way the engineer mixed. This system has excellent sonic integrity because, unlike the VCA system, there is no need for another amplifier in the circuit; it is understood that fewer amplifiers means less distortion.

MS mic technique: A coincident stereo microphone technique. "M" stands for mid and "S" stands for side. The mid mic is aimed at the middle of the stereo image and can be a cardioid or omni polar pattern. The side mic is bidirectional and is aimed to the sides. The mid mic is sent equally to left and right. The side mic is also sent equally to left and right but the phase is inverted on either the left or the right side. In stereo, the result of this configuration sounds very similar to the X-Y configuration, offering a very good stereo image. In mono, the result of the side

mic being reversed in phase between left and right is total cancelation of the side information, leaving the mid mic sounding as if it were the only mic used.

nanoWeber: a billionth of a Weber (10^{-9}). Operating levels for analog tape are measured in reference to the amount of magnetism, in nanoWebers per meter, that a tape produces on playback. Standard reference tapes (reproducer calibration tapes) are made at exacting specifications. Sine waves are recorded onto the tape at precise magnetic levels (fluxivity), letting the engineer adjust tape machine playback levels in accordance with an industry standard. Different tape requires different operating levels so check the manufacturer's suggestions regarding specific setup.

natural sound: Sound that could possibly occur in real life. Sound that's comfortable to listen to in that it reminds the listener of a familiar acoustical setting.

NOS Configuration (Nederlandsche Omroep Stichting): A stereo miking configuration that uses two cardioid microphones aimed 90° apart and at the sound source. The centers of the two mics are typically 300mm apart.

ORTF Configuration (Office de Radiodiffusion-Television Francaise): A stereo miking configuration using two cardioid microphones aimed at the sound source but 110° away from each other. The center of the two mics are traditionally 170mm apart.

overtone: Similar to, and often used synonymously with, harmonics. Related to the fundamental by interval rather than purely mathematical formula. Whereas the overtone series consists of the fundamental, the octave above the fundamental, the fifth above that, the third above that, etc., the harmonics are whole number multiples of the fundamental frequency.

P-Bass: Slang for a Fender Precision Bass, the industry standard bass.

partials: Overtones that aren't related by mathematics or natural interval. Bell sounds and other percussion sounds have very different and abstract overtones that fall into the *partials* family. Partials can be below as well as above the fundamental.

passive direct box: This direct box only matches impedances; it doesn't add anything to the sound. In fact, passive direct boxes typically decrease all or part of the signal. These are the simplest and least expensive direct boxes.

ping-ponging: see *bouncing, bouncing down.*

pizzicato: On a stringed instrument, this indicates that the notes are to be plucked rather than bowed.

the player's touch: The way the player plays the instrument; the physical strength of the picking technique; the amount and consistency of left hand pressure on the strings; the emotional control of the physical action of performing a piece of music.

plectrum: A playing technique for guitar or bass using a guitar pick.

plosive: A hard consonant like "p" or "b." These consonants are sometimes difficult to record. Enunciating plosives clearly results in an abundance of air projecting from the singer's mouth. This abundance of air can push the diaphragm of the microphone past its normal range of motion, causing a loud pop on the vocal track. This pop can be very difficult to eliminate in the mix.

plucked: Picked with the finger or a guitar pick.

pop filter: Another name for a wind screen. Diffuses air from the singer that will cause a pop if it hits the microphone capsule with too much force.

print: To record to tape. To *print* a mix means to transfer it with all of the changes and modifications that the mixing engineer has devised, from the multitrack, through the mixer and onto the mix recorder.

psychoacoustic enhancers: Effects processors that use combinations of varied phase, delay and simulated acoustic information to give a recording either a larger than real life sound or a more interesting and naturally occurring sound.

punch-in: The act of switching a recorder into record mode while the tape is moving. Typically the track is heard in playback mode until the instant the track is switched to record mode. Once the track is in record mode, the track is heard as it's being recorded.

punch-out: The act of switching the recorder from record mode to playback mode while the tape is moving.

reference tone: A sine wave that is recorded onto the master tape at 0VU. The standard reference tone of level setting is 1kHz; this frequency gives a good representation of basic recording and playback level. If the master tape has 30 to 45 seconds of 1kHz at 0VU recorded on it, then any other engineer can play that tone on his or her system and adjust playback levels to read 0VU, therefore optimizing the integrity of the playback machine. 10kHz is frequently used as a high-frequency reference tone; 100Hz is often used as a low-frequency reference tone. With 1kHz, 10kHz and 100Hz recorded on your master tape, it is easy for another engineer, or the duplication facility, to adjust their equipment to match the playback level and record EQ of your system, especially if your system has been accurately and properly adjusted.

Rhodes: A brand of electric piano made by the Fender Musical Instrument Company. See *electric piano.*

riding the fader: The process of manually adjusting the record or playback level while a track is being recorded or played back.

safety copy: A copy that is made in case the first generation master is damaged.

samples: Digital recordings.

short stick: On a grand piano, the shorter of two support posts that prop the lid open over the strings.

sibilance: Sibilance is what we call the sound produced by a sibilant consonant. A sibilant consonant is any consonant that has a hissing sound or includes a phonetic sound with a very fast attack. "S" and "t" are examples of sibilant consonants. "S," "t," "sh," "see" and "ch" are examples of the sound of sibilance.

SMPTE: The abbreviation for the Society of Motion Picture and Television Engineers. This society developed a binary numerical code that's used as the standard time reference in the synchronous control of transport systems for audio tape recorders, video tape recorders, film machines, sequencers and computers. This time code is generated in the form of a continually changing series of square waves that can be recorded onto a tape recorder track.

soundscape: Similar in concept to a landscape. The visual picturing of sound ingredients in a recording and the mental map for positioning those ingredients.

Steinway Grand: The brand name of a piano considered to be one of the best available. Steinways typically have a warm, smooth and clear sound throughout the entire range of the instrument.

stereo imaging: The realization of specific points of origin across the listening panorama for each ingredient of a recorded work, providing the listener with an accurate and controlled mental picture of where a sound comes from and the acoustic space that surrounds it.

stock: Original factory equipment; just as it comes from the factory. Many musicians like to hot-rod their gear by installing souped-up, after-market components designed to increase the efficiency and/or power. They often reject original stock components as being not quite good enough for their high standards. Sometimes these concerns are valid, sometimes they are not.

string buzz: The sound of the string rattling against the frets of a bass or guitar. This is caused by poor adjustment of the instrument or by a heavy and forceful playing style.

striping: The actual recording of time code onto one track of an audio tape recorder or video tape recorder.

It's most common and efficient to record time code throughout the full length of the tape at the beginning of the session.

submaster: A copy of the master, often made as a safety copy in case the master is damaged. This term is typically used when referring to analog copies.

surround sound: Multi-channel and multi-loudspeaker audio (typically four or six channels and speakers) that uses speakers placed around the listener. Often this system uses separate and discrete information sent to each speaker, which is useful for filling an acoustical environment with several audio points of interest. This approach is very good for high budget, high quality film work, filling a theater with interesting sounds that engulf the audience. Simpler surround systems use the normal two front speakers with a stereo mix, supported by two back speakers behind the listener. These two back speakers contain the normal stereo mix that's been processed through a chorus, delay, reverb or any combination of these processors.

sweet spot: In equalization, the center point of a boosted curve that makes a particular range of a particular instrument sound best.

take: In recording, a take is one successful completion of a performance. This applies to recording the complete song or rerecording part of a track. A "bad" take is not usable for the song. A "good" take includes a good technical recording, a good sounding recording, a good technical performance from the artist and a good emotional interpretation by the artist.

tone oscillator: A sine wave generator. Tones are used to make electronic level adjustments; the most commonly used tones are 100Hz, 1kHz and 10kHz. Many tone oscillators produce frequencies—infinitely variable and sweepable—from the lowest frequency we can typically hear (20Hz) to the highest frequency we can typically hear (20kHz). Some oscillators generate sine waves from 0Hz up to several times the highest frequency that the human ear can hear.

treble strings: The upper third of the strings on a piano (approximately the upper two octaves) when talking about treble, mid and bass strings. Also, the upper half of the strings on a piano, when only referring to the treble and bass strings.

vari-speed: A control on a tape recorder that can speed up or slow down the transport system. Slowing the tape down on playback lowers the pitch of the music. Slowing the tape down during recording results in a track that sounds higher and slightly more rhythmically precise when played back at normal speed.

VCA automation: Automation system in which the pertinent moves in a mix (faders, knobs or buttons) are feeding voltage controlled amplifiers (VCAs). Different moves represent changing voltages to the VCA. The computer remembers the voltage changes to the VCA and re-transmits them to the VCA on replay of the mix. The VCAs then duplicate the action in accordance with the voltage changes, but the actual controllers (faders, knobs or buttons) don't move.

vertical piano: Pianos in which the strings lie vertically and are attached from the top to the bottom of the soundboard. There are four basic sizes of vertical pianos based on the longest string length. They are:

    console: maximum string length of 40-42".

    spinet: maximum string length of 36".

    studio: maximum string length of 45".

    upright: maximum string length of 52".

visual balance: Creating a mix that gives the listener a mental impression of balance. Good mixes are often conceived from a visual standpoint because the mind's eye can control and place musical ingredients within a visual reference that's typically easier to understand than audio balance.

voicing: In relation to piano setup, this refers to the process of fine-tuning the sound of the instrument. Voicing is accomplished by adjusting the hammers for uniform sound and volume throughout the range of the piano. A piano can be voiced to sound brighter by applying a type of shellac to the hammers to make them harder; they therefore produce a stronger, more metallic attack. A piano can be voiced to sound warmer by roughing the surface of the hammers. This reduces the attack, resulting in a smoother, mellower sound. Another kind of voicing involves putting thumbtacks into the hammers at the striking point. This produces the most metallic sound and is referred to as *tack* piano. Voicing is best left to a trained professional!

Weber: A unit of magnetism. A unit of magnetic flux.

wet: Containing reverb or delay. A setting on an effect that adjusts the output to only contain the effected signal (reverberated, delayed, etc.) with none of the original (100 percent dry) signal.

wind screen: A device used on a microphone. Outside, the wind screen is used to shield the mic capsule from the wind. Inside, the wind screen is used to diffuse air as it comes from the singer's mouth.

X-Y configuration: Stereo mic technique that uses two microphones. The capsules of both condenser mics must share and rotate on the exact same vertical axis. The mics should be at a 90° angle (± about 20°) to each other on a horizontal plane. This is the most common form of coincident stereo miking technique.

Index

A Music Bookstore At Your Fingertips...

FREE!